SEXUALITY BEYOND CONSENT

SEXUAL CULTURES
General Editors: Ann Pellegrini, Tavia Nyong'o, and Joshua Chambers-Letson
Founding Editors: José Esteban Muñoz and Ann Pellegrini

Titles in the series include:

Sexuality Beyond Consent

Risk, Race, Traumatophilia

Avgi Saketopoulou

NEW YORK UNIVERSITY PRESS

New York

NEW YORK UNIVERSITY PRESS
New York
www.nyupress.org

© 2023 by New York University
All rights reserved

References to Internet websites (URLs) were accurate at the time of writing. Neither the author nor New York University Press is responsible for URLs that may have expired or changed since the manuscript was prepared.

Please contact the Library of Congress for Cataloging-in-Publication data.
ISBN: 9781479820238 (hardback)
ISBN: 9781479820252 (paperback)
ISBN: 9781479820276 (library ebook)
ISBN: 9781479820269 (consumer ebook)

10 9 8 7 6 5 4 3 2 1

Also available as an ebook

Για την γιαγιά μου, την πρώτη φεμινίστρια της ζωής μου και την πιο σημαντική

CONTENTS

Introduction

Erotics of the Terribly Beautiful

What is the meaning of art, architecture, music, painting, or
poetry if not the anticipation of a suspended, wonder-struck
moment, a miraculous moment?
—Georges Bataille, *The Accursed Share*

Culture is the precaution of those who claim to think
thought but who steer clear of its chaotic journey.
—Édouard Glissant, *Poetics of Relation*

Carmen opens her analytic session as follows: "Many people had slapped
me before Ava, but no one ever like her. No previous slap had landed so
precisely. It was the right angle, the right amount of force, the right part
of my face. It was so exceptional my body felt like it was liquifying."[1] In
her five years of analysis thus far, Carmen has returned to this arresting slap a few times, so singular did it feel to her. But this time she adds
something new, and her relationship to it now seems more fraught: "The
moment I felt it, I immediately wanted to take back my consent. Yes, I
had asked Ava to slap me, but I didn't mean for her to do it so well. What
I had wanted was a mediocre, manageable slap, not one this exquisite."

I start with a clinical vignette for two reasons. First, I am a practicing psychoanalyst, which means that both my database and my skill set
come from the consulting room.[2] Second, throughout this volume, I rely
on a series of case studies from the clinic and beyond—from theater and
film, to texts, podcasts, and interviews—as a way to think about consent,
trauma, racialization, and the currents of sadism.[3] My approach to these
case studies is somewhat unusual. For one, I use clinical case studies as
springboards to make more universal claims about some processes (e.g.,
consent, sadism) and their operational mechanics that extend beyond

the particular dynamics of the individuals discussed. For the discussions of these case studies, I lean on the metapsychology of the psychoanalyst Jean Laplanche, who offers a distinctive psychoanalytic theory that is not often encountered by academics or, in fact, by most trained analysts.[4] Laplanche brings something novel to the understanding of the unconscious and to the theorizing of the ego, which permits him to ask unusual questions of psychic time and to put generative pressure on repetition.[5] I deploy his thinking *and* stretch it further to reflect on trauma, racialization, and the erotic. One of the premises of this book is that a theorization of sexuality and trauma that understands the unconscious as a granary of unbearable affects and intolerable experiences hamstrings our thinking about traumatic experience and, importantly, about race. Pushing back against the fixation with discourses of trauma, I argue that a theorizing of traumatic inscription that assumes trauma to be unchanging and immobile is traumatophobic. Traumatophobia keeps trauma inert, and that poses a problem because trauma that is not inserted into circulation does not wither and disappear: it stalls and it controls us. Trauma, I argue, *needs* to circulate; it *needs* to be revisited. I describe this approach, of maintaining a hospitable attitude to the revisitation of trauma, as "traumatophilic." Traumatophilia does not overlook or diminish the impact of trauma but offers, instead, a way of working with the recognition that we cannot turn away from our traumata, that we are strangely drawn *to* them. To recognize that traumatic experience is not possible to eliminate takes mental fortitude, as the human impulse is to cling to the idea that trauma can be resolved. But sustaining such illusions is not humane. Much as we would want to think otherwise, the impact of traumatic experiences cannot be eliminated or repaired: at best, we live in their aftermath on different terms than when they were inflicted on us. Relinquishing the idea that trauma can be repaired opens paths to thinking about what subjects do *with* their trauma.

Another distinctive element in my use of psychoanalysis is that my reading of Laplanche's work is refracted through my engagement with performance theory, philosophy, critical theory, queer studies, and queer of color critique. Consequently, the Laplanche I bring to you is a bit idiomatic and, in a word, "queer." This is not to say that you are getting a spoiled Laplanche, only a (re)purposed one that is especially exciting for thinking about erotics and aesthetic experience. With his conceptual help, I intervene in ongoing conversations about affirmative consent to argue a point that runs through this book: while violations of consent are real and deserve our attention, affirmative consent does not. There is no such thing as consent, at least not in the way that affirmative consent paradigms imagine it or in the way it is sold to us as a metric that can subtend ethical relations or inform our sexual politics—though there *very much is* such a thing as its violation. I introduce a different kind of consent paradigm, which I call "limit consent." Limit consent has ties to the rousing of the sexual drive and entails a nuanced negotiation of limits that belongs neither to the domain of activity nor to the sphere of passivity. Limit consent is not something we "exercise" or something that is "done" to us: it has more to do, rather, with surrendering *to* an other or, more precisely, with surrendering to the opacity in the other and to the opacity in ourselves. Consent, we will see, is not only something that we offer to another; it is also an internal affair. While the usual paradigm around consent is about maintaining control of a situation, limit consent is more about giving up control. If consent is not a way to take control but, within a certain given context, a way to let go of it, we cannot rely on the outcome of an encounter (what happened or how someone felt about it) to decide whether the encounter was ethical. Other variables have to come into play, and aesthetic experience, as I will discuss, is a critical variable in this process with ties to the ethical domain. To explore how limit consent ties to thinking about sexuality, aesthetics, and ethical relations, I put Édouard Glissant in conversation with Laplanche.

Last, there is a rich and important body of theory in queer studies and queer of color critique that has already engaged psychoanalysis to think about racialization, eroticism, and performance (Eng, 2001; Musser, 2014; Pellegrini, 1997; D. Scott, 2010; Stockton, 2006). This work has been enormously influential for me for my own thinking *and* my clinical practice. What I want to bring to these conversations as a clinical psychoanalyst is the benefit of case studies not as hermeneutic projects but as disorienting encounters between embodied subjects, each with a sexual unconscious that *acts on* the other. Let me explain what I mean by the phrase "acting on" here: Freud initially theorized the unconscious as a psychic structure that developed in order to house repressed traumatic memory. Recovering these memories, his early thinking went, could empty the unconscious of its contents—which implied that one could be "cured" of one's unconscious. This idea was eventually abandoned, but it continues to haunt the discourse on trauma to this day—as, for example, when we talk about something being "worked through," about "processing" one's trauma, or, more colloquially, about exorcizing one's demons. The deceptive promise that trauma could be drained from the psyche (through recollection or insight) was drastically revised when Freud (1915a) discovered that the unconscious never stopped flaring up in the embodied relation with the analyst (what we call "transference"). The unconscious was thus recast from something that could be extinguished (if we better understand ourselves) to an ever-persistent force that never dissipates and that we encounter in what the patient does *to* the analyst, not just *what* the patient tells them (Kahn, n.d.).

Part of a clinical psychoanalyst's training thus involves learning to discern where, in what form, and with what possible effects the unconscious *appears* phenomenally—rather than focusing (only) on what information about the past or the patient's fantasy are disclosed when the unconscious shows up (in symptoms, dreams, etc.).[6] I bring this sensibility to my discussion of performance and art, to investigate the mechanism through which some theater may have the transformational potential claimed on its behalf. To explain how performance touches us, we usually turn to the interior elements it evokes: for example, we may say that it reminded of us something or that it resonated with something we have experienced or that it spoke to a particular part of ourselves. I want to highlight what is usually disregarded by this overemphasis, to draw our attention to how art or performance acts on us and away from which part of the self/memory it evokes. Those who do not just suffer through difficult art but who savor the anguish and vulnerability that some performance engenders may endure aesthetic experience (Doyle, 2013). Such experience can leave one transformed.

With that said, let us return to Carmen.

Carmen

For Carmen, eroticism has always been inextricably bound to the aesthetic; it has never been about a consolidated or identitarian form of sexuality. What usually compels her libidinal attention is the domain where the erotic gives chase: in the fiery encounter with one's own opacity that is accessed through the quality and intensity of experience—in experience, that is, that steps off the ledge of representation, where the aesthetic unifies the beautiful with the morbidly strange, the pleasurable with the unexpected. There is a long tradition in literature, film, and performance that links the aesthetic realm with lustful suffering and libidinal ferocity that leaves one spent. To me, Carmen specifically brought to mind the Marquis de Sade's explorations of how principles of aesthetic judgment are implicated in perverse desires (1795/1966c; 1797/1966a). In Sade's novels, the beauty of suffering and the aesthetic dimensions of brutal licentiousness are used to demonstrate—repetitively, logically, and exhaustively—the threat that aesthetics posed to the prized Enlightenment subject's autonomy and reason (Horkheimer & Adorno, 1987; Lacan, 1963/1989). "Exercising aesthetic judgment precisely in order to undermine and critique [Enlightenment] ideologies" (Byrne, 2013, p. 17), Sade produced an aesthetic philosophy that resisted an essentialized ontology of sexuality. Its subject, universalized as White, is not Carmen, who is a Latinx femme dyke. Still, Carmen operated unaware of but entirely in sync with this counter-Enlightenment tradition, pursuing the intensification of experience that can draw one closer to oneself, offering brief yet piercingly impactful bursts of *self-sovereignty*. In chapters 4 and 5 of this volume, I dedicate lengthy sections to this concept of self-sovereignty, derived from the philosophy of Georges Bataille (1954, 1957), and elaborate how it differs from the notion of sovereignty as used in political theory. For now, briefly, self-sovereignty displaces the notion of sovereignty from the domain of power to resituate it to the domain of experience. Self-sovereignty is an intimate experience wherein one's energies are not split by the demands of capitalism (to constantly invest in ourselves and in the world around us) and in which the subject can be transiently relieved from the demands of relationality. It is a rare and transient state.

Carmen's reaction to Ava's slap was very unexpected given her usual attraction to the aesthetics of being undone. I was, therefore, surprised to hear her say that she had wanted to retract her consent because the slap had exceeded her expectations.[7] Carmen's "consent-regret," if we can call it that, is not about having granted it to Ava—that is, Carmen did not feel that Ava violated or mistreated her, nor was she "blaming"

Ava for slapping her so excellently. It has more to do with her *relationship to having consented* in the first place—but not because the slap was too much (as in injurious or traumatizing) or too little (as in unsatisfactory or disappointing) but because in surpassing her imagination, *it overcame her.*

The kind of consent Carmen is referencing does not belong to the interpersonal realm of drawing boundaries, communicating them, having them be respected, and so on: it is an internal affair. Carmen experienced something she did not anticipate—though she had signed up for it—and was then unable to surrender herself to the distance between what she expected (a "mediocre" strike) and what she received (an "exquisite" one). This difficulty with surrendering is the last point of defense against becoming overwhelmed and shattered by experience— and chapters 3 and 4 examine what can arise when one moves past the brink and becomes overwhelmed. Notably, Carmen has the integrity— and psychic capacity—to own her regret without attributing it to Ava's conduct.[8] Rather, it is Carmen's confidence in herself that is shaken. The risks entailed in such encounters, then, also involve a kind of personal responsibility that cannot be outsourced to the other. That is, it does not matter how well Ava "holds" Carmen's emotional experience—though such care is neither irrelevant nor insignificant. Carmen is also responsible for the vulnerability she has invited—and these themes are discussed in chapter 2. What Carmen wishes she could have staved off is how humbled she was by the sensations and the cravings the slap unleashed in her. Said otherwise, the experience seems to have brought Carmen into contact with her opacity—a concept that Glissant describes as "subsistence within an irreducible singularity" (1990, p. 190) and that, as chapter 1 argues, has interesting affinities with the unconscious. Consent, we begin to see, does not only encompass conscious processes unfolding *between* people; it also implicates our interiority. When we consent to something, we open ourselves up to encountering the otherness in ourselves.

I am thus making an argument for limit consent, a type of consent that is conceptually grounded in negative dialectics. Affirmative consent emerges out of the tradition of reading the Hegelian dialectic as giving us an ethic of recognition, wherein wishes and boundaries are communicated and negotiated, recognizing each other's needs so as to reach a synthetic conclusion (for example, what kind of sexual contact both are assenting to).[9] But in this volume, I explore a different ethical terrain than the one we are accustomed to, which arises in the confrontation with the irreducible opacity in oneself and in the other. Where affirmative consent imagines a subject that can be fully transparent to herself, the kind of psychoanalysis you will find in this volume acknowledges that the self cannot be fully known, that we are always somewhat opaque to ourselves, and, therefore, that consent negotiations always involve more than we think we bargained for: they involve a confrontation with what is irreducibly alien to us about ourselves. This confrontation assumes risk, as chapters 2 and 3 will elaborate, and that risk can enable different relational possibilities. Where Hegel gave us a vision of self-consciousness that exists because of the other, Bataille gives us an understanding of self-consciousness as the unknowable in us, which is an experience of a strange order, in that it does not appear phenomenally. What my psychoanalytic take adds to this thinking is a theorization of how that can then be rendered into the material realm so that it can become perceptible, that is, appear phenomenally into the world, where it may leave a lasting impression. Under the aegis of limit consent, relating can thus approximate what Maurice Blanchot described as "infinite conversation" (1969) and what Glissant called "being-in-relation" (1990). Both were referring to the radical potential for self- and world-making that arises when we meet the other without trying to exercise our will over them and when we surrender to our own foreignness to ourselves. Insofar as affirmative consent promises to close the gap between ourselves and the other, it trades in the opaque for recognition, exchanging the unintelligible for the transparent. Affirmative consent does not give us opacity; it insists that the self can be deciphered. But grasping the other—or our hope that the other will grasp us—is neither harmless nor politically neutral: "*to grasp*," Glissant writes, "contains the movement of hands that grab their surroundings and bring them back to themselves" (1990, p. 192).

In thinking with Glissant, for whom opacity is "that which cannot be reduced" (1990, p. 191) to the terms by which Western thought demands transparency; with Christina León, who sees opacity as a necessary supplement to ethical curiosity (2020a, 2020b); and with Laplanche, for whom the otherness in ourselves is not "ours" but arises through "the intervention of the other" (1991, p. 557), I propose that an understanding of consent as affirmative interpersonal negotiation fails in that it does not take radical alterity into account. My aim in this volume, is to think about forms of consent that work alongside alterity and to argue for the ethical urgency of consensual paradigms that reach beyond the transparent and the communicable—both of which may be too restricted for sexual politics and minoritarian intersecting identities.

Turning toward Opacity: The Ego's Resistance

Turning toward opacity, however, is neither easy nor effortless. Why? Because opacity, as León notes, "materializes as a resistance" (2020a, p. 172). Her phrase alerts us to how intransigently difficult it may be to be receptive to the opaque, as León seems to imply that some resistance to it will have to be overcome. But what she also seems to be saying is that opacity is *itself* a resistance. Thankfully, we might say, something in us always resists being grasped and understood, and in that sense, opacity may be seen as a sturdiness in us—and that, as we will see, connects to self-sovereignty. This sturdiness in us is always there. The question is what relationship we can develop or maintain with it—or, seen from a different angle, what relationship with it we can bear or endure.

Chapter 1 examines in granular detail how Laplanche's theorization of the psyche can help explain why recoiling from opacity is far easier than giving oneself over to it. For now, epigrammatically, here are the main ideas: For Laplanche (1987), the adult's contact with the infant injects into the infant indecipherable elements from the adult's sexual unconscious. Some of these will eventually lead to the formation of the child's own sexual unconscious, which will henceforth be experienced as an "internal foreign body that must at all costs be mastered and integrated" (2003b, p. 208). These attempts are always partially incomplete and thus doomed to failure. The unconscious derives from this failure to master the turmoil introduced by the other's sexual deviance (the adult's sexual unconscious).[10] This internal foreign body will forever remain an "internalized exteriority" (Fletcher, 2000, p. 101) that is never quite fully metabolized, which is to say that it never becomes ours in the sense of being something we can decipher about ourselves.

The implantation of the other's sexual unconscious into the infant is traumatic, but it is also critical to subjectivation. Why? Because to cope with this enigmatic disturbance, the infant "translates" these messages, which means that the infant coats them with meaning. The ego is the aggregate effect of these successive coatings accruing over time. The raw materials that the infant reaches for to draft these meanings/coatings come from their excitable, libidinal body and from the socius: concepts, ideas, and myths about how the world works, including gender, race, ethnicity, and so on, all become tools for the building of the ego. Adding to Laplanche's theory, I will argue that what this means is that the prejudices, stereotypes, and bigotries that underlie concepts such as gender, race, and so on and that, to some degree, are what gives these their density will also become threaded through the ego. In other words, our very sense of the self and of our functional stability is, to varying degrees, also reliant on problematic social values. The significant implication is that White supremacy, male superiority, heteronormativity, and so on reside not in the unconscious but in our egos—and as such, they cannot be eliminated through insight or self-knowledge. If this seems like a big claim, it is because it is—and we will go over it in detail in chapter 1.

The ego thus develops "around a kernel of things that it cannot understand" (Cimatti, 2016, p. 207), becoming invested in its own stability and in maintaining its equilibrium. Once it is formed, one of its central functions henceforth is to master this tumult that enigma—a term I return to shortly—constantly generates. Understanding itself as the sovereign, the ego will mount formidable resistances when it senses that its authority is questioned or that it may be deposed—which is what contact with the sexual unconscious and with the opaque threatens to do. The ego, that is, tries to keep the energetic irreverence of the unconscious at a minimum—if not at bay. This is not to malign the ego as a conservative force, which it also is: we need our ego to feel stable, to enjoy a sense of basic psychic cohesion, and to feel "at home" with ourselves—many aspects of our day-to-day functioning depend on it. But it does mean that the ego's investments lie in the direction of resisting the foreign—in the other but also the internal foreignness in ourselves that originates from the other's effraction into us—by appropriating it into its structure. This is the mechanism by which the ego resists opacity. We begin to see, then, that the ego's default orientation is to maintain its homeostasis by preventing anything it perceives as introducing dysregulating turbulences into the psyche.

This default orientation has interesting implications for intersecting minoritarian identities because while the ego is universally invested in its structural stability, which it defends fervently as a way for subjects to feel "at home," the raw materials it is made out of are not equally hospitable for all subjects. As such, those for whom dominant social values "work" better because the world makes a home *for* them are better served by the ego's investment in maintaining the status quo. Those who are minoritized by virtue of their sex, race, nationality, gender, and so on may more readily be willing to risk disturbing the conservative forces of their own egos. To put this differently, is it possible that persons who do not get to be "at home" in the world may be more susceptible, more readily receptive to the disquiet of their own opacity?[11] Further, because the social can provide a bolstering of one's narcissism, it can also operate as a fortification of one's resistance to encountering one's opacity. In this sense, dominant social location (e.g., Whiteness) works on the side of resistance: by giving the illusion of being at home, it may embolden the subject's narcissism, creating the (fragile) sense that problems need not be encountered—an illusion that requires constant reinforcement to be maintained. Chapter 5 explores the particular form of ethical sadism, *exigent sadism*, that is required to put pressure on such illusions.

The fact that the ego will not relinquish its stabilizing investments willingly or, to say it differently, with its consent is why aesthetics and eroticism (perversity in particular) can be such powerful nursemaids for the psychic and political transformations that the ego's rupture can enable—and endure. Chapters 2 and 3 take up this shattering of the ego through the analytic concept of "overwhelm." Both the aesthetic realm and the erotic operate in ways that are alien to the ego, which is another way of saying that they can disrupt the ego's complacency.[12] When this disruption escalates beyond what is bearable, the ego may shatter—a phenomenon explored in chapter 2. Such contestations of the ego's hegemony are not welcomed, which is why erotic and aesthetic experiences that are most likely to unsettle the ego are harder to give oneself over to.

To be clear, by "unsettling," I am not referring to experiences that may be upsetting, where the upset is actually compatible with one's ego investments—as, for example, when a White person feels upset that they did something racist but nonetheless focuses on their upset, thereby resisting reckoning with how their racist act could rework their sense of themselves. Rather, I am discussing experiences that challenge the ego by jeopardizing its economic stability. Such challenging of the ego's reign requires that one pushes back against one's own ego's self-conservation. I call this countering of the ego's resistances *bending one's will*. If we loop back to Carmen with this in mind, her appetite for erotic aestheticism and the usual susceptibility she brings to coming up against the strange in herself may now be seen as a facility in bending her will. Such facility is always fleeting and short-lived, which is another way of saying that the bending of the will is not a durable capacity that one develops but a receptivity that has to be wrested each time, again and again, against the objections of the ego. The latter is what happens for Carmen around the experience of the slap: she does not respond to it in the way she does during other encounters, in which she is usually able to surrender to the experience. In this case, Carmen is unable to bend her will: she resists encountering her own opacity.

Lest this is misunderstood, let me emphasize that in talking about the bending of one's will, I am *not* talking about a willfulness of the kind that solidifies one's experience of agency, which is more the domain of the ego. Nor is the bending of the will about willing a specific outcome but, rather, about what it takes to step into the fray of the unknown. Such bending of the will is not isomorphic to masochism. If anything, what is on the line when the subject bends their will is not a diminishment of the self but its expansion.[13] In chapters 2 and 5, I will specifically elaborate on, and argue for, the utility of some forms of sadism and show how in exigent sadism, the "sadistic" subject also has to bend their will. We will go over these ideas from multiple angles, but what I want to underscore here is that the bending of the will involves having to overcome a gradient of internal resistance. In fact, the more heterogeneous to the ego the encounter feels, the higher the gradient of pushback one will encounter and have to overcome. And let me also be clear that what I am describing involves the bending of one's *own* will, not the other's, which would amount to sheer violence and which is not related to my project.

The Economic Regimes of the Erotic and the Aesthetic

Let us linger in the interstices of what occurs as the unconscious is pressing for translation before its energies are coagulated into meaning, that is, in the space of opacity that the ego so fervently resists. I argue that this "interval between reach and grasp" (Carson, 1986, p. 30) is the domain of aesthetics: herein one is exposed to the energetic fervor of the enigmatic, a site of excitement but, also, of our sheer vulnerability. Accessing this domain requires, as already discussed, the bending of the will, but such bending cannot be an intentional undertaking, as is the case, for example, with willfulness, since the pooling of intentionality with action is in the province of the ego. When we bend our will, we make ourselves subject *to* something, we endure the rousing of something in ourselves that "does not have the character of calculation or strategy . . . [and that] requires that one can risk . . . put[ting] oneself blindly into play" (Hollier, 1979, p. 321). Encountering opacity means that we dwell in such spaces without giving in to the impulse of trying to master the experience—for example, by seeking to understand or to interpret or to symbolize what is unfolding—and without trying to turn the experience into a project, as in "the philistine demand that the artwork give [us] something" (Adorno, 1970, p. 17). What comes out of this form of aesthetic experience is not intentional or willed.

If we tarry in this interval, it is not through deliberate choice or willful decision—*nor it is with the ego's consent*. Some subjects develop a taste for such experiences, gorging themselves on it through performance, art, or the erotic—and in chapter 4, where I use myself as a case study, I describe my own relationship to Jeremy O. Harris's *Slave Play* as such gorging. But for now, and with these ideas in mind, we may recast Carmen's verbalization in the following terms: the fantasy of retrospectively withdrawing her consent may be about mastering the perturbation that Ava's jolting slap introduced.[14] It is only when one resists the possibility of mastery or when the urge to master is taken away by someone else (which, as we will see, is what an exigent sadist does) that one gets to experience—a word that, tellingly, in French also means "experiment." In chapter 5, I introduce and elaborate on the concept of "exigent sadism" as a type of sadism that involves considerable work on the part of the exigent sadist. Exigent sadism, we will see, is a form of care that can foster encounters with opacity for those who, despite everything, are willing to embark on such a voyage. My hope is to stimulate conversations about sadism that deepen our critical engagement with a concept that is mostly demonized. Sadism does indeed have a demonic dimen-

sion, but exigent sadism, as I will show, is also a form of absolute exposure (on the part of the sadist) and performs important work related to
caring for another.

In speaking about these phenomena, it is very hard to be precise or
clear—in fact, clarity threatens the opacity of the very processes I am
trying to describe. Perhaps poetry can help us here. Anne Carson turns
to Zeno's paradox; "Zeno's runner," she writes, "never gets to the finish
line of the stadium, Zeno's Achilles never overtakes the tortoise, Zeno's
arrow never hits the target . . . [Each of these distances] contains a point
where the reasoning seems to fold into itself . . . [and each time] it can
begin again, and so the reach continues" (1986, p. 81). Now, if you happen to be someone who can enjoy the suffering of such a process, "you
are delighted to begin again" (Carson, 1986, p. 81). The aesthetic, I would
say, resides precisely in the luxuriating bittersweetness of this exercise.
For those who "like being situated at that blind but lively spot" (Carson,
1986, p. 87), some erotic engagement, much like some art and performance, may put such experimenting in motion—though which erotic
moment, which theatrical piece, or which artwork will have that singular effect on any of us is impossible to tell ahead of time. The form of
aesthetic experience this book focuses on, in other words, is not something we attain by plan or determination, nor is it arrived at through
the formal elements of the artwork. Not all art is equally likely to spur
such movements. The sort of aesthetic experience I am concerned with
is the province of art that refuses to offer understanding or resolution,
frustrating the expectation it also cultivates and disappointing the hope
of a cathartic outcome (chapters 4 and 5 illustrate and expand on these
ideas). In *Aesthetic Theory*, Theodor Adorno explicitly urges us to refrain from "burdening artworks down with intentions" (1970, p. 27) so
that we may let ourselves experiment, instead, with what may await us
when "content becomes more opaque. Certainly, this does not mean that
interpretation can be dispensed with as if there were nothing to interpret." What Adorno advocates for is exposure to an "increasing opacity"
that does not get "replac[ed] by the clarity of meaning" (1970, p. 27).

As you can see, I am not interested in theorizing the interior psychological features that can enable some subjects to develop a taste out of
this interstitial space between enigma and translation or to examine art
as an inquiry of what it revives *about* the past. My project, rather, seeks

to map how some art stuns, at times even slaps us, in order to explore how some performance works on us not by kindling the past *as memory* but by revivifying it *in the present* as a force in the here and now. One of this book's organizing premises is that the aesthetic may have less to do with meaning and more to do with the imprint of pleasure that is suffered, an imprint that can deliver us beyond the reach of the everyday and into "the marrow of experience" (Adorno, 1970, p. 31).

Aesthetics of the Terribly Beautiful

The term "experience" is commonly used to describe the distinct, subjective sense we may have of an event: as in, "I experienced x person as thoughtful" or "my experience of y event was traumatizing." In this usage, "experience" refers to discrete moments or to a series of impressionable moments. In this volume, following Adorno (1970), I steer away from the reduction of experience into psychological subjectivism. Instead, I rely on the term "aesthetic experience" to reference experience that is not the property of the subject but that arises out of an encounter with the other's and our own alterity. Aesthetic experience relates to the enigmatic quality that extends beyond what the subject intends or aims for. It is a dynamic form of experience that involves an interaction with an object outside the self—a person, a piece of art, an encounter—and the interior process it sparks. For that to happen, the outside object "must treat the other in a non-dominating, non-subsumptive, non-homogenizing manner" (Jay, 2005, p. 356), and when that happens, the effect can be transformative. Chapter 5 explores the critical role that exigent sadism can play in curating aesthetic experience that draws into/makes us confront opacity, but, for now, let me turn to my understanding of aesthetic theory as framed by Fred Moten's powerful discussion of Emmett Till and "Black Mo'nin'" (2003).

"How can this photograph challenge ontological questioning?" asks Moten, meditating on the aesthetic possibilities that may dwell in looking again and again at the photograph of Emmett Till's destroyed face (2003, p. 62). It may seem odd that anyone would think to summon aesthetics at the site of an atrocious crime committed against a Black child who was shot in the head and thrown in the river for allegedly whistling at a White woman. What Moten is trying to do, as I read him, is to intervene in the way Western political philosophy (through Kant) and aesthetic theory (through Barthes) have argued for the beautiful in ways that historically exclude people of color, in order to explore aesthetics that encompass the terrible. To the inquiry of how Emmett Till's photograph challenges ontological questioning, Moten offers that this may be accomplished "*by way of a sound*, and by way of what's already there in the decision to display the body, to publish the photograph, to restage death and rehearse mo(ur)nin(g)" (2003, p. 62). For Moten, such a decision "is never disconnected from an aesthetic one, from a necessary reconstruction of the very aesthetics of photography, of documentary, and, therefore, of truth, revelation, and enlightenment as well as of judgment, taste, and, therefore, the aesthetic itself" (2003, p. 62). What Moten poignantly flags is that the aesthetic is neither synonymous with the beautiful nor is it a depoliticized pleasure. Invoking the sonic dimension in the site of this torture scene, he seems to want to defamiliarize us from the usual ways in which we might have otherwise engaged with Till's image, prying us away from "the ocularcentrism that . . . shapes theories of the nature of photography and our experience of [it]." Moten wants to reorient our attention toward the photograph's "phonic substance" (2003, pp. 62–63).

How, though, does one listen to a photograph? And what does one listen for? There is, we might say, an opacity to Moten's call, which leaves the space open for his readers to fill this in themselves. For me, Moten's call to tend to the sonic may be read as an incitement to fantasize *about* the photograph, to hear in it not some latent, previously undiscovered sound that resides *in* the image but to allow the photograph to act on us, to rouse a sonic response (the essay's titular "mo'nin'" and perhaps other sounds too). For that to happen, we have to let "what we thought we could look at and hold, hold[] *us*, capture[] *us*" (Moten, 2003, p. 64, emphasis added). Moten thus directs us toward "a general disruption of the ways in which we gaze at the face and at the dead" (2003, p. 64). His move entails an ethical call: not to look in order to master but to let oneself be acted on by the photograph's dysregulating force. This, in turn, might rouse something in us over which we have no willful control but for which we will nonetheless be responsible. His asking us to return to the photograph again and again is not staged as a demand, even though that does not make it any less of an ethical imperative: to stay sutured to the photograph, we will have to bend our will and resist the impulse to look away—because it is too hard to look at, because it hurts one's soul to look, because it is too bizarrely compelling to look. We have to resist, that is, the ego's inclination to easily assimilate the photograph into the a priori it expects to find in it. This is where Moten's inventiveness regarding the acoustic register comes in: a less trod path than the visual, the sonic is, perhaps, less appropriative, less given to "grasp" the photograph to bring it toward oneself and one's preordained meanings. Why do we listen in the first place? Because the opaque pulls us in; it draws us into the image, and it is in following that exigency that we stand to listen to it.

Listening to the photograph as an incitement to fantasize *about* the photograph opens us up to the gap between the photograph and ourselves, not so that we see it more clearly, as if there were some previously undiscovered detail to take in, but to eavesdrop on what gets roused in us. Listening makes us attentive, though not for something specific, because no matter how hard we listen, there is no sound to tend to, but to turn toward the hollow, toward opacity—and it is that turn that motors us to fantasize. Here, then, is a form of listening that is not about perceiving or grasping something but about dispossession. To listen this way, to listen for the "gap," we have to give ourselves over to our own unconscious, which is another way of saying that listening to the sonic is also about giving ourselves over to the perverse in us. It is worth remembering here that Till's murder was set in motion by the sexual fantasies recounted by a White woman. They were sexual in that she reported that he had "grabbed her around the waist and uttered obscenities," and they were fantasies, because, in 2017, the woman admitted to having made that up. In other words, she fantasized about it but reported it as a factual event. To listen to the photograph, then, would also have to involve listening for the way in which the perverse may be commandeered—in this case, by racist fantasy. Such listening may feel unpalatable, even horrific, because we do not know what our unconscious will produce or, thus, what we will encounter. Therein lies also the difficulty with which one must contend: even as the unconscious is never "ours," in that its force is not under our "command," it is also *of* us, which means that we are responsible for its effects in the world. Because the unconscious is an alterity that can never be integrated into the ego, it is not subjectively ours (that is, we do not possess our unconscious), and yet we are still responsible for its effects in the world (Laplanche, 1994/2015d).

We listen to Till's photograph, then, not just with our ears but with our entire body, including the libidinal body, which is also a racialized body. The libidinal and the enigmatic, that is, participate in our response to the aesthetic object; they contribute to this dispossessed form of listening that can lead to our own disruption. If we can bend our will to give ourselves over to the *"terribly beautiful"* (Moten, 2003, p. 74) in this photograph, we are also ethically obligated to listen attentively so that we may eavesdrop on ourselves for what arises out of such an encounter. It is this odd blend of self-relinquishment and ethical responsibility that can make being engrossed with Till's destroyed face not gratuitously voyeuristic but deeply ethical: to stay tethered to the photograph not as an epistemological project to be mastered but to expose ourselves to its force is to experience the limits of our being. This has profound political implications that will be expounded on in chapters 4 and 5. And the invitation is itself risky, because there is no way of ensuring that if what is roused in us turns out to be ugly, we will have the integrity to engage it in an ethically and politically accountable way. Part of the danger in turning to opacity is that although it opens up the space for thinking about ethical engagement, it also requires that we think about the menacing and the horrid. Opacity, that is, is not a guarantee of "good" politics, nor are the ethical and the horrid antithetical; they belong to the same order.

Emmett Till's photograph, like the art and performance I discuss in this book, denies us the comfortable distance of spectatorship, propositioning the viewer "to lose himself, [to] forget himself, [to] extinguish himself in the artwork" (Adorno, 1970, p. 17). This volume thus takes up aesthetic objects that do not operate under the Aristotelian regime of a cathartic, resolutive release, but follow the economy of the sexual drive, procuring intensely lived experience and acute intoxications. My interest lies in the way some art and performance achieve their effects on us not because they make contact with some formed content or memory in us that they activate but by creating dizzyingly intense experiences that meet us at the core of our being.

Bringing Adorno into contact with Laplanche and Glissant, we may thus begin to understand what Adorno meant when he talked about approaching art objects not to make the artwork like ourselves but, rather, to make ourselves more like the artwork (1970). Performance, art, and eroticism do not ask for our consent: we either give ourselves over to them or we do not, which is a different way of saying that these regimes operate under the aegis of limit consent. This brings us to Mia.

Mia

Mia arrived to our first consultation session "six years too late," which is how long it took her to be able to ask for help. Not only, she told me, was she afraid that she would "be made to talk" about her traumatic childhood, but as a Black trans woman, she could not imagine "feeling safe" with *any* therapist—so fucked up is, really, the world.[15] Her three previous consultations with other analysts had confirmed her concerns. So, if she was sitting in my office at this moment, she wanted me to understand, it was not because she wanted to but because she had to: her relationship was declining and transitioning was proving harder than she had expected. It did not take a psychoanalyst to sense the deep vulnerability lurking underneath the surface of Mia's matter-of-fact, no-bullshit demeanor. I instantly liked her.

I listened carefully, asked a few questions, and made a comment that she seemed to find relevant. She softened a bit as we talked. At the end of our first meeting, which I thought had gone well, I asked her if she wanted to return to finish the consultation. She said she did. She asked about my fee. At the time, I was a second-year candidate building my private practice, which means that my fees were comparatively low.[16] I told her my fee, anxious that it would betray how green I was. Instead, it made her angry. She could easily afford it—and, she now revealed, she was in possession of some wealth—but she said that it was more than she wanted to pay. She asked if I had sliding-scale slots available. I said that I did but that I reserved them for people whose need was financial. Predictably, this did not land well. Mia shot back that she found "politically problematic" my asking her to pay more simply because she had money. I was taken aback by her sense of entitlement. I started wishing I had brought up the fee myself on our initial call, even though she had not asked about it.[17] Mia was now acting as if I had somehow tricked her by exciting a craving that came at too high a price. Then, as if something previously obscure had become illuminated, she pointed her finger at me and said, "I *did not* consent to this. I *do not* consent to this. *You screwed me.*" I was momentarily frozen, watching myself, as if in slow motion, shape-shift in Mia's mind into someone who violated her. I did not agree with her assessment of what had occurred. I wondered, and told her, if the *this* to which she had not consented was more than just my fee—which, by this point, she had disdainfully informed me she intended to pay. Might it have something to do with her *wanting* to come back? "That's *some* bullshit!" she replied. Time was up, we had to stop. I was more than a little relieved.

The night prior to our second session, Mia had a sexual dream about me. She had been unable to dream in years, so this dream made her unexpectedly hopeful—convincing her that she should work with me. But this also intensified her feeling of vulnerability, so my having "screwed" her in the first session now took center stage. She recounted the dream and then explained the predicament I had put her in: had I mentioned my fee on the phone, she would have never made a first appointment, she would have never met me, she would not now be finding herself in the position of wanting to work with me, and, therefore, she "would have never gotten into this mess," where her "only option" was to pay me "an uncomfortable amount." But now it was too late. The damage was done. Since she now did not want to see someone else, she would have to "submit" to me. Furiously silent, Mia weighed her options.

Finally, she said she could only see one way forward: she was willing to begin an analytic treatment with me, meeting four times a week, but only on the condition that we both understand that she would be entering analysis against her consent. Suffice it to say, this did not thrill me. The work is hard enough as it is, and starting an analysis with someone who already felt that I had "screwed" her made me nervous. In all honesty, I had somewhat soured to the idea of working with her. If you are thinking that that is already a lot of drama for two sessions, that is because it is. But, I hasten to add, it is also how the work proceeds, through the patient's dynamics becoming dramatized—that is, enacted and lived out—between the patient and the analyst through the action of the unconscious. Usually, however, it takes much longer for this kind of intensity to develop in a therapeutic relationship, and, as such, these two sessions forecast a tumultuous treatment.[18]

So it may surprise you to hear that I accepted Mia's condition.

There were several reasons. First, I was utterly fascinated by the way consent was being problematized so early on in the treatment. When referring to something becoming "problematized," we usually mean that it is being turned into a problematic, converted from something self-evident to something that may be queried. In psychoanalytic work, something becomes problematized not in the verbal, dialogic exchange but, rather, in the way it becomes inserted in the transference: not through words but in the way it gets under the analyst's skin, in the way it *acts on* the analyst—in this case, then, on me.[19]

Second, although Mia and I had not yet explicitly spoken about our racial difference (and would not until later in the treatment), I sensed— not yet able to articulate why—that Mia's insistence that the treatment was starting against her consent was less about the fee per se. Could the "drama" around it have been the medium through which something about race was getting played out in the session? (In fact, the work that followed proved that that was the case.)[20] Racial difference entered the consulting room not through language about race or racism but encoded in our discussion about consent.[21]

Last, I was especially intrigued that, in Mia's experience, I had somehow *seduced* her by arousing in her the longing to work with me. In those early meetings, Mia had not yet used the word "seduction," as she later would. But the idea was presaged in her sexual dream of me: in the dream, she met someone who shared some physical features with me for a blind date; the woman teased and then left her "hanging out to dry." Mia was not right about my "tricking" her, but she was also not wrong. The analytic situation, in its promise of deep listening, in its offer of an unusual and outlandish intimacy, and in its careful guarding of the asymmetry between analyst and patient, always involves an inadvertent "ethical seduction" (Chetrit-Vatine, 2014).[22]

Seduction, however, as the term is used by Laplanche, is not unique to the psychoanalytic situation; it is part of the process of human subjectivation overall. In other words, it is not a deceitful ruse by which the other is entrapped, though it does involve an unauthorized trespass—in that the adult's perverse effraction into the infant is beyond "consent" and leaves behind an imprint that indelibly marks the child. We will revisit seduction in chapters 1 and 2 of this volume, and it will help us discern how subjectivity and the subject-object relation are inaugurated through encounters that materialize at the border of our consent, encounters that create a messiness from which we can never fully extricate ourselves and that, to boot, vibrate on an erotic frequency.

Accordingly, although Mia's "dramatic" beginning comes to us from the consulting room, it raises issues that are not unique to psychoanalytic work. We are all routinely humbled by how our experience of autonomy and sense of sovereignty are delimited by the unexpected and the unforeseen arising in our encounter with the other. Such contact with opacity and with the unknown may whet appetites we did not know we had, embroiling us in situations we may have not chosen to get tangled into. We do not always get to draft the conditions of our interpersonal encounters, encounters to which we have to sometimes submit, sometimes surrender, to get part of what we need or want. Such surrender, Mia's case underscores, is not necessarily welcome or relieving—that is, Mia was not thrilled with the circumstances of our origin story, and neither was I. But let us also note, recalling Carmen from earlier in our discussion, that while Carmen did not blame Ava but recoiled from the experience, Mia accused me but did not recoil. Her inventive solution (that we work together against her consent) could be seen as an effort to find a way to stay in relation with me, not to move away from but to move *into* the gap-space between us. We could say that I, too, in agreeing to start analytic work under this peculiar premise, relinquished my hold over the way I understand how the work should begin.[23] To enter the analytic relationship at all, then, Mia and I both had to suspend our expectations—and both of us did so against our consent, having to bend our will. Of course, Mia's dynamics inform what she brings to and how she handles her feelings about my fee.[24] The same applies for me and my handling of the situation—however good I think my reasons may be. An "ethical relation to alterity," writes León, does not "sediment difference into a domesticated realm" (2020a, p. 169), which means that Mia's original presentation was not a hurdle to be cleared but the very site of our ethical engagement. Such ethical engagement will not always be easy, uncomplicated, or generous, which is one reason why we may not come to it willingly but despite ourselves—as was the case with Mia and me.[25] To surpass this resistance, both Mia and I had to bend our wills, to step not just into the unknown but into terrain that felt somewhat tricky or dangerous to both of us.

***

Psychoanalysis has treated racial, gendered, and sexual otherness atrociously, so if even the invocation of the term sets off red flags, you are in good company. And even when more inclusive, psychoanalysis remains easily caught in the stranglehold of neoliberal logics, inculcated in prioritizing thinking about productivity or value. In chapter 4 I discuss how the concepts of sublimation and creativity offer themselves as alibis for this capitalist slant. To me, however, the analyst's job is not to heal: it is to resist the narrative of restoration or repair, to refuse the idea that anyone ever returns to some prelapsarian moment, to the restoration of innocence before trauma, or to a harmonious reconciliation toward a utopian future. The analyst, in other words, cannot afford to be traumatophobic; she needs to be traumatophilic. Much more important than repair is a nondominating relationship between the subject (the ego) and her unconscious, which also means a nondominating relationship between the subject and the object. What this requires is a frustrating of the subject's desire (her will) to master the world through conceptual and practical activity, including understanding and "insight." The psychoanalytic attitude involves, rather, signing up for the unexpected, for surprise, and for contradiction. That makes psychoanalysis into an aesthetic practice. It is also what makes it an adventure.

I wrote this book in that vein. I was drawn to writing it as my way of coping with the strain of watching *Slave Play*, a play that, as you will read in chapter 4, overwhelmed and startled me. I wrote this book because I could not look away, because I wanted or, more precisely, because I *needed* to forge a relationship with the aesthetic experience that *Slave Play* roused in me. The risk of reading this book, no less than the risk of writing it, is to experience what happens when we expose ourselves to something unknown, not knowing where it will take us—including to unfamiliar concepts and texts or to defamiliarized uses of concepts and texts we thought we already knew.

I also wrote this book for you, not the plural you but the singular you. You can read it for its ideas, and I hope you will. But this is not only a book about ideas; it is a book that also wants to give you an experience. Writing this way is a risk. It has required a great vulnerability of me. Writing this book has also led me to places I did not expect to go, to experiences I did not expect to have. It has taken me to places that scare me. More than once, I found myself before something much bigger than myself, towering over me. I have written this book so that you can follow me there. You do not know what you will experience, what you will encounter, how it may disturb you, what it might set in motion in you. But if you stay with me, if you go slowly, if you linger in the interstitial spaces between reach and grasp, this book can give you more: it can demand something *of* you. Perhaps you will have an experience yourself.

More than anything, I wrote this book for readers who savor their experiences, who are willing to push themselves to the limits of self-understanding, who are able, and eager even, to bend their will. For readers willing to be pulled out of reason to tread into something raw and tender, for readers who yearn to go beyond the sensible, there is an elsewhere in yourself to which these pages may take you. I have, in fact, written this book imagining you giving yourself over to me, which is a strange thing to say given that I do not know you. Neither do you.

Let us begin.

1

To Suffer Pleasure

Limit Experience and Transgression

But, we have to ask, can there be experiences worthy of the
name, experiences without the robust, integrated subject,
which deny presence, plenitude, interior depth, and narrative completion? Can there be a non-phenomenological notion of an experience that isn't so much actively "lived" as [it
is] suffered and endured?
—Martin Jay, *Modernism and the Retreat from Form*

Abjection, a Sexual Lure

In the fourth year of Adam's four-times-weekly psychoanalysis, he
described the following experience to me: he and his lover were in a foreign country, visiting a bathhouse. Adam was in a sling when a stranger
walked into the room. The stranger's whole being screamed abjection:
he wore a yellowed, stained jockstrap; his hair was noticeably greasy;
and he reeked of cigarettes. Adam found this man ugly, instantly repulsive. He began to feel queasy. His lover left the room in disgust. Adam
hesitated. He, too, had the urge to leave but felt himself strangely compelled "torn between my repulsion and the desire opening up in my
body." Adam stayed in the room, "transfixed by this filthy man." My
patient not only had sex with this abject stranger—though what exactly
he meant by "sex," I never found out—but the experience, he told me,
was intensely memorable. When orgasm came, he said, "I exploded into
thousands of tiny pieces, was hanging out in space like overheated pieces
of dust."

Adam savored this experience. In its aftermath, however, he became
considerably distressed that the suffering of disgust had so voluptuously

potentiated his pleasure. In having stayed in the room and given himself over to the experience animated by his revulsion, Adam had violated something that, to him, was taboo. Adam had made contact with something opaque in himself: staying in the room with this man had felt absolutely necessary to him. His sexual contact with this man also markedly contrasted how Adam understood himself to inhabit his White, middle-class gayness: clean, organized, "together." Straining to account for the way his lush repugnance animated the intensity of his orgasm, he vaguely recalled that this appalling, malodorous man was extravagantly endowed. I was not convinced that size was key and wondered if size were not being retroactively revised to spare Adam the mortification that such a phenomenal orgasm could be caused by the welding of pleasure with disgust.[1] I mention this to underscore that while the theoretical notion that revulsion quickens the erotic was not new to me, my conceptual familiarity did not help me to have something cogent to say about how or why *his* sexual pleasure had become so erotically ionized. At the time, Adam and I were both looking for explanations that would make his desires more legible and his motives more transparent—which is another way of saying that when I was working with Adam, I was still an inexperienced analyst.

For the anthropologist Mary Douglas (1966), revulsion issues from the impulse to purify oneself. Establishing a taxonomy of cleanliness versus dirt and contamination, she argued that something is kept pure and untainted (clean, hygienically organized, together, like Adam) by systematically expelling anything deemed to be out of place (soiled, greasy, abject, like Adam's stranger). For the psychoanalyst Muriel Dimen, sexual disgust has to do with affect: "when passion runs high," she writes, "the balance between love and hate swings nauseatingly" (2005, p. 16). This is where abjection comes in. Within abjection, the psychoanalyst Julia Kristeva intervenes, loom "dark revolts of being, directed against a threat that seems to emanate from an exorbitant outside or inside, ejected beyond the scope of the possible, the tolerable, the thinkable. It lies there, quite close, but it cannot be assimilated" (1982, p. 1). Resisting such revolts is ego-constitutive, helping to consolidate the ego's durable belief in its dominant power over others *and over the rest of the self*. Critical to abjection for Kristeva, as well as for Bataille (1934), is the relationship to our bodies' excess—mucus, snot, puss, pimples, menstrual blood, shit, saliva—which is one of disavowal. We are drawn to these bodily excrements and where we repudiate that draw, disgust arises. For Bataille in particular, the excision of such appetites came hand in hand with human beings becoming "civilized," in our moving away from our animality. On the larger landscape of social relations, abjecting the heterogeneous "other" from the body politic establishes (the illusion of) a homogeneous social order—a project with gender, racial, and class undertones (Tyler, 2013). This, Davis and Dean argue, is also where the problem with democracy and the problem of the sexual converge: both involve elements that are antithetical to the orderly way in which we like to think democratic politics and ethical sexuality (2022). Becoming objects of revulsive hatred as well as ecstatic attraction, the unpalatable elements are excluded, but this exclusion is not "successful" once and for all. It requires constant monitoring. Consider, for instance, how "the invocation of 'Mexican rapists,' 'nasty women,' and a news anchor accused of 'bleeding from her wherever' can aid in restoring the ultimate sovereign white male subject" (Hennefeld & Sammond, 2020, p. 2). The abject trades in repudiation; it traffics in turning away from opacity—and that makes a sustained inquiry into abjection politically necessary. These ideas helped me think about Adam's experience more complexly—for example, I now wondered about how he had read this man's race. This offered the analysis the possibility to probe Adam's Whiteness, and we began to see how he relied on it to consolidate a sense of himself as fundamentally good and pure.

It soon became clear that Adam's sexual encounter had been more than just sensually intoxicating: something transformative was unfolding. Humiliated, yet intensely curious about how the pleasure of abjection spiked his erotic enjoyment, Adam brought to his analysis bits of sensation that were strewn into the moments when he had come undone. These experiential fragments could not be gathered into language well: there was a semihallucinated impression (a fuzzy black object), a distantly reverberating sound (a voice? a cry? he was not sure), a skin sensation he could not place (not a shudder, more like a jolt). Elusive, these surplus meanings set in motion an exploratory process, which revealed them to be momentous for Adam.

Adam's clinical story, in its conjunction between eroticism and abjection, starts us out in the midst of the mess that the sexual is—or, rather, in the midst of the exuberant, generative, unsettling, and challenging mess that sexuality can become when the undecipherable occurs, when one bears the unease of having enjoyed the indignities of sensual pleasures whose memories do not cave under the most strident superego chastisements, delights whose intensities refuse to shrivel under the thick crust of shame. Maintaining a hospitable proximity to such experiences involves resisting the more ordinary tendency to drag them out of their opaqueness to shine on them the light of "insight." This tendency is not unique to the clinical situation: it permeates much theorizing around the erotic overall. To be clear, I am not arguing that nothing can be gleaned from querying what enthralls us erotically, just that such inquiries can only produce intelligible answers that have first passed through the bottleneck of what can be psychically represented ("translated," as we will soon see). The sexual, however, is not meaningful but precisely that which cannot be organized through meaning. The erotic, we might say, has more to do with what appears as an *effect of the unconscious*, when we bend our will to allow ourselves to be disarmed in the encounter with our own and the other's opacity. Said differently, Adam probably found himself disarmed, exploding into pieces of dust, because he was in that friction zone between the opacity of the other (the man was literally a stranger to Adam) and his own. The sexual unease of his disgust, we might say, defamiliarized him *from himself.*

This friction zone between opacities is critical: an exclusive preoccupation with the other's opacity, without the implication of one's own, is a turning away from the erotic. This is one way to think about the ethics of sexual objectification: the problem is not when the other is treated in a sexually objectifying way—being turned into a part-object rather than a full human being, as we will see, is how the sexual drive operates, and many people enjoy being treated that way in sex—but in an objectification of the other that is accompanied by a refusal to come into contact with one's own opacity. The fact that Adam remained in the "friction zone of opacities" is what makes his encounter deeply ethical—but no sooner do I say this than I feel anxious. I am not interested in instituting universal laws to steer ethical relations but in how we may become receptive to our own alterity when relating to others. If there is something deeply ethical about such moments (and I think there is), it has less to do with these encounters being drafted mutually and consensually and more to do with what arises spontaneously in the encounter, not as deliberate, planned action or to evidence "good politics." Such intentionality is actually at odds with the state of being disarmed of one's ego that is critical to the ethics of such experiences. My goal is to navigate perversity's foothold in the unconscious and the way that the bending of the will—remember that Adam wanted to leave the room—can open us up to aesthetic experience.[2] Such experience, as our discussion of Moten in the introduction presaged, has deep ties to the ethical not as legislative attempt but as a susceptibility to our own unconscious.

Polymorphous Perversity

In Freud's early drafts of *Three Essays*, polymorphous perversity is integral to infantile sexuality, and infantile sexuality is the lining that runs through all psychic life (Van Haute & Westerink, 2016). The infantile sexual is not genital: it is dispersed across the skin's surface; it is not organized heteroprocreatively but has diffuse aims; it has exchangeable objects; it is not concerned with the other as a whole person but is oriented, instead, toward body parts ("part-objects"). If the sexual drive, in its very ontology, is concerned with part-objects, we begin to see that infantile sexuality complicates questions around the ethics of objectification or fetishism. Further, its temporality cannot be plotted in chronological time but proceeds, rather, in repetitive spurts and in nonlinear movements. In that sense, perverse sexualities pulsate on "the temporal tangle," they ask "about the temporal leak, and about the many questions that attend time's returns" (Schneider, 2011, p. 10). I purposefully invoke Rebecca Schneider's work to underscore the imbrication between the force of the infantile sexual and some performance. The polymorphously perverse, I argue, surges through some theater—though not so much through the themes it tackles but via the exigency with which the art and its themes *act on us*. In that sense, some performance re-presents the infantile sexual (Scarfone, 2015b), though not in the citational sense of "twice-behaved behavior" (Schechner, 1985, p. 36) or as in reenactment (Pellegrini & Shimakawa, 2018; Schneider, 2011) but by exciting us. By "exciting," I do not mean that it enthuses us or that it turns us on, though these may also happen, but in the etymological sense: to excite, Jean-François Lyotard writes, comes from *citare*, which means "to set in motion, to arouse," and from *ex-*, "to bring forth, . . . to awaken" (2002, p. 23). That action, as we will explore in chapters 4 and 5, is especially pronounced in forms of performance that excite our perversity. Putting the erotic in conversation with the iterative modalities of time (Chambers-Letson, 2020; Colbert, Jones, & Vogel, 2020; Pellegrini & Shimakawa, 2018), I zero in on the kind of art that Jennifer Doyle has described as difficult and as provoking moral outrage (2013).

Restless and pervasive, the infantile sexual is not something we outgrow or mature out of (Scarfone, 2014), it remains boundlessly energetic inside us. Beyond the limits of gender, sexual difference, and reproduction, it is not a sexuality that seeks climax but ever-intensifying tension. I am recuperating the quintessentially psychoanalytic idea of polymorphous perversity because staying connected with the theory of infantile sexuality will help us refrain from futile efforts to understand the force of perversity by reducing it to a behavioral set of sexualities that need to, or can, be explicated. Rather, I argue for perversity as an erotic possibility with political potential, the vicissitudes of which deserve the effort and nuance of our critical attention. In making this claim, I follow the psychoanalyst Ken Corbett, who, in 1997, urged us not to ask "why" homosexuality but "how" homosexuality, an intervention more recently repurposed by the psychoanalyst Griffin Hansbury in regard to trans experience (2017). Hanbury asks not "why" trans (that is, what "causes" or "explains" trans) but what do people do with their transness and to what effects. Arguing in favor of "how" perversity may seem outdated in today's academic landscape—even in some (small) pockets of the psychoanalytic world. But I insist on it because the press to locate origin stories that account for the nonnormative is nowhere near extinct even in progressive circles (if you are unsure that this is still the case, wait until we get to the discussion of *Slave Play* in chapter 3 and to the conversation of *The Night Porter* in chapter 5). Asking "why" exceptionalizes perversity when perversity is ever present. To me, the more interesting questions regarding perversion ask after the forms in which the perverse manifests itself and after the way it acquires its particular shape. For Freud, perversion "is something innate in everyone" (1905b, p. 171); what varies is only its intensity and the shape it takes to appear phenomenally. By that statement, Freud did not mean that everyone is a behavioral pervert (not that there would be anything wrong with that) but that all sexuality, independently of its behavioral expression, has the alien and the perverse swirled in it. If the perverse underwrites all sexuality, rather than ask perversity to account for itself, we might, instead, ask after docile, tame, and subdued sexualities that may suffer from having *lost their footing* in the perverse.

Adam's vignette provides a framework that will help us investigate how erotic experience may be further quickened by racialization and how perversity can help us imagine audiences "who *don't* want closure, whose readings practices are not fueled by a penetrative, epistemic drive moving always towards 'deeper' levels of meaning" (Doyle, 2013, p. xiii). I propose a set of psychoanalytic tools that offer a vantage point routed through the perverse that shifts the weight of our attention from hounding for causative chains and chasing after meaning to exploring what happens when we allow ourselves to become subject to the force and to the impetus emergent in perversity. That there is potential in perversity is, of course, not a new idea at all; queer theory (Bersani, 1986; Davis & Dean, 2022; Dean, 2008, 2009, 2012; Halperin, 1995; Stockton, 2006) and queer of color critique (Chambers-Letson, 2020; Cruz, 2016; Musser, 2014; Rodríguez, 2014; D. Scott, 2010) have already argued these points convincingly. My Laplanchean approach adds to these conversations by showing *how* some erotic practices build their transformational density, by showing that some types of aesthetic experience have important ties to the perverse, by naming some of the resistances that arise in us in the encounter with the liminal forces of the infantile sexual which turn us away from encountering opacity, and by offering a different approach to perverse pleasures that evades perversion's conceptual fate of being either pathologized or kneecapped by incurious, liberal acceptance.

My hope is to whet an appetite for theorizing the alien and the bizarre in sexuality not from within a state of alarm or from the rubric of tolerance (Jakobsen & Pellegrini, 2004) but by sitting with the *force* of shock that can facilitate (through processes I discuss) an encounter with opacity. "Opacity," Perry Zurn describes, "insists upon a space for curiosity, marked not by clarity but complexity . . . where histories break, and incommensurability cracks open" (2021, p. 206). Even the most progressive and capacious queer thinking can run aground in theorizing the perverse—and nowhere do we hit this impasse with more difficulty or urgency than in the domain of race and racial difference. Consider, for example, how even as capacious a thinker as the queer theorist José Muñoz strained to make sense of Gary Fisher, a gay Black man whose erotic desires were organized around wanting to be sexually dominated by an older White man. That Fisher's eroticism elided the "anticipatable calculus of equivalence ending in some recognition of the self in the other" (Muñoz, 2019, p. 199) effectively stripped previously relied-on conceptual tools of their explanatory power. "Gary Fisher's writing," Muñoz admits, "is a challenge for those of us who toil in the archives of collective historical dispossession" (2019, p. 197). Fisher's sexual perversity, quickened through the accelerant of racial trauma, becomes thematized in chapter 3. What I want to highlight here is that desires like Fisher's might be easier to navigate if we try to approach them not to "grasp" what motivates them but to respect the inassimilable strangeness of the infantile sexual (what Muñoz calls the "incommensurable"). This directs our attention, instead, to the way perversity's thrust appears phenomenally. Desires that embroil the trauma of the Holocaust in the erotic, as is the case with Liliana Cavani's *The Night Porter*, pose a similar difficulty, waging important conceptual battles about "the future of the past" (Schneider, 2011, p. 4).

While I mostly focus on racial and larger historical traumata, the points I raise can also, with some modifications, be considered for other kinds of trauma. Dorothy Allison, in her autobiographical novel *Bastard out of Carolina* (1992), points us to the way her sexual abuse becomes knitted into her masturbation fantasies and her erotic sensibility. In my classes on psychosexuality, I also read with candidates the anonymously authored *Incest Diary* (2017), a memoir discussing father-daughter sexual incest. Contrary to most such personal accounts, the narrator opens with descriptions of the author's erotic response to her father that are startlingly pornographic, disrupting the genre of memoir-writing on incest. Both these books discuss perverse erotics that cannot be discounted as residual scar tissue without also callously knocking down the ways in which Allison and the anonymous author have fashioned their erotic lives: not by trying to "overcome" trauma but by folding it into their erotic complexion, a traumatophilic approach that we will discuss in depth.

Toward a Theory of Perversity

From a behavioral standpoint, I use the term "perversion" to designate a polymorphous sexual process—rather than circumscribed sex acts—that issue from the materiality of the body, which involve internal experience and which engage, rather than resist, the exigent forces of the infantile sexual. Interembodied, encounters that are experienced as transgressive move toward the "more and more" of experience—and when this escalation becomes unbearable, they can shatter the ego (more on this shortly). Which acts will be experienced as transgressive varies widely: lines of prohibition are perched on the highly personal divide between the intrapsychic, the social, and the historical—that is, who does what to whom, in what context, and at what point in time. And they are also liable to being judged differently based on subject positionality and the degree of privilege accorded them by the socius (Dimen, 2005; Kulick & Rydström, 2015; Srinivasan, 2021). But here I am interested in what is *felt* to be transgressive, because it is that experiential excess that will ultimately contribute to the subject's feeling overwhelmed enough for anything new to occur: for one, it may be the shame of anal penetration; for another, the longing to be reduced to begging one's lover; for a third, a forced feminization script. What makes one's sexuality perverse is not the precise script enacted but the imbrication of transgression with the intensities of the body's libidinal excitability. The former lures the self into crashing through its own regulatory walls, one's idiosyncratically sutured line of prohibition, while the latter inundates the subject with indecipherable messages from the other: What does this person want from me? What did that look/gasp/touch mean? (Laplanche calls these "enigmatic," as we will soon see.)

I am advocating that we accord more serious attention to perversion rather than treating it as an unfairly misunderstood set of nonnormative sexual practices, an approach that too readily forfeits the importance of engaging perversion's reach. Delving more deeply into such practices can help us sidestep the dipole of perversity as either pathology or benign variation—a concept we find in Freud, who noted "the human need for [sexual] variation" (1905b, p. 151), and in Gayle Rubin, whose plea to acknowledge a wide range of possible sexual appetites in human psychosexuality first put this notion on the queer theory map (1984/2011).[3] Rubin's intervention was an admirable, path-clearing effort to carve space for diverse sexual expression, but thirty-five years later, it may now look to us somewhat asthenic—not because its mission has been fully realized (it has not) but because we can now afford to ask more nuanced questions after sexual desires.[4]

Conventionally, we tend to see pleasure and suffering as belonging to ontologically disparate spheres, but Adam's example illustrates that an erotic arc links the two. Psychoanalysis has not fared well when it comes to exploring the coextensiveness of suffering and eroticism, though this snag is not psychoanalysis's problem alone. In *Three Essays*, Freud articulated the sexual as ontologically deviant, considering sadism and masochism as the most important of the perversions.[5] "As regards active algolagnia, sadism," he wrote, "the roots are easy to detect in the normal [person]"; all sexuality "contains an element of aggressiveness—a desire to subjugate" (1905b, p. 156). Freud, of course, was not unambivalent about the revolutionary nature of his propositions. He thus darts back and forth between the notion that sexuality is definitionally polymorphously perverse and the idea that a postpubertal, mature sexuality will eventually remand the perverse to a sexual sidekick. Provided, says Freud, that one does not linger in foreplay, forgoing "the real thing" (penetrative heterosexual sex), perversion can furnish that "extra" momentum to get you to your real destination, which is none other than orgasm. In (the normative parts of) Freud's developmental theory, therefore, the sexual efflorescence of infantile sexuality (masochism, sadism, scopophilia, exhibitionism, and homoeroticism) becomes compressed into genital and procreative coherence. The terms "developmental theory" and "developmental stages" are, of course, psychoanalytic jargon for normalization: by telling us how things are expected to evolve, they direct the analyst's clinical attention to where intervention is needed.[6] Freud's wavering notwithstanding, his daringly original insight argued that sadism, masochism, exhibitionism, homosexuality, and even "attraction . . . that overrides the barriers of the species" (1905b, p. 148) are all elements of the sexual.

Has Freud gone too far in this passing reference to bestiality? If so, this is our reminder that for him the perverse really does involve the objectionable and the utterly unthinkable, not just the socially abjected. Even as Freud has given us this list, the question of where we draw the ethical line, and, most importantly, based on what principles, continues to be up for debate. If the example of bestiality made you uncomfortable, you are not alone. The psychoanalyst Dominique Scarfone helps put some of the complexities of polymorphous perversity in context by clarifying that when it comes to polymorphous perversity, the stress should be placed not on the perverse elements alone but also on the polymorphousness by which the infantile sexual makes itself known to us (2014). For an example of what a polymorphous erotics of bestiality could look like, think of Sophie Lewis's commentary on the Oscar-winning documentary *My Octopus Teacher* (2021). The documentary's protagonist begins to "visit" an octopus, a voyeuristic visitation that vibrates on an erotic frequency with colonial undertones. This voyeurism is awash in perversity; in fact, it is, in some sense, queer because it is so vertiginously perverse.[7]

Still, while Freud's formulation that polymorphous perversity is endemic to our sexual constitution is much cited, it is usually quickly passed over. For the most part, perversion is read as sexuality con-scripted into dismal repetitions of the traumatic past (Bach, 1994; Kern-berg, 1995; Novick & Novick, 2012) or as the death drive's cooptation of the sexual (Joseph, 1971, 1982; Steiner, 1982). Even analysts who have been thinking more expansively about the multivalent nature of sex-ual perversions, like Robert Stoller (1975) and Joyce McDougall (1995, 2000), gloss over the fact that sexuality is de facto imbricated in per-versity. Treating the interimplication of suffering with pleasure as a failure of the sexual function that requires therapeutic restoration (e.g., Holtzman & Kulish, 2012) leaves out experiences like Adam's. Adam was not self-destructive or reckless, and his experience only enlarged him. Rumbling in the background are sex panics (Rubin, 1984/2011), as well as what Corbett has called the anxiety of regulation (2009): a set of ecstatic anxieties that obtain from the encounter with nonnormativity and that animate the anxious press to regulate the other so as to soothe oneself. Under the aegis of such anxieties, it is easy to get caught in the defensively mobilized quicksand of colonizing the other's sexual par-ticularities by "confus[ing] what the[y] . . . mean to [us] with what the[y] mean" to themselves (Dimen, 2001, p. 833). In the clinical setting, such responses foreclose the analyst's genuine curiosity, blocking important queries into the psychic uses of pleasure that is suffered. In the nonclinical domain, they can give rise to censorship and shaming or, alternatively, to the patch that is identity and that covers our opacity. One might think that such theories are nowadays mere historical artifacts, relics of a time long gone. But we need only to turn to the way sexuality is regarded today in the larger culture, as something that requires legal fervor and suffocating specificity, and to note the relentless push for an increasingly antiseptic administering of sexuality, to which affirmative consent is stipulated to offer a remedy (Fischell, 2019).

Thinking about perversion is rife with pathologizing discourses. To avoid reflexive pathologization, some authors rely on the relational arrangement within which perversity manifests itself. Perverse sexual relations, some propose, should be considered "normal" when they are mutually enjoyed within the contours of emotionally intimate relationships (Slavin et al., 2004). Similarly, the influential psychoanalyst Otto Kernberg recasts behaviors that are otherwise deemed perverse, such as bondage and domination, into playful sexual adventures as long as they are performed within matrimony's normativizing confines (1995). For Jessica Benjamin, it is mutuality, equality, and intersubjective recognition that spare polymorphous pleasures from being seen as pathologically perverse. What is wrong with emphasizing equality, you may reasonably wonder. Discourses that stake the permissibility of perverse desires on equity are oblivious to the effects of social asymmetries issuing from racial difference, class disparities, citizenship standing, disability status, and so on. To demand equality as a precondition for sexual variation to be deemed "benign" is to effectively exclude relations between subjects with intersecting minoritarian identities from the captivating affinities between pleasure, pain, and anguish.

These affinities have been heatedly debated in feminist circles, producing political rifts as well as invigorated thinking (Duggan & Hunter, 2006; Hollibaugh, 2000; Lorde, 1982; Rubin, 1984/2011; Vance, 1992; Walker, 1982). And they have also shown that while lessons in good politics can leave us gasping with shame, they do not leave us breathless with arousal (see also Duggan, 2021). Consider, as an example, how many women, straight and queer, entertain rape fantasies or enact play-rape scenes with lovers. Such desires are often interpreted as indexing women having become conscripted into participating in their own violation (e.g., MacKinnon, 2007).[8] We are still at an impasse as to how to understand them otherwise. It is that lacuna that makes politically vexed desires vulnerable to the perennial "why" that we cannot stop asking of them. My project looks for another entry point into these debates, one that neither denies the historical and structural circumstances that condition such desires nor surrenders perverse sexual appetites to the cold shower of ethics or good politics. Suffering is often experienced alongside pleasure not only because the material sexual body can become a lightning rod for psychic pain but also because the transgressive blend of flesh and intersubjective engagement can render the pain/pleasure matrix a portal for experience. Again, I am using the word "experience" here not in its ordinary meaning, as in having an experience *of* something as when we take the reins of subjectivity, but as something that we risk when we soften our grasp on those reins, to undergo something the coordinates and effects of which can not be secured or anticipated. When we are talking about pleasure and pain, there is no universal; experience varies widely, and what is aesthetic experience to one person may not be so for others. The ethical is thus not about legislating what is right or wrong, it is about acknowledging that in the erotic domain there are no universals. Experience so defined stands to bring us into contact with our raw being. This is what Adorno called "experimentation": rather than something we can name, understand, explicate—as Adam and I initially tried to do—such experience throws us off balance.[9]

Attachment Theory, a Normative Theory

To explore why thinking about sexuality alongside trauma is so difficult theoretically, we will need to understand first the ideas that underwrite the presumption that sexuality is about love or about feeling connected and bonded. Two theoretical currents contribute to this: The first, to be explored in chapter 2, has to do with Freud having "go[ne] astray," as Laplanche describes it (2006b, p. 185), in eventually settling on theorizing sexuality as operating centripetally, that is, as oriented toward linking and organizing. This fastened the erotic to love, to relationality, and to interpersonal connection—that is, to relating to the other as a whole object even though the sexual drive operates according to part-object logics. This move drained sexuality from its more discomfiting and disruptive dimensions. The other theoretical current that has made it very hard to think about sexuality outside of relationality per se has to do with attachment theory, a set of theories that exclusively situate all human functioning, including sexuality, in the quality of the bond developed between the child and their primary caretakers. Situating the sensual lusciousness of the mother-infant dyad at the constitutive epicenter of psychosexual life (Seligman in Slavin et al., 2004), attachment theory argues for sexuality as an expression of relating that privileges connection, deep bonds, and mutuality. This yielded a rather impoverished theory of sexuality in which the mysterious plenitudes of the erotic, not to mention the erotic frisson of power differentials, go limp (see Mitchell, 2003). Unsurprisingly, such mother-infant dyads are heedlessly imagined as White, middle class, cis-gender, and able-bodied, and are usually imagined as nested in a heterosexually organized normative family structure. This blanched-out, homogenized thinking persists despite the fact that its normative strivings have been heavily critiqued both inside and outside psychoanalysis (Davis & Dean, 2022; Dimen, 2001; Edelman, 2004; Eng, 2001, 2010; Eng & Han, 2019; González, 2020).

Desexualizing the parent-infant dyad sidesteps many of the difficulties that arise when visceral eroticism surfaces in relationships of care. More specifically, research shows that while caretakers name and mirror children's affect when it comes to anger or sadness, sexual affects are almost always ignored (Fonagy, 2008; Target, 2007)—the adult looks away, breaks eye contact, refrains from offering language, and so on. This is not mere avoidance (though it is also that); it has to do with the difficulty posed by the sexual. What, after all, asks the psychoanalyst Jody Davies (2001), would be the equivalent response to an empathic registration of a child's sexual arousal that would not amount to sexualizing the relationship? We may say to a child, "you must be sad," mirroring their sadness, but we cannot say, "you must be turned on," and certainly cannot mirror their excitement. Anxieties about how dizzying erotic affect can be also arise in the consulting room as hibernating desires can awaken in the erotic heat of the therapeutic relationship. The same goes for the classroom, where things can also become vertiginously erotic.

Importantly, attachment theory has not been merely a theoretical turn but has become the predominant theoretical paradigm that organizes thinking around the sexual—and not just in psychoanalysis—

though thankfully, within psychoanalysis, some authors have continued to write about the astonishing libidinal power of pleasure. For example, the influential analyst Ruth Stein notes the extraordinary poignancy of sexual experience, giving us an understanding of psychosexuality as always already dysregulated (1998, 2008). Muriel Dimen also has urged analysts to think alongside arousal (1999) and not to recoil from the excitements of disgust (2005) and perversity (2001). Her work queries the analyst's squeamishness, noting the multiple ways in which personal anxieties about the intensities of sexual experience get churned into theoretical formulations that are then elevated to orthodoxy. Even this more expansive thinking about the psychosexual, however, is quick to qualify the "dangers" inherent to sexuality and can see excitement and arousal as swarming with menacing risks. Stein, for example, warns that libidinal thrills may get out of hand, cautioning us as analysts to ensure that our patients' libido not feed on exploitation (2005b). Concerned that the erotic may "deteriorate into obscenity" (2005a, p. 26), Stein emphasizes the importance of working with the patient to regulate the intensities of the patient's sexual passions lest they get out of hand. The normative dangers of such regulation are obvious, but, to list them shortly here, we can easily imagine that some subjects' racialization or gendered embodiment may unevenly "select" them for such regulation and that, similarly, nonnormative desires may also more readily be diagnosed as being dangerously voluptuous and out of control. As for Stein's caution about sexuality becoming exploitative or entailing the other's erasure, I want to call attention to how violation and trauma seem to be the only imaginable possibilities when one treads beyond the well-regulated domain of the sexual. When it comes to the erotic, limits of one sort or another always slip in as critical to the preservation of order. The role of the limit in this context is one of guardianship: to ensure that pleasure will not disband the Law or throw the subject into disarray.[10] Pitting the limit against pleasure, however, overlooks that psychosexuality is amplified through prohibition.[11] This lesson, handed down to us by the Marquis de Sade (1795/1966c, 1797/1966a), appears in its more contemporary iterations in the work of Georges Bataille (1957) on transgression. We will turn to that work shortly. But first, we will need a theory of psychosexuality that is less panicked about the intensities of sexual excitement.

Jean Laplanche: *The Fundamental Anthropological Situation*

For Laplanche, the other has a foundational and, in fact, inaugural impact on psychic formation.[12] Critiquing the Ptolemaism dominating analytic thinking, which positioned the self at the center of its own psychic universe (with the sun going round the Earth), he fleshed out a Copernican theory that privileges otherness (1992b). In emphasizing the primacy of the other in the constitution of the unconscious and the ego, he thus shares with Glissant an interest in allocentrism. Here are the main tenets of his theorizing regarding the constitution of the psychic apparatus.

Let us consider a father who, in cleaning his son during a diaper change, applies slightly, but identifiably, less pressure on the infant's anal area.[13] Why might that be? The short answer is that we do not know. But we could guess: it could be that incest anxiety kicked in or that homoerotic anxiety inhibited him or that he got worried that such touching would be in some way "inappropriate," too sexual, and so on. Whatever the case may be, we see that the adult's attachment-message to the child (e.g., "let me clean you and make you comfortable") was surcharged with something else. This spillover, which "contaminates" the message, as Laplanche described it, issues from the adult's own sexual unconscious, which is awakened through the adult's contact with the child's profound embodied vulnerability. For Laplanche, the adult's exposure to the infant's radical helplessness specifically awakens the adult's perversity (i.e., his sexual unconscious), though it is important to note that Laplanche does not have in mind a disturbed adult but, rather, speaks to the kindling of the normative perversity in all adults. In fact, he considers this unintended and inadvertent "intervention of the other" (Laplanche, 1987, p. 143) on the child so universal that he calls it the "Fundamental Anthropological Situation" (FAS). Returning to the diaper-change scene, the infant senses this surcharge in the adult's message. How? He senses it through the embodied relation, precisely because this surcharge has produced a shift in *how* the father touched his skin (the "identifiably less pressure.") The infant registers this change in a very rudimentary way; the infant senses that "something" happened, but what that something was is unclear to him. It is, in Laplanchean terminology, enigmatic. It is enigmatic not because it represents an intellectual challenge to the child's yet-undeveloped mind (though that is also true) but because, having issued from the father's sexual unconscious in the first place, its meaning is unknown *and unknowable* even to the father, who, as is often the case, may not even be aware that he touched the anus differently.

The infant receives the adult's enigmatic surplus *as* a message, as something *meant to communicate something to him*, even as enigma is not really a message addressed to anyone but a spillover of the parent's unconscious.[14] Enigma, then, functions as an "internal foreign body." Having pierced the child's psychophysiological surface (the skin) through, in this example, the "identifiably less pressure," enigma is a question mark without an answer: What was my father trying to say to me? Why did he touch me differently there? and so on. This process (of enigma's effraction into the infant), which Laplanche called "implantation," is strangely traumatic, and the interference it introduces "must at all costs be mastered and integrated" (2003b, p. 208). Implantation's indelible trauma, to be clear, is not in the order of meaning. That is, the infant is not traumatized because he senses the father's homoeroticism or picks up on the father's incestuous anxiety (remember, it is I who made the hypothesis that the father struggled with that). What the infant is traumatized by is the implantation of something unknowable (enigmatic) in him. Implantation, then, is traumatic because of its indelible *effect* on the infant's psyche. The son in our example is left with this enigmatic implant that is "'stuck' in the envelope of the ego like a splinter in the skin" (Laplanche, 1999, p. 209).

The infant is impelled to make meaning out of these enigmatic implants to cope with the strain of the way the adult's perversity has "broken into" his psychic envelope. Laplanche called this meaning-making process "translation," and it is important to remember that translation is not about "translating" the secret meaning of enigma but about coating its opaqueness with an ascribed meaning. For Scarfone (2016), translation is akin to fantasizing. The ego develops out of the cumulative layerings of these translations, that is, through the aggregate effects of enigma's meaning-filled coatings. As such, the ego is established as an apparatus that constructs meaning (symbols, fantasies, etc.) and that binds (organizes) enigma. Enigma, said differently, is organized into fantasies and representations. I cannot emphasize enough that these translations are neither correct nor incorrect decodings of the adult's intentions but simply efforts to master the unintelligibility of the adult's communication (Scarfone, 2021). To put it simply, the ego is made up of psychic representations that are more energetically stable (more bound psychic energy), while enigma is energetically charged and, thus, more mobile and less stable (unbound energy). Unbound energy threatens the coherence and stability of the more bound form (the ego, identity), and translation—the binding of unruly energy into more durable forms—is a reduction in intensity that works to reduce that threat. Fantasy and representation, to put it differently, are a form of management.

This self-theorizing is what also distinguishes humans from nonhuman animals: the human subject, writes Laplanche, "is a self-theorizing being . . . humans are self-symbolizing" (1987, p. 14). The notion that our humanity inheres in our capacity to wrest meaning out of trauma, means that humans are not just driven to symbolize but that we *become* human by engaging in the activity of symbolizing. It is our capacity to translate again and again that furnishes our humanity and this, we will see in chapters 3 and 4, has significant implications for thinking about racialization in general and about Blackness in particular.

Translation, Laplanche believed, never quite fully manages to coat enigma with meaning, and, as such, no translation is ever complete: an ineffable, untranslated remainder always remains. These "unworked chunks" (Laplanche, 1992a, p. 12) float inside the infant's psyche. Unbound by the ego, they dwell inside us *on a somatic register* that exceeds psychic organization. "Resistant to all metabolization" (Laplanche, 1999, p. 136), these remainders become repressed (Laplanche called this "primal repression"), which is how the unconscious is formed. Repression congeals these highly charged elements, reifying them into what comes to feel alien and opaque to us about ourselves. This is what Laplanche calls the unconscious, and we see that, for him, repression *creates* (rather than populates) the unconscious. Repressed enigma will continue to press for translation, constituting the sexual drive. The sexual drive will henceforth exert an exciting, compulsive power, a sense of exigency (Laplanche, 2006b). This exigency, I add, both propels and frightens us: following it draws us closer to ourselves but also involves overcoming a gradient of resistance *to ourselves*.

For Laplanche, the unconscious is sexual through and through, and it is synonymous with infantile sexuality.[15] The unconscious and infantile sexuality are, thus, established as fundamentally alien to the self, as persistently and hauntingly other (Laplanche, 1999), always "resistant to straightforward intelligibility" (Davis & Dean, 2022, p. 19). By definition that which we cannot possess, sexuality is never "ours": it is, rather, the way in which we become "dispossessed through the address of the other" (Butler, 2005, p. 54)—though by "address," Laplanche does not refer to the other addressing us but to the way in which we respond to the other's enigmatic intervention by imagining it to address us. If our sexuality is never fully ours, if it is constituted through the inevitable failures of translation, we see that sexuality is not a domain where we may ever have sovereign control or reliable self-understanding.[16] To the contrary, it is a part of ourselves that we can only be drawn closer to, and that drawing closer happens through our opacity. That, as we will see, has considerable implications for thinking about sexual politics and raciosexual trauma. For now, however, let us stay with noticing how a Laplanchean unconscious is ontologically opaque from the outset: not a treasury of repressed memories, fantasies, and affects but an energetically unsubordinated realm that resists the ordering force of the ego.

Memories, fantasies, and affects also get repressed, and that process Laplanche calls "secondary repression." Secondary repression is what other analysts (and everyday language) mean when we say that something was "repressed"—the removal from consciousness of unbearable memories, traumatic experience, or ideas that are incompatible with the way we view ourselves. For Laplanche, however, secondary repression is secondary in the sense that what it represses has *already* been translated, that is, has already been subjected to some degree of psychic organization. Secondarily repressed material does not get "stored" in the unconscious (remember, the unconscious is of an order that definitionally resists all psychic organization) as fantasies, memories, and the like but in what Laplanche called the "pseudo-unconscious." The prefix "pseudo-" is not meant to imply falsity of content (repressed memories, fantasies, affects, etc. are always true on the level of psychic reality) but that it is not a truly dynamic, reconfigurable entity. Material that has been repressed secondarily is not part of the unconscious (as a psychic structure); it is unconscious only in the sense that it is not consciously accessible to us and cannot be called up at will.

There are interesting affinities between Laplanche's notion of the unconscious and Glissant's thinking on opacity. Glissant explains that opacity resists "enclosure within an impenetrable autarchy" (1990, p. 191). Like the unconscious, which cannot be recovered but only coated with meaning, opacity also requires that we "give up this old obsession with discovering what lies at the bottom of natures" (Glissant, 1990, p. 190). Similar to Laplanche, Glissant also stays attendant to what resists capture, as "seizure or grasp is the very thing [he] seeks to undo with his notion of opacity" (León, 2020a, p. 182). Importantly, Glissant understands this desire/urge/impulse to capture as being deeply rooted in the tradition of Western philosophical thought and as giving rise to colonial violence. For Laplanche, the urge to seize and grasp is more rooted in the psyche's need to cope with the dis-order introduced by the intervention of the other's sexual unconscious. So while Glissant and Laplanche share an allocentric focus, they have a different understanding of where the impulse to dominate over the external other comes from. For Glissant, "seizure or grasp" is an appropriative impulse that involves the imposition of a Western framework on other cultures that seek to rapaciously assimilate the foreign into its own systems of thought.

Even though Glissant thinks with coloniality and worldliness and Laplanche stays in the domain of interiority and the self (as the psychoanalytic tradition problematically often does), it is possible to put them in conversation to profitably expand both. What Glissant adds to Laplanchean metapsychology is a way of thinking more critically about psychoanalysis's seemingly benign preoccupation with "understanding" our patients and trying to exhaustively account for the patient's psychic productions.[17] What Laplanche's thinking may add to Glissant's formulation about opacity is that the opaque may not be languid but restless, and that it has a force and an impact that may be specifically energetically sexual. That would situate the opaque in an energetic regime that stands to unsettle the ego's homeostatic hold, helping us understand why opacity "materializes as a resistance" (León, 2020a, p. 172)—to think of opacity both as generating resistance and also as introducing an energetic disquiet that can itself resist established meanings of world-making. Let us bracket this issue for now to loop back to Laplanche.

An especially important aspect of Laplanche's theory is that parental implantations, even when pleasurable—or, I would say, perhaps especially then—involve in their excessiveness the experience of painful shock: "The necessarily traumatic intervention of the other must entail," he notes, "most often in a minor way but sometimes in a major one—*the effraction or breaking in characteristic of pain*" (1999, p. 123; emphasis added). This space between the parent's enigmatic leak and the infant's translation is necessary for the emergence of the ego, and, thus, of the subject. We see, then, that subject formation originates from the other's enigmatic effraction into us, an effraction that is inevitable (rather than intentional) and that happens without regard for our consent. (There are implications here for thinking about consent which I forgo until chapter 2.) Insofar as the intervention of the other is, per Laplanche, psychosomatically registered as pain, what this means is that implantation welds pleasure with pain: the process, to borrow a phrase from Michel Foucault, both "consumes and consummates us" (1977, p. 44). Sexual excitement originates in this gap between the caretaker's excess and what the infant's ego can bind; the misalignment between the two is riveting. Add to this the bodily sensations that arise later in life through the excitations of the bodily surfaces, and we end up with a veritable powerhouse of experience, at the foundation of which lies the other's trespass into us—a trespass to which we also owe our subjectivation.

When amplified, the literary theorist Leo Bersani proposed, this interimplication of pleasure/pain can leave the subject "momentarily undone" (1986, p. 100). This unraveling of the self "disrupt[s] the ego's coherence and dissolve[s] its boundaries" (Bersani, 1986, p. 101), an experience that Bersani famously described as the self's shattering.[18] Bersani's theoretical move was arresting, dealing a decisive blow to the prized notion, in psychoanalysis and beyond, that psychic life rests on continuity, integration, and synthesis. From a Laplanchean perspective, ego shattering amounts to the ego's links, organized through translation, being broken down. As an unstitching of the meaningful threads that compose the ego, the self's shattering would be akin to what Laplanche called "detranslation," "a dismantling and a reversal of translation" (1989, p. 413). This is nothing less than a "scouring, a scraping away, of the existing translation" (Laplanche, 1989, p. 415), which is another way of saying that detranslation de-links the chains that the ego forged in crafting its translations and, thus, itself. We could think of detranslating as pulling on a dangling thread left behind when a sweater has snagged: if one keeps going, the sweater will be reduced to mere string. This is a good metaphor for what happens as the ego's breakdown brings down the self, in the undoing of the subject. To appreciate the implications of detranslation and ego shattering, we will want to examine more closely the processes by which the ego is formed. This will help us understand better Laplanche's claim that detranslation can turn us "toward the *past*" to attempt "a better translation—one more inclusive, less repressive, with new possibilities" (1989, p. 420).

Translation: Ego, Mastery, Power

The question of how the infant forges her translations is an important one for Laplanche—and for my thinking in this book. Since there are no "real" meanings to be recovered, the infant must seek codes with which to organize the ways she will make sense of enigma. The infant "doesn't invent these from nothing" (Laplanche, 2003b, p. 216), but uses what is already available to her: her experience of her body (e.g., the experience of inside-outside) and what is made available to her from the domain of the mythosymbolic. The mythosymbolic includes significations that circulate in the larger social milieu and the familial environment: these are meaning-making templates that have to do with myths, symbols, and stories. These exist in the "adult cultural world in which the infant is completely immersed from the outset" (Laplanche, 1984, p. 303), and they permeate the parents' embodied lives, which means that they are conveyed to the child both verbally and nonverbally. "Codes, knowledges, languages, and structures of feeling," Teresa de Lauretis explains (2017, p. 1921), all get called into this process of translation, and they all participate in making the production of the ego.

The infant, however, does not just passively introject the mythosymbolic. Picking up elements of this and that, she combines these elements inventively and of her own accord, which means that our translations are assembled by each of us idiomatically. The word "assembled" may give a false impression, as if this were a conscious, deliberate process, which it is not; what I am trying to highlight, rather, is that there is some range in how the mythosymbolic may be put to use by each of us to yield our ego and our translations. As a result, even though the ego that gets churned out of this process is threaded together through "found objects" that are not of our creation, because it arises through personal innovation, it comes to feel *genuinely ours*, not what others think about the way the world works but *our own knowledge* of the way the world works. Translation, that is, gives us our fine-grained individuality. Laplanche specifically addresses gender as such a meaning-making template. As a cultural object that is readily made available to parents and the larger family circle and that appears as simply "natural," binary gender circulates in the mythosymbolic as a tool with which to tame the enigmatic excess of the parents' communications.[19] Others have extended this thinking to race, to argue that enigmatic signifiers "colonize the unconscious" (Evzonas, 2020).

If translation rests on existing mythosymbolic codes, what this would also mean is that all the problematic elements in the concept of race (and any other social category, really, that may be used as a translational tool) will also infiltrate the ego's translational efforts. These problematic elements, therefore, play a role in ego formation. This would connect processes of racialization to translation, thereby situating "race" and racism as part of the ego, which, we will recall, Freud described as being primarily bodily (1923). As such, dominant ideologies and prevalent understandings of the world and how it works, as well as the troubling assumptions baked through them (prejudices, preoccupations, stereotypes, symbolic conflations, and so on), which subtend the categories of race (and gender), would also participate in the ego's formation.

For example, let us imagine a Black mother sitting in a pediatrician's waiting room with other mothers, most of them White. Let us also imagine that her infant, exploring the space, crawls toward a White person's belongings. The mother may quickly pick the child up, urging him to stay closer. This urging may be about him respecting others' private space, but it could also be about the mother's concern about how White people would respond to her child's approach. Such communication conveys to the child much more powerfully than words ever could that there is something about him (the infant) nearing White people's belongings that may become difficult, even dangerous. Even as race may not enter the mother's verbal communication per se, her intervention is awash in the mythosymbolic register. That is, the mother is functioning aware of race and racism and the ways both are affected by gender. She may have particular concerns due to racist stereotypes of Black masculinity and the way they shape how the world perceives her son. The mother's communication to the child has messages about race and racism in it, but it is not enigmatic in the Laplanchean sense because even though it is nonverbal, it is still based on some organized "code[], knowledge[], language [and] structure[] of feeling" (de Lauretis, 2017, p. 1921) that circulates in the mythosymbolic space (i.e., about how White people respond to Black bodies), of which the mother probably has personal experience. The meanings conveyed implicitly to the infant become available as translational tools, and they include a web of symbols and myths about race and gender, myths about safety and dangerousness, about racial difference and the perils of interracial encounters, and so on. The infant may use these to format his own sense of his racialization and to forge a sense of the raced world around him: the problematic myths about race, then, will also form part of his ego.

The implications for thinking about translation in the social world are that the prevailing systems that organize the adult world—and that are permeated by patriarchy, ableism, racism, heterosexism, normative gender ideology, and so on—also become part of the ego's cohering glue, getting swirled into our very sense of self from the get-go. I purposefully use the word "swirled" to underscore that these problematic ideas do not layer themselves atop an otherwise pristine, unbiased subject. This means that they cannot be simply removed from the rest of the self as if peeling back an outermost, tainted layer of soiled film, as is imagined by discourses that urge us to "become aware" of unconscious racism, tend to sexist presumptions, mind heterosexist prisms, check one's privilege, etc. Because the ego is largely oriented toward protecting its integrity and cohesion by inhibiting the disturbance that change ushers into it, and because many of these defensive operations happen outside our awareness or, at least, without our conscious control, becoming, say, more educated about one's privilege or learning to better discern White-supremacist logics will only touch the more logical, outermost layers of the self, leaving untouched the more visceral inscriptions. Education, in the sense of knowing the history surrounding these oppressions and being able to "read" where and how they are ongoing, is important; but such interventions, while important, do not penetrate the deeper levels of psychic structure. Tragically, these "-isms" are not pollutants of an otherwise pure psyche but the very materials through which one's sense of self is constituted—for both majoritarian and minoritarian subjects. They are baked into how we are subjectivized.

Of course, the specific contents of these elementary translational building blocks vary from culture to culture—and from subculture to subculture—across chronological epochs, and from one family (whatever its kinship structure) to another. In other words, the concept of racial difference does not circulate in different adult worlds (from which the infant will pluck for their translational efforts) in the same ways or with the same meanings. But the point I want to make is that because the translations become the basic units out of which our sense of self coagulates, whatever -isms and biases saturate the cultural surround may become baked into *who we become*. Counterintuitively, then, all subjects, even those who inhabit intersecting minoritarian identities, like the infant in the pediatrician's waiting room in our example earlier, may develop ego structures that are, to some degree, organized through ideas (in this case, about race and racism) that serve dominant ideologies.

Putting Glissant's insights side by side with Laplanche, then, we could say that the ego is, to a certain degree, if not coextensive with power structures, at least sometimes working on a colonial, appropriative logic. "Assimilation, appropriation, aggression, infantilization, or emasculation—all the psychical strategies commonly associated with racism," Homay King explains, could be seen through Laplanche's theory as "driven by the desire to eradicate or bind the *internal* otherness, implanted in the form of the enigmatic signifier and revived by an encounter with an other" (2010, p. 32). But we need to remember that the agent responsible for conflating the concrete external other (that is, the other human being) with this perturbing internal foreign body in ourselves is none other than the ego itself. In others words, this conflation is not ontological—and, thus, is neither fixed nor immutable. And this conflation is also not something good politics or intentions can eradicate, at least not on the psychic level. "Not so easily segregated," writes King, "their eradication would be tantamount to the destruction of the self" (2010, p. 32).

I hope that this theorizing, which will be revisited throughout this book from different angles, begins to convey the high stakes accompanying the ego's undoing—and why its detranslation can have such incredible personal and political ramifications. Understanding itself as the sovereign, the ego will dedicate all of its energies to resist contestations of its sovereignty. This is why contact with the sexual unconscious and with opacity is threatening. To preempt this, the ego can produce varied narcissistic crises, some of which may be more "dramatic" (think White fragility and White tears), or more emboldened—and institutionally supported—pushbacks (think of the war waged against critical race theory and trans children), or genuine mental health emergencies (think of a man who becomes suicidal when his sexually harassing behavior becomes public) and so on.

The psychoanalyst Dominique Scarfone describes the ego's efforts to transduce the disquieting energies of the "internal foreign object" to a more tranquil regime as a reach for mastery (2021, in press). That this attempt will always "egregiously fail" (Scarfone, 2021) does not discourage the ego, which remains dedicated to trying to churn meaning out of the enigmatic and to wrest transparency from opacity. What this means is that binding is also about making the other predictable, never surprising, never a source of curiosity or excitation. (Stereotypes, for instance, do a lot of work in this regard.) The ego's energies are organized toward binding the strangeness of the enigmatic and thus dissipating the alterity in oneself and in the other (where it arrives by projection). But translation, thankfully, cannot achieve complete mastery over extraneous elements of our own and the other's alterity; both besiege us. In a subject with an engorged sense of narcissism, this failure can feel so humiliating and wounding that mastery transmutes to a drive to power and control of the other (Scarfone, 2021). Social positionality, group membership, and cultural capital can also embolden one—and procure the resources with which—to act over others in destructive ways. So, while the drive to mastery is universal, its mutation into a drive to power is contingent.

The ego resists the energetic turbulences of the sexual. The notion that we are shattered not only in infancy but, if we are lucky, again and again and again paves the way to our being able to think about traumatophilia—that is, our attraction to the site of the traumatic. A return to the site of our constitutive trauma can thus be understood not as a rote and mechanical recursion that is too hackneyed to escape iteration but as a way of touching inaugural wounds, opening up new possibilities. In Adam's experience, suffering and pleasure amalgamated to blow him up "into thousands of tiny pieces . . . hanging out in space like overheated pieces of dust." We may now understand that moment as having to do with how the rise in excitation arising out of Adam's visceral revulsion and erotic enthrallment overrode his ego's organized surfaces, rupturing it. Such shatterings may sound traumatic, but they are not necessarily so.

Thinking With, Not Against, Pain

To explore further the kinds of experience that may enable the self's dissolution, we have to be able to bear thinking *with* pain and abjection. To accomplish this, I turn to ideas from French philosophy, specifically to the notion of "limit experience." The roots of this concept originate in the eighteenth-century pornographic, eschatological, and philosophical work of the Marquis de Sade and were subsequently elaborated in the philosophies of Bataille, Blanchot, and Foucault.

The Marquis de Sade lived and wrote during the period of the French Revolution. Imprisoned and confined in psychiatric institutions for most of his adult life, he acquired his reputation for writing books of sexually sadistic and masochistic content that he mostly wrote from jail, sometimes on toilet paper, shielding them from his censors by hiding them in cracks on the walls of his cell.[20] Much scholarship has proliferated around his pornographic writings, wherein libertines, in the pauses between their debauches, deliver long philosophical treatises on state power, human nature, sovereignty, erotic subjectivity, and the subject-object relation. These philosophical musings, and their implications for political theory, have been densely theorized (Bataille, 1973; de Beauvoir, 1953; Klossowski, 1967; Lacan, 1963/1989; Lély, 1966; Hénaff, 1999; Phillips, 2001). Sade's oeuvre captured philosophers' and political theorists' attention because of the meticulous attention he paid to how political institutions (e.g., the French aristocracy in its excesses and debauchery and the church) at once defined the limit and invited its transgression. Deeply affected by and inspired by Sade's work, Bataille posited that the possibility for a very particular kind of experience lies at the transgression of the limit: inner experience.[21] For Bataille, the limit marks the line between life and death, a death that we deny and the reality of which we refuse to confront—though by death, he did not (only) mean the end to organic life but a return to uninterrupted being. In his thinking, the limit and its transgression are also connected to the taboo. For him, the institution of taboo, credited as the beginning of civilization, in fact led to the loss of our base humanity, disconnecting us from our animal nature, throwing us in the machine of capitalist production. For Bataille, transgression is thus also a political gesture.[22] By bringing us into contact with the base and the abject, it ecstatically erupts back into our humanity, where energy is not conserved in the name of a capitalist future that needs preserving but is, instead, extravagantly wasted in the present. In his writings, he sought to reinstate the central importance of a "general economy" of expenditure (*dépense*), waste, excess, and base materialism to offer a critical response to the focus on scarcity (and its remediation through accumulation), associated with the "restricted economy" of local capitalism. As such, what compels Bataille's attention are human activities (sacrifice, festival, eroticism) that cannot be rationalized as productive and that offer no functional or utilitarian value. Because eroticism is economically wasteful (aka nonproductive), it is well positioned to disrupt the subject's continuity and claim present time, wrenching the subject from herself to hurl her toward such an uninterrupted state. Bataille's contemporary, Maurice Blanchot (1969) described such experiences as what one encounters when one has "decided to put [one]self radically in question" (1969, p. 203).

Foucault was profoundly influenced by his encounter with the works of Sade and Bataille. He theorized experiences of the edge as trying "to reach that point in life which lies as close as possible to the impossibility of living" (Foucault, 1991, p. 31), a "wrenching the subject from itself . . . bringing it to his annihilation or dissolution" (Foucault, 2000a, p. 241). Sexuality, he thought, is in a privileged position to elicit the subject's tear from herself because, even though bodies are constituted through discourse, they also exceed it (Foucault, 1991).

Not all sexuality is created equal in that regard: the perversity inherent in the sexual makes sexuality that runs on the energetic charge of infantile perversity (as opposed to sexuality that is more tame) ideally suited to bid the ego's unraveling. Transgression's insatiable appetite for intensified stimulation can produce paroxysms that override homeostatic controls, thus contesting the ego's sovereignty. Key to transgressive pleasure is not tension reduction but "the *pursuit of excitation* even to the point of exhaustion" (Laplanche, 2000b, p. 41, emphasis in original)—a luxuriously wasteful and unproductive consumption of energy. This welling up produces pleasure that is suffered unproductively (expenditure), and it is what furnishes perversity with its queer and anarchic potential. Courting the limit is not about triumphing over boundaries or intending to shock or to omnipotently triumph over limits (Nigro, 2005)—such triumphing, after all, would be about mastering (binding) when at stake is the ego's contestation (unbinding). This is important because the ego's contestation has ties to opacity, whereas narcissistic triumph is about the refusal that there is anything outside the ego's reign. If the practices that are more conducive to limit work are scandalous or subversive, this is not for the sake of shock per se but because their exuberant energies are more likely to kindle the escalating economy of the sexual drive.[23] We should heed Tim Dean's caution that "simply accept[ing] or, indeed, celebrat[ing] perverse sexuality" by folding it into an ego/identity structure may itself "be a way of avoiding what is so intransigently difficult about [perversion]" (2014, p. 269).

Rather than the homeostatic regulation that attachment theory idolizes (Lyons-Ruth, 1999, 2006), this vigorous pursuit of experience pushes past the limit to become overwhelming, threatening the ego's integrity. Although when we speak of sexuality, we refer to a set of representations and/or to conduct relating to sex, the erotic is always infiltrated by the sexual drive, by the more rogue, unintegrated, radical root of the infantile sexual. Importantly, varied kinds of experiences can be arrogated by the infantile sexual, including art. Activities annexed by the drive's perversity may thus bring the subject against her limit—and this is more amplified with practices that have an energetic affinity with the infantile sexual: the erotic, repetition, and trauma are especially apposite for such experiences. When such energetic extravagance overruns homeostatic controls, the ego can become unmoored and break open, to hurl the subject into a state of uninterrupted belonging (Bataille, 1957).[24]

Instead of focusing on identifying and maintaining optimal levels of stimulation that protect the subject from being overwhelmed or arguing for relying on the other as a way of ensuring that injury and trauma are avoided, this volume asks after eroticism and performance that flows not away from but *toward* overstimulation. Therein, in what I call the "more and more" of experience, in experience that presses into the unbearable, a state of "overwhelm" may arise. What is often read as compulsiveness in repeated enactments of perverse sexual scripts (Bach, 1994) and what Freud (1905b) thought of as the quality of "fixity" in perversion can, instead, be seen as a path to the ego's unraveling. This unraveling may, in turn, bring down previously established meanings in favor of new ones that might replace them. To think of perversity this way is to grant it considerably more psychic heft than implied in the concept of "benign variation," without seesawing into pathologizing perversion.

Interembodied sexual experience that is powered by transgression's search for escalating excitations has the extraordinary potential to recapitulate the scene of implantation, that is, to undo the links between enigma and its translations. This breaking open of the ego will animate the ego toward new translating work. In the following chapters, we will encounter how experiences that usher such ego ruptures are subtended by an unusual type of consent that is not of the affirmative kind and that has more to do with making oneself susceptible to something unknown and unpredictably opaque in oneself. But let us now briefly loop back to Adam.

Adam

Recalling Adam's experience of feeling like overheated bits of dust, we can now see that moment as the phenomenological correlate of ego shattering. Adam was disrupted in encountering the abject in himself and in experiencing the desire that was "opened up" in his body by his repulsive stranger. What occurred after that was not an explosion of unbridled energy that got out of hand. Adam did not dissociate; he did not have a psychotic break; nor was he traumatized. Trying to approximate what happened for Adam, we might say that he was in an altered state of consciousness (Ghent, 1990; Epstein, 2004), a state of heightened attention whereby he experienced an unusual sense of presence, a fleeting state of self-sovereignty.[25]

Exploring this state in Adam's analysis suggested that the moment of unraveling behaved like a portal. Incomprehensible fragments of experience leaped forward—Adam's semi-hallucinated black object, the reverberating sound, the jolting skin sensation he could not place entered the analytic space. These were not objects to be dissected for meaning.

Rather than vivisect, to cut them open in the hope of discovering some hidden truth, and thus killing off their vitality, we followed their intensities.[26] Instead of asking what messages might have become encysted in the sound that was neither voice nor cry, whether the "fuzzy black object" pointed to an entombed memory, whether the jolting sensation was a faint mnemic trace, which would treat them as something to master, we came to appreciate that his sexual encounter had somehow rendered the ineffable into something that appeared in the world. Becoming something that could be apprehended by him in the moment and by us in the session, the enigmatic thus came to have the effect of presence.[27]

With time, Adam and I relaxed our grip on trying to grasp these appearances and gave ourselves over to the emerging realization that we would have to work *with* this opacity rather than against it (i.e., trying to make it transparent). With this implicit admission came something else: new associative chains began to form between these sensory experiences and parts of Adam's history that wrenched our attention from its previously habituated focus. Stories that I had never heard before began to emerge, and others that had been repeated lifelessly for months began to stir with life. Something new and enlivening was happening.

2

The Draw to Overwhelm

Limit Consent and the Retranslation of Enigma

There subsists in us a silent, elusive, ungraspable part. In the region of words, of discourse, this part is neglected [and] usually escapes us . . . Language . . . is [therefore] dispossessed, can say nothing, is limited to stealing these states from attention.
—Bataille, *Inner Experience*

A colleague, whom I will call Imani, is playing with her four-year-old daughter, Lumi.[1] "Be the monster!" Lumi instructs her. Instantly transforming herself into an imposing ogre, Imani leaps forward. She snatches Lumi. "I will eat you!" she growls menacingly. Lumi squirms from within Imani's firm grip, squealing with delight. She fights back, giggling in abandon. Then suddenly, she yells, "Stop!" Imani stops immediately. They look at each other; a moment passes. Clearly, they have done this before. "Again!" Lumi commands. Imani instantly leaps forth. Again she grabs, again the scary monster, again ominous and frightening. Lumi is laughing. "Stop!" she commands anew. Imani stops. They rehearse this scenario a few times. Several repetitions later, Lumi looks vaguely unsatisfied. Then, a solution! "We'll play a different game," she announces. "I tell you to be the monster; you grab and scare me; I say stop; but this time"—she punctuates each word—"You! Don't! Stop!" "I don't?" Imani now hesitates. "No," Lumi replies confidently, "you go on and on, more and more." "What if it gets too much?" Imani asks anxiously. The little girl, however, seems utterly disinterested in this adult question of safety and careful calibration. The question of safe limits does not appear to worry her: "You have to not stop, or else it won't work!" she says impatiently. "Don't worry, let's just go on and on, more and more."

In this chapter, I take up this playful exchange to discuss the links between consent and the psychic economy of the infantile sexual. In chapter 1, we saw that the infantile sexual is multiple and polymorphous, more of a force rather than something that appears phenomenally, while sexuality is the set of behaviors, fantasies, acts, and identities that, though inflected by the infantile sexual, are more psychically organized. The infantile sexual, that is, is not locked into sexuality; it gives an account of something else entirely (Fletcher, 2000). Freud's fundamental discovery, infantile sexuality is "the object of psychoanalysis" (House, 2017, p. 796), and in this chapter it will help us explore states of dysregulation that I call "overwhelm," in the action of retranslating enigma (after it has been detranslated via the ego's shattering). I am pointedly using overwhelm as a noun. This unexpected use is aimed to defamiliarize us from its more common use as a verb and from its adjectival form, as when we describe something as problematically "overwhelming"—that is, it is meant to dissolve the links between the word and how we are accustomed to understanding it in a negative way.

This chapter is organized in three sections. The first section explores the psychic topography of consent, a concept that has garnered needed attention through the visibility of the #MeToo movement. The notion of affirmative consent understands consent as issuing from a subject who is fully transparent to themselves and who, in thinking consciously and deciding rationally, can anticipate the probable effects of their assent. Affirmative consent is said to foreground clear communication to avoid misunderstandings in the hopes of fostering mutually satisfying experiences in adult sexual encounters—and it is rooted in Hegelian dialectics of recognition that have been taken up in contemporary psychoanalysis. Such consent, I propose, is an epistemological project of dubious usefulness; one never knows what one signs up for and what one will get until after the fact, however carefully, dutifully, or earnestly one communicates. I introduce a different type of consent negotiation, "limit consent," that, as I argue, can bear more of the weight of the complexities of the sexual. Limit consent does not center on (re)producing an experience of satisfaction but, instead, works to facilitate novelty and surprise. Grounded in negative dialectics, limit consent recognizes that even careful interpersonal negotiations leave behind a remainder that cannot be eliminated. As such, limit consent offers us a way of thinking about consent as also pertaining to our interiority, as ushering encounters with the strange and with the opaque in ourselves—and we may think here of Mia and Carmen from the introduction. In contrast to affirmative consent, limit consent hinges not on respecting limits but on their ethical transgression. Limit consent runs on nonlinear time, blurs the divide between active and passive, and comes dangerously close to the line of something going wrong. Why play with fire at all? Because, I propose, limit consent enables the pursuit of the states of overwhelm that I discuss in the second section.

The second section shares the sensibilities of Muriel Dimen (1999, 2003) and Ruth Stein (1998, 2006, 2008) regarding the compelling power of sexuality and its transformative potential, and it heeds Stein's plea (2008) that we rehabilitate the notion of excess in sexual experience. In this part, I argue for the conceptual and clinical utility of the psychic territory I call "overwhelm," which is brought about when escalating excitations are pushed to the limit. Overwhelm is a dysregulated state; it is not in the purview of repetition compulsion and is not necessarily destructive, though it does court risk, which means that it can, in some instances, become perilous. Overwhelm differs from dysregulations that issue, as attachment-based theories would aver, from a history of parental misattunement (Benjamin & Atlas, 2015; Lyons-Ruth, 1999, 2006), overstimulation, or trauma (hereafter, to distinguish them from overwhelm, I refer to these as "malignant dysregulations"). Unlike malignant dysregulations, overwhelm is a driven state that issues from within an attuned dyad. While its phenomenology of surplus excitement makes it appear similar to malignant dysregulations or to traumatic overstimulation, it is best understood in terms of the economic regime of infantile sexuality. Overwhelm is an extreme state that can bring about ego shattering, a radical unbinding of the ego, as discussed in chapter 1, that could unravel previous translations that may be at an impasse, opening up space for new ones. But unlike self-shattering, which presumes a quick, and better, reconstitution of the subject, as in Bersani's work (1986), overwhelm opens us up to actual risk, not just the thrill of it. Overwhelm involves varied pathways and persistent, effortful repetitions. In chapter 1, I already suggested that sexuality, especially sexuality in its transgressive and perverse renditions, may be ideally equipped to incite overwhelm. In this chapter, I explain the mechanics of why that is so.[2]

In the third, clinical section of the chapter, I also place the term in the context of attempts made in some queer communities to resignify and empower a range of different sexual practices, expanding on my reasoning for retaining the term perversion despite its fraught and problematic history. To that effect, I offer a clinical illustration of what the implications of these ideas may be for thinking about the role of infantile sexuality in experience. I ask you to travel with me through an account of clinical process that may feel foreign to non-analysts and that sets the stage for the exploration of similar processes that later chapters take up vis-à-vis performance and race. I describe a patient's transgressive sexual encounter, the state of overwhelm it generated, the radical unbinding of her ego it produced, and how that then, in turn, incited a state of overwhelm in me as her analyst. The work around this material led to a transformation in domains that were previously untouched by the analysis and that may also help illustrate what is at stake (outside of analysis as well) in considering the workings of limit consent and overwhelm states.

Limit Consent: Risk, Nonlinear Temporality, and the Blurring of Active and Passive

Lumi and Imani's play depicts a rather ordinary, albeit complex, scene of adult-child play. In the first segment ("be the monster," "stop," "start again"), a negotiation occurs that directs the game and that makes the starting and stopping points explicit. Imani follows Lumi's instructions. The interaction proceeds well. Insofar as Lumi scripts it, she decides what it looks like, how far it goes, and when it stops. Imani, though, is not merely following Lumi's directions. For the play to work as it should, she has to be inventive and imaginative in the way she renders them. And, as is true of all good play, what ensues is both real and not real. Insofar as Imani has to perform her growls and grabs monstrously enough for Lumi to be at least startled, even somewhat scared, the play is real. But it is also not real, as Imani becomes a monster, and stops being one, on command. As long as this exchange is enacted with delicate attunement, it remains in the sphere of playful, well-regulated interaction. It has a rhythm and emotional pace that thrills. But it does not tip into malignant "too-muchness" (Benjamin & Atlas, 2015, p. 42), that overstimulated state of damaging overexcitement. It is pleasurable but manageably so.

The game, however, turns a corner when Lumi asks Imani to "violate" her limits going forward—though the word "violation" is in quotation marks here to mark its oddness. This new directive requires Imani to override Lumi's consent in a future moment when Lumi *will* be asking her to stop. Temporally speaking, the new game is nonlinear: Lumi is preemptively authorizing Imani to disregard her command to cut the game short, a command that Lumi anticipates she will be making *later* and that she directs Imani *now* to ignore. This is, in part, what makes it risky. How can Imani be sure that Lumi will still want her prospective "no" to be overruled at the time that she pronounces it? How will she know the precise point at which Lumi's softer "stop" may crystallize into a hard limit if words cannot be relied on as the rudder?

The paradoxical semantics of these complex negotiations—I am asking you to take my "no" not to mean "no" and not to stop at your "no" either, so that by trespassing them both, you may take us into a state of "more and more"—involves relinquishing the ordinary ways in which boundaries are patrolled in everyday life. Such relinquishment courts a state of receptivity that can be easily mistaken for passivity. I say "mistaken" because Lumi's receptivity is not equivalent to, and should not be confused with, passivity. There are marked differences between being susceptible to the other and capitulating to the other's will: the latter is not what is occurring here.[3] Lyotard (1988/1991) has coined the term "passibility" (in French, *passibilité*) to express this crucial distinction. Passibility is not opposed to activity; it is, rather, a state by which alone we are fit to receive and, as a result, to modify and do, and perhaps even to enjoy (Scarfone, 2011). Passibility is akin to the radical receptivity that the psychoanalyst Emanuel Ghent (1990) described as surrender, which he carefully distinguished from masochism and submission. For Ghent, submission is not about resigning oneself to passivity and can be thought of as a "defensive mutant of surrender" (1990, p. 111). Said differently, submission is heavy and weighs one down, whereas surrender occurs more spontaneously.[4] Surrender involves a giving of oneself over to the other; it is a sort of relinquishment of power that comes about under the aegis of certain "facilitative circumstances" (Ghent, 1990, p. 111), to yield states where one is besieged, dispossessed of oneself, sub-

THE DRAW TO OVERWHELM | 61

ject *to* the other.[5] To be clear, such surrender cannot be demanded from the other as in sexual harassment and assault, where someone tries to impose their sexual will on the other, as it also involves a succumbing to something in oneself.

From Imani's angle, too, complying with Lumi's request is not simple. So much can go wrong, largely because agreeing with Lumi's new directions will court a certain kind of edge. If Imani plays along, she could go too far, traumatizing Lumi and herself in the bargain. It is precisely because Imani understands this risk that she now hesitates when she was previously all in. How, then, to go forward? To privilege Lumi's temporally scrambled request—Lumi is telling Imani now what she will want later, and that could change—Imani would have to enact a strange version of mindful attention in which obeying the new game's rules means that Imani will act in violation of Lumi's order to stop. To do that, Imani will have to suspend her own, conscious preference to "play it safe" and to keep things contained; she will have, that is, to bend her will too. On a less conscious level, to effect this deliberate crossing of limits, Imani will have to bear the rousing of something inside her that will in turn fuel her "forcing" Lumi. That is, if the play is to feel "real" to her and to Lumi, Imani will not just be "innocently" playing along: she will not be entering the interaction mimetically (*as if* she were "all in") but as a full participant. The force that will be roused to effect Imani's participation is linked to the mother's infantile sexuality, to her own sadism—which, alongside masochism, is, for Freud, "the most common and the most significant of all the perversions" (1905b, p. 157). This force subtends all psychosexuality, and while it is not necessarily destructive, it is a force that can get out of hand. The risk entailed, we might say, is ordinary, but depending on how it is handled, things can become precarious, painful, or traumatic—and it is worth noting that chance has a share in this as well. The "decision" to "chance" it is not about carelessly taking risks at the other's expense, though the chance obviously has implications for the other; it is about putting oneself at risk beyond strategy, calculation, or insurance. I describe the risk as ordinary not to minimize its dangers but to dedramatize it in the sense that Lauren Berlant and Lee Edelman use the term "dedramatization": "not to deny [the] drama[tic element] but to address it tenderly" (2014, p. 14). We only partially understand, they continue, "what we are doing when we take up a position" that brings us closer "to becoming undone" (Berlant & Edelman, 2014, p. 14). In fact, the experience of the unforeseeable may actually be exactly what this dyad is negotiating. Imani's normative sadism (which, as we saw in chapter 1, belongs to the domain of the infantile sexual) will, of course, have to be balanced against Imani's concern for Lumi's well-being, which is another way of saying that the exchange is not one Imani can fully control. Accordingly, to agree to this new game, Imani will have to assume two kinds of risks: On the more conscious level, she will have to agree to push past her worry that she may upset or even hurt Lumi. Less consciously, she has to be willing to tolerate a largely unconscious tide of sadistic desire surfacing in her, a desire that is not pathological but ordinary, without inhibiting it as a good mother is wont to do, for it is this normative sadism that will ultimately drive the push past Lumi's "no." To let it course through her, Imani will have to bend her will (her wish to stay in the "safe zone"). It is this bending of the will that stands to convert a normative sadistic current into an ethical one.[6] It may sound paradoxical to say that such sadism is a form of care, but we see that if Imani is to enter this new game, she will be holding quite a bit—even as she will also not be fully "in control" of herself or of the situation. Neither Imani nor Lumi know what comes next, what opacities may lie ahead. That, in fact, may be exactly the point.

In the game's original version, we might say that the dyad operated along the lines of affirmative consent: clear, precise, and consciously un-ambivalent communication that aimed to yield a desired outcome by outlining what was permitted and what was not. Affirmative consent and its medical counterpart, informed consent, have emerged from long histories of boundary crossings and abusive practices in personal rela-tionships, the social world, and medical contexts.[7] Both are tasked with protecting people with diminished power (Faden & Beauchamp, 1986) by emphasizing open sharing of information, communicative clarity, and the setting and respecting of limits (Archard, 1995; Haag, 1999). The importance of affirmative consent has come to the fore in the United States with the unfolding torrent of sexual abuse allegations brought forth by the #MeToo movement—but it is by no means a new issue.[8]

The affirmative consent model, however, is insufficiently nuanced: it problematically imagines desire to be autonomous, unconstrained, and possible to separate from social inequalities that, in fact, condition who gets to withhold consent and who does not. Premised on and trafficking in appetites and erotic acts that are intelligible and socially palatable, it "often buttresses normative sexualities and sexual hierarchies" (Cruz, 2016, p. 46). From a psychoanalytic perspective, then, affirmative consent is revealed to be but a ruse: the discourse on affirmative consent presumes individuals with distinct centers of subjectivity who inform, negotiate, and reach agreements to minimize misunderstandings and manage expectations (Haag, 1999), which overlooks that we cannot know, except after the fact, what we will enjoy or not and how or what will pain or traumatize versus growthfully challenge us. So while violations of our boundaries and a disrespect of our limits absolutely deserve our attention, affirmative consent is illusory and thus not a useful concept.[9] Further, the affirmative consent discourse does not sufficiently account for the varied types of different consent negotiations (Butler, 2011; Fischel, 2016, 2019; Fischel & O'Connell, 2015). In Lumi's new game, for instance, neither her consent to be trespassed nor the consent solicited of Imani is of the affirmative sort. They differ in several ways: the stopping point is not explicit; the communication has some built-in vagueness; the game has no precise aim. Moreover, if the game is to proceed, Imani also has to consent to its new iteration: to do so, she will have to bend her will (to overcome her inhibitions against embracing the sadistic impulses animated in her) and, at the same time, keep the same impulses in relative check as part of her ethical responsibility toward Lumi.

Thus, Imani's consent paradoxically requires a tentative surrender to Lumi, to Lumi's desire, and to the unknowability of what is coming next. Lumi, too, is setting up the conditions of her surrender—though as a child, she is obviously less aware of (or responsible for) the complexities she is inviting. Imani's and Lumi's consent, we might say, involves a mutual, though asymmetrical, letting go. What they are implicitly agreeing to in this negotiation is to be subjected to something unforeseeable, to being vulnerable, and to being surprised. Why does Lumi make this strange request? One possibility—though we cannot know for sure—is that, sated with the repetition, she wants to experience something new, something that will lead her into what she describes as "more and more." We need a different concept for this type of consent, one that, unlike affirmative consent, is predicated not on setting and observing limits but on (Lumi) initiating—and (Imani) responding to—an invitation to transgress them. To mark how closely such consent approaches the limit, I call this kind of consent "limit consent." I am also choosing the term "limit consent" to mark this type of consent's proximity to limit experience and the self's shattering—links that I will explore shortly.

Limit consent's interpersonal syntax does not entail the assertion of one's sovereign boundaries but centers, rather, on surrendering to another—risking coming up against one's own and the other's opacity. To the extent that Imani is also letting herself be taken over by an internal force that she cannot fully control, limit consent involves a surrender to herself as well, which makes consent an internal affair (and we may remember Carmen here and her inability to surrender to the unforeseen experience of Ava's exquisite slap). Such surrender can enable experience—though this is not an experience we have but an experience we risk, and in that sense, it is also an experience that can wound us. But unlike affirmative consent, in which being wounded has to do with an explicit disregard of the other's stated limits, if injury occurs in limit consent, it is inadvertent; it results from infantile sexual urges that have gone too far, gone beyond play, with neither party knowing it until after the fact. That is, the injury is realized only après-coup. Limit consent necessarily involves straddling the murky line of something going seriously awry, and that makes limit consent onerous. For example, something could go awry because Imani does not "read" Lumi well; because Lumi may be unable to signal; because she is unable to know when, on balance, she really wants Imani to stop, realizing it only after the fact; or because Imani's infantile sexuality takes over, becoming too inflamed and resulting in Imani losing control.[10]

Imagine a related but different scene in which two adults agree to enact a play-rape scenario. The person in Lumi's position, the "bottom," appears to be powerless since she hands over to the other the power to determine the stopping point. As the authorized arbiter of limits, the person in Imani's position, the "top," may be seen as the person with power as she is the one who "calls the shots." Obviously, a sexual scene of this sort derives its frisson and erotic charge precisely from this top-bottom power differential, that is, from its asymmetry. Inversely, one might see the bottom as being in control, since she, after all, is the one who decides when things stop and what goes or does not. The top, in this reasoning, is merely executing orders, "servicing" the bottom. But, for several reasons, we would not be correct to view this encounter as one in which power is totally split—with one person having it and the other person not. The idea that the top is ultimately in control naïvely overlooks the top's vulnerability: in consenting to act as the top, she has engaged the bottom's invitation for her to move past her own limits. The fact that she may also be pleasured by the experience does not diminish the fact that, in overcoming her internal resistances—that is, in bending her will—the top has to assume some responsibility if something were to go wrong. The top, therefore, makes herself passible to the bottom and to the bottom's desire, which means that she is not the sovereign in the dyad. Nor is she sovereign in herself since, in accepting the vulnerability of bending her will, she permits the calling up of things in herself that she cannot predict ahead of time. To enact the rape play, she will have to engage with the rousing of her sadism to let it flow, while also keeping some relative check on it. At the same time, the popular opinion that because the bottom conceives of and directs the play she is ultimately the one in control is not correct either. While it is true that the top's authority is granted—and can be revoked—by the bottom, the bottom also assumes the risk of being exposed to something going awry, which is also what makes the erotic engagement "hot."[11] In other words, limit consent gives us an understanding of consent in which power is not dichotomously apportioned—as in, one has it and the other does not —but elaborates a vision of consent in which power, vulnerability, and responsibility are more complexly distributed, not only between the participants but also in the texture of their encounter. Dichotomous power is in the purview of affirmative or informed consent.

Consent in the Psychoanalytic Situation

Of note are some parallels between limit consent and the analyst's role and the patient's anticipatory, largely implicit authorizing of the analyst to push the patient's limits.[12] As we saw in my early sessions with Mia (in the introduction), the patient cannot fully appreciate what it is that they are consenting to when seeing an analyst (Furlong, 2005; Gentile, 2015) or as they begin to recount dreams, emotions, physical sensations, and so on.[13] It is only *as a result* of the analysis that the patient may better appreciate the affective and mnemic currents that will have been stirred by the treatment, what the transference will have brought, and what traumatic eruptions will surface. The patient's original consent in that respect is in large measure naïve—though in what way precisely one will only be able to tell in retrospect.

In different ways, the analyst too is unaware of what she is really consenting to when starting a treatment (Dailey, 2014; Saketopoulou, 2011b, 2015; Saks & Golshan, 2013). That is, though the analyst is equipped with theoretical and experiential knowledge gained from other treatments, including her own, regarding the intensities an analysis can awaken, she does not know how these will manifest themselves in any particular treatment. Neither can she anticipate how she will become unconsciously entangled with a particular patient, how her exposure to her analysand will kindle her own infantile sexual, and what currents or maelstroms of affect will arise that are well beyond what the analyst thought she was consenting to. Analysts are better aware of these constraints than most patients are and more knowingly step into the unknowns of consent when beginning a new analytic treatment: we do not know *what* the treatment will bring, but we do, at least, know *that* we do not know. Still, as analysts, we are also, to some measure, naïve as to what our consent will come to mean.

The analyst makes the offer of analysis (Laplanche, 2006a; Morris, 2016) sensitive to the constraints on the patient's consent and her own. And she also "accepts" a different set of constraints, ones relating to the patient's originally stated limits. Imagine a patient who seeks treatment to address relationship problems but declares from the outset that she will not (or cannot) discuss her history of sexual abuse. The analyst accepts this condition, in the hope that as the analytic work progresses, this limit may shift, making exploration possible. The hope that time will erode stated limits is standard analytic practice. In some cases, it would be poor technique even to intimate to the patient that limits may shift in the course of the work.[14]

This is a simple but illustrative example of why psychoanalytic work may not fall under the purview of informed consent as understood in the medical profession, as in "the informed exercise of choice, and [the ability] to evaluate the options available and the risks attendant upon each" (Saks & Golshan, 2013, p. 6). In some respects, it may make sense to think of psychoanalytic treatments as proceeding along the lines of limit consent. (The same, as we will see in the next chapters, is true in some art and performance.) The analyst's decision-making is implicitly authorized by the patient; the skilled analyst registers the patient's limits—both those explicitly stated and those discerned through the analysand's refusals, symptoms, and defenses—and makes judgments regarding when to persist and when to ease up. Of course, the analyst's best judgment is not a guarantor of good outcome; there is no technical fiat to ensure that (Greenberg, 1986). But if, as analysts, we let up when we feel the pushback of the patient's discomfort, the work would remain stagnant. Not to let up, however, is not easy either; as analysts we have to counter our will telling us to not to upset the patient and not to take a risk that might injure them, which is to say that we have to bear some, at times considerable, discomfort in evoking painful affects and memories. We cannot anticipate what will be evoked in ourselves and with what strength. Things can (and sometimes do) go off the rails. The analyst is "working with highly explosive forces," warned Freud (1915a, p. 170), but that risk, he also insisted, should not deter us; it must be engaged, even dared. In some of those high-octane moments, the analyst has to try to resist the impulse to recoil and make the judgment call as to whether they will persist despite knowing that things could go wrong. The analyst must themselves take risks: analysts who only work to maintain safety in the consulting room give evidence to what has broken down in psychoanalysis, they point us to where psychoanalysis has gone astray. The analyst's attentiveness is nowadays too often oriented to the closing of wounds when the work of the new resides in "reopen[ing] the wound of the unexpected" (Laplanche, 1999, p. 280).

However judiciously the analyst's decision is made, things could get derailed, and the patient may be hurt or traumatized, or the treatment may end prematurely. These are considerable vulnerabilities for both parties. The vulnerability of the patient is the more obvious and the most important. But there are vulnerabilities for the analyst as well. It is never easy for the analyst when the patient feels hurt or leaves treatment prematurely. The analyst is also vulnerable, though, of course, the responsibility is asymmetrical. And, to briefly return to Imani, let us remember that it is actually Imani and not Lumi who worries about things becoming "too much." It is, ultimately, Imani's responsibility, as it is the analyst's and not Lumi's, or the analysand's, to safeguard Lumi's, and the patient's, well-being. And it is Imani's and the analyst's job to manage whatever gets (over)excited in their own self.

Preconditions of Limit Consent

But, you may ask, what about safety and trust? It might appear that I am arguing that these have no role to play in limit consent. On the contrary, I believe they are the very conditions of possibility for limit consent to come into play in the first place. Lumi, we may reasonably assume, is able to ask to have her prospective "no" trespassed only because Imani has proven herself trustworthy up to that point. Imani is an attuned, lively adult with whom ruptures get easily repaired. In the earlier version of the game, she has respected all of Lumi's limits. These are crucial preconditions for Lumi's wish to be pushed to the limit and into this peculiar and unpredictable unsafety to arise in the first place. In that sense, although both affirmative and limit consent hinge on being negotiated within the protective envelopments of safe relationships, the work of safety is very different in each case. In affirmative consent, safety's promissory note is that the top will respect the bottom's expressed limits. In limit consent, the relative safety of the relationship is what puts in place the "facilitative circumstances" that Ghent (1990, p. 111) suggests can enable passibility and the risking of an encounter with opacity. The safety in question, however, is not that things will not go wrong but that if they do, which they could, both parties will stick around to process and hold the injury together. As opposed to legal frameworks that take up the question of responsibility, in this model a negative outcome is not necessarily evidence of bad will or intent, as is the case in affirmative consent. Limit consent's twinned emphasis on mutuality *and* asymmetry takes responsibility out of the judicial framework of culpability, ushering us into a different register of how to think about risk. This register is more about a holding of the other and a trust that one will bear what happens—without knowing *what* is going to happen. In this unusual type of trust, the top too is vulnerable, and in that sense, limit consent opens up both parties to the unforeseeable, which is another way of saying that there is no guarantee as to what comes next, only a commitment to undergo it together.

Whereas affirmative consent aims at eliminating risk and liability, limit consent is open to both. Why step out of affirmative consent and into its limit counterpart given the risks involved? Why might Lumi want to leave the earlier, well-regulated game? And why would Imani even consider Lumi's convoluted request when it would just be safer to stay with "no means no"? I propose that the request to have one's limits overrun and the willingness to consider that request are both driven by infantile sexuality's economic tendency to seek escalating excitations toward more stimulation. The move into the "more and more" of experience can produce states of overwhelm that, as discussed next, may catalyze significant psychic transformations.

Overwhelm: The Psychic Economy of More and More

As discussed in chapter 1, Freud, determined to disabuse his Victorian peers of the notion of sexual normality, famously proposed that the sexual drive is by nature polymorphous and perverse, using the term "perverse" to "enlarge the sexual beyond the limits of the difference between the sexes and beyond sexual reproduction" (Laplanche, 2000a, p. 19). Irrespective of perversity's cause or derivation, for Freud it was the foundation of "infantile sexuality" (the title of the second essay), which gave rise to "the sexual aberrations" (the title of the first), with the remainder of sexuality arriving with "the transformations of puberty" (the title of the third).[15] Perversity, thus, was not a deviation from "normality" but sexuality's very foundation. Freud taught us to expect that the sexual drive will attach to objects opportunistically (i.e., there is no predetermined "right" object); that while it sources from specific body parts (erotogenic zones), it has transferrable potential and can therefore proliferate in unexpected sites (e.g., an armpit, the big toe, and the navel can be as likely sites as the genitals); that it will be constituted by component instincts and, as such, that masochism, sadism, exhibitionism, and voyeurism are endemic to the sexual rather than being the defensively sexualized debris of trauma or overstimulation; that it will not be teleologically organized (i.e., it will not necessarily seek the climactic or reproductive end); and that it operates with part-objects (e.g., objectification), rather than with persons being treated as whole subjects. Then, seemingly recoiling from his radical ideas, he shifted course to propose that the irreverent and unobliged character of the infantile sexual acquires in puberty the "mature," normative shape of heterogenitality.

But Freud was nothing if not ambivalent about the relationship between the infantile sexuality of the first two essays and the more "civilized" sexual instinct of the third, which is to say that he did not entirely backtrack. In *Three Essays*, this ambivalence shows up in his theorizing of sexual tension: on the one hand, he writes, "a feeling of tension necessarily involves unpleasure" (1905b, p. 209), while on the other, "the tension of sexual excitement . . . is also undoubtedly felt as pleasurable" (1905b, p. 209). This contradiction yields two registers in the ontogeny of sexuality: forepleasure, the pleasurable buildup of tension, is deemed to be the purview of "perverse" infantile sexuality and begets further pleasure. In the domain of mature sexuality, accumulated excitations produce unpleasure, thereby impelling action to bring about release— the end-pleasure of orgasm. Muriel Dimen (1999), Leo Bersani (1986), and George Klein (1961) have all noted that this theorizing of fore- and end-pleasures sets up a two-tier system of discrepant economic sexual genres. In the perverse regime, tension continually escalates, while the mature rendition runs on a discharge economy of dissipating tension.

Insatiable Appetites of the Drive

As discussed in chapter 1, for Laplanche the sexual drive is not innate but epigenetic, constituted through the "intervention of the other" (1991, p. 557), and it does not seek a moderation of tension but its escalation, "even to the point of complete exhaustion" (2000a p. 11). We encountered these ideas in chapter 1, so I will only summarize briefly here: the parent's acts of care surcharge the conscious messages of attachment emitted to the child with unconscious sexual conflicts/contaminants that derive from the parent's sexual unconscious.[16] This surcharge slips in like a "stowaway passenger" (Scarfone, 2013, p. 550), compromising, as Laplanche puts it, the intended message. This renders a portion of the message enigmatic, and the infant perceives this enigmatic surplus as a message addressed to *her*. Enigma installs on the child's psychosomatic surfaces (e.g. the skin or the orifices) a question mark without an answer (e.g., "What did this look mean?" etc.). The infant is propelled to make meaning of these enigmatic messages by generating, for example, a fantasy (Scarfone, 2017). Laplanche called this meaning-making process "translation" and emphasized that, since the excess charge of the parent's original message is unconscious to the parent, the infant's translations cannot be—and therefore never are—veridical transcriptions. Translations, thus, do not interpret accurately or inaccurately, they only attempt to cope with the disturbance produced by enigma (Scarfone, 2015a). Further, this translational process is always incomplete, leaving untranslated residues behind. What happens to these residues? They get repressed, constituting the unconscious, which, for Laplanche, is tantamount to infantile sexuality. "'Stuck' in the envelope of the ego like a splinter in the skin" (Laplanche, 1999, p. 209), this untranslated remainder can never henceforth be eliminated. It is constantly pressing for translation, giving rise to the sexual drive. The sexual drive can never be observed in unmediated form; it only makes itself known derivatively, that is, by borrowing a representational form from elsewhere that will vestigially bind it. More like a force than a carrier of cloistered meanings, the unconscious has an impact rather than a concealed signification— and, as such, it has the density of opacity.

The Taming of the Infantile Sexual

When Freud (1914a) introduced the concept of narcissism, Laplanche (1995) argues, he set the stage for a radical shift in the theorizing of sexuality. By suggesting that "the ego unifies the sexual drives . . . adopt[ing] as its own the interest of the self-preservative functions" (Laplanche, 1995, p. 169), Freud made the ego—an ego that became homeostatically focused and whose work was to bind—the seat of the sexual drive. Lodging sexuality in this docile terrain meant that Freud's original emphasis on the infantile sexual of *Three Essays* as a force radically contrary and hostile to the ego was considerably dampened (Laplanche, 1995). Thus, in *Beyond the Pleasure Principle* (1920), in which Freud posited Eros as a less fierce concept, Freud obscured its destructive and destabilizing aspects (Laplanche, 1995, p. 170), a shift that resulted in the conceptual taming and domestication of the sexual. Laplanche referred to the fragmenting dimensions of the sexual that were thus excised from the sexual as a "demonic aspect" (1984a, p. 360). Since the demonic aspects of the sexual could no longer be ontologically housed in the domain of Eros,

Freud was then forced to relocate it elsewhere: hence the new conceptual space that Freud called the "death drive," which also established Eros and Thanatos as two warring factions.[17]

Laplanche's reading of Freud's theoretical pivots allows us to see how the assimilation of sexuality under the tranquil and unifying aegis of the ego paved the way to the sexual's normalization. Having been divorced from the force and disruptive properties of the sexual drive, Eros now became exclusively nested within object relations and, from there, further usurped by attachment theory (as discussed in chapter 1). This domestication may also have contributed to the sexual's eventual capture by sexual identity. In any case, Freud's move effectively ousted "the sharpest edge of analysis . . . the 'plague,' in short" (Kahn, 2018, p. 3) from psychoanalytic theorizing. As a result, sexuality came to be understood as far more pacified, organized, and defused than what infantile sexuality would have led us to anticipate; it became organized around establishing links, that is, bonding, connecting, feeling loved, feeling seen as a full object, and so on.

A less noticed, but important consequence (especially for thinking about queer sexualities) is that this excision of the "fragmented and fragmenting" order of the sexual from sexuality (Laplanche, 1995, p. 168) meant that sexuality could no longer be seen as having ontological claims on component instincts, relegating sadism, masochism, voyeurism, and inversion (the old lingo for homosexuality) to the sphere of disturbance. As such, entwinements of pain/suffering and pleasure were now placed under the banner of pathology or symptom, which is another way of saying that their very presence now required a dynamic explanation. To put it differently, if the demonic sexual is not seen as a natural part of the sexual but as belonging to a separate domain (aggressivity and destructiveness), special accounting will be required to explicate their pairing. This would apply independently of whether we view aggression as endogenously derived (the death drive) or exogenously produced (e.g., as a reaction to traumatic events). Gone, then, is the room for anything opaque to dwell in the sexual, which is now newly composed of the synthetic elements of Eros and answers only to full objects (love, respect, connection, recognition). The usual suspects we then turn to for explaining the pairing of sexuality with aggression are psychic trauma, early overstimulation (e.g., a parent who was too sexual, emotionally overbearing, or intrusive), and early object failures in containment (Fonagy et al., 2002). Subsequent analytic theorizing, therefore, regarding excessive and overexcited sexual states or sexualities that blend pain or humiliation with pleasure follows one of two trajectories: these phenomena are seen either as inventive or defensive sexualizations of early psychic injury (Khan, 1979; McDougall, 1995, 2000; Stoller, 1975) or as attempts by the psyche to cope with early parental misattunement, overstimulation, or overexcitement (Benjamin, 1988; Benjamin & Atlas, 2015; Meltzer, 1973). Few scholars resisted this grain of theorizing, but those who did vociferously protested how such formulations "seem to 'forget' . . . how different we are when we are sexual and how great the discrepancy is between sexuality and daily life" (Stein, 2008, p. 44), insisting on the ubiquity of the perverse (Dimen, 2001).

Laplanche, for his part, remained steadfast on the original formulation of the sexual drive as an anarchic and intractable force. Because he thought that the process of translation can never be exhausted (the definitive meaning of the enigmatic can never be pinned down), he gives us a way of understanding why the sexual drive is ontologically never sated, and the fact that it is always pressing for more is not exceptional, nor does it require accounting. Even he, however, did not explore what psychic states we might expect to encounter if we followed the sexual drive's appetite through its paroxysmal buildup. It is as if, like Freud before him, he became frightened of the revolutionary implication of his ideas, hesitating to follow the sexual drive's dizzying escalation to track the phenomena that appear there.

Let us venture into that space next.

Into Overwhelm

For Freud, the force of the repetition compulsion is a "daemonic force" (1920, p. 35) that takes over in cases of trauma in ways "more primitive, more elementary, more instinctual than the pleasure principle" (1920, p. 23). But the repetition compulsion's demonic force is not the same as the sexual drive's normative push to escalation/intensification, though the similarity of their energetic pulsions may cause them to be confounded. It may help to remember that Freud's formulation of repetition compulsion followed on his already having doctored the sexual into a more pacified urge, of having stripped it of its more savage elements. But because Laplanche (1995) is critical of such a defanging of sexuality and because he insists that the sexual drive involves the synergy of binding properties (what he calls the "sexual drives of life") with unbinding properties (which he calls the "sexual drives of death"), it would be reasonable to assume that he would not see such a state as the exclusive province of trauma or self-destructiveness. To put it differently, the sexual drive's frenzied economy may not always mark the workings of destructiveness; nor would it necessarily have to issue from compulsive or traumatic repetitions.

To think about what may take place as the sexual drive reaches into the "more and more" of experience, we would need a new concept. This concept would not assume that the buildup of excitations always issues from the compulsion to repeat: such an assumption would be tantamount to treating aggression as always already desexualized—and as if its pairing with the sexual is not natural but requires particular circumstances. In contrast to this, then, we would need a concept that admits of a sexualized aggression that does not arise from the compulsion to repeat. This new concept would also recognize that because the demonic sexual coexists with the sexual life drives, self-destructiveness cannot be de facto assumed. And it would also admit the real risks invited by the demonic aspects of sexuality and the unbinding of the sexual death drives. To embrace the way this concept reaches into overstimulation and into the more and more of experience, let us give it the name "overwhelm." In using "overwhelm" as a noun rather than its common usage as a verb or an adjective, I am purposefully devising this neologism so that, as a term, "overwhelm" may maintain its ties with the quality of feeling flooded that the phrase "being overwhelmed" or the expression that something is "overwhelming" usually conveys, while also defamiliarizing it from the habit of thinking that such flooding is necessarily problematic or traumatizing.

Whereas Stein cautioned against pathological excess, writing that a "breach of one's boundaries" involves "the experience of being flooded or overwhelmed" (2008, p. 63), I am, in fact, arguing in favor of exactly such a breach, though not one arrived at through malicious intent and purposeful and/or mindless boundary crossings (which can very much be traumatizing) but through limit consent, where boundaries are

crossed not out of carelessness or disregard but by way of a paradoxical respect for the other's wishes that invites a trespass, as in the case of
Imani and Lumi. Such a trespass involves following the exigency of the
sexual drive (which will be our focus in chapter 5), to facilitate the emergence of aesthetic experience in the other and in the self. To put this
differently, overwhelm is not inherently destructive or self-destructive.
If it incubates precarity and risk, it is because overwhelm draws on the
unbinding, eruptive elements of the sexual drive. We should, therefore,
expect that it will run the risk of crossing into unsafety, where things
can go off the rails. This, we might guess, could be why Imani hesitates
to participate in the new game: becoming genuinely engaged in pushing
past Lumi's limits would expose Imani—and, of course, Lumi—to the
dangers of Imani's normative sadism. This could happen not because of
some problematic dynamic in Imani but due to the unregulated nature
of the sexual drive.

The Shattering of the Ego: Radical Unbinding through Overwhelm

Overwhelm occurs when the sexual drive escalates with negligible
interruption or modulation. Excitation stockpiles beyond the pleasure
principle, into pleasure that is suffered (through pain, humiliation,
abjection, etc.). If this escalating excitation becomes so excessive that it
reaches past the brink, it can threaten the ego's coherence producing the
shattering of the ego (Bersani, 1986).[18] The shattering of the ego occurs
when a certain threshold of intensity is reached, disturbing psychic continuity by sensations or affective processes "beyond those connected with
psychic organization" (Bersani, 1987, p. 213). Bersani's notion of shattering shares key features with Laplanche's notion of the ego's unbinding,
which amounts to *de*translation. Detranslation is the delinking "of the
myths and ideologies through which the ego constructed itself in order
to master" enigma (Laplanche, 1996/2015b, p. 198). What this means
is that ego shattering stands to unweave the subject's previously established meanings, "calling into question narrative structures" (Laplanche,
1998/2015c, p. 251), stripping enigma bare. For this delinking to occur,
excitation needs to transgress the boundaries of the ego, creating a
turbulence, a crisis that has some interesting implications. In this inter-
mediate space between detranslation and retranslation—that is, after

the subject has come undone and before enigma either gets bundled up into a new translation or becomes repressed—enigma is untethered to signifiers, existing outside psychic representation. In it, language breaks apart, and experience is no longer communicable (Bataille, 1957). This is as unmediated as the drive can ever be, which means that in ego shattering, previous translations come undone, exposing us to the presence of the drive. This state is very short-lived; a state of unbinding quickly and urgently gives way, either producing new translations or yielding to repression. The unstitching of translations, disorganized and disorganizing though it may be, opens up to particular kinds of luxuriating experience (i.e., "sovereign experience," which is the focus of chapter 4) and possibly to the fashioning of new translations. Overwhelm can thus deliver the subject to states of radical unbinding, disturbing the psyche and "disorganizing accustomed ways of being" (Berlant & Edelman, 2014, p. 38).[19]

Paths to Overwhelm

From a behavioral standpoint, we might expect that any human activity commandeered by the sexual—any activity, that is, that follows the drive's frenzied economy to its apogee—may plausibly become a path to overwhelm. Consider, for instance, the range of exploits in which one can become engrossed almost to the point of losing oneself, exploits that chase a rush and that can appear—and at times be—reckless, obsessionally pursued, or self-destructive: extreme sports (e.g., skydiving), psychedelic drugs like ayahuasca, high-risk/high-voltage sexual practices, purposefully pursued mystical experiences (e.g., silent retreats), ascetic religious practices (e.g., extreme fasting), and other practices that may appear extreme and excessive. Theater and some performance art can also have such impacts, as for example in the performances of Ron Athey (Johnson, 2013), and we will encounter this in the context of race and racialization in chapters 3 and 4.

A wide range of behaviors can galvanize the escalating excitations that may lead to overwhelm, provided that the infantile sexual surges through them. Perverse and transgressive sexualities, however, have a privileged relationship to overwhelm, because perverse sexualities are especially likely to be arrogated by the sexual drive. This is because they share some of the drive's constitutive key features: they are embodied, nongenital organizations that involve the body's excitability; they are often ordered around component instincts, tarrying in sadism, masochism, voyeurism, and so on; they transgress norms; they recruit affects like humiliation, shame, and terror; and, as we saw in chapter 1, they operate on the logics of part-objects.

Isabela

Isabela was in her mid-thirties when she started a four-times-weekly analysis. Her professional and social worlds seemed rich and exciting, but what unfurled in our sessions felt private, remote, even vacant. In my office, she was overly poised and highly selective in her choice of words. Over time, I gleaned "information" about her: she had grown up in a working-class family of color that immigrated to the United States for "a chance at a better life"; her parents had had considerable difficulty adjusting to the new culture and never learned English, which meant that Isabela grew up partly translating for her parents; and their persistent melancholia and a stifled longing for their homeland saturated her childhood.[20] Isabela had always been transfixed by her parents' magnificent pain and nostalgia, which vibrated on a frequency that she could not fully access or share in. Much of this was communicated to me as data, with no deeper meaning, as if not deserving further exploration. Suffice it to say that the work was protracted and the progress slow. Against Isabela's otherwise affective grays, her relationship with her lover, Raven, a White trans woman, stood out, pulsating with life.

   Isabela described herself as a pervert. My patient did not use this word with its usual, condemnatory connotations but in keeping with the way some queer communities reclaim and resignify pathologized meanings to articulate sexual and gendered possibilities and build communal ties (Clare, 2015). In psychoanalytic discourse, "perversion," as already discussed, is a weighty term with a long and injurious history (Dimen, 2003, 2005). I continue to use it in my thinking and in clinical work with patients who identify this way because it captures an edge and a phenomenological dimension that more neutral descriptors like "nonnormative sexuality," "atypical sexual practices," "BDSM," and "kink" do not. Further, I am extremely reluctant about phrases like "erotic games" (e.g., Celenza, 2000) not only because I find them conceptually limp but also because they ground their legitimacy in the relational arrangements within which transgressive sex occurs, oftentimes privileging normative relational forms (heterosexual, state-sanctioned, long-term, monogamous, dyadic). But, more importantly for the wager that this volume makes, terms like "erotic games" and "kink" usually rely on the notion of affirmative consent to draft the parameters of perverse encounters, when limit consent may be a more useful angle in considering perversion's transgressive reach. Conceptualizing such sexual encounters as merely "enlivened erotic play" (Weinstein, 2007, p. 124) denies them the darker and wilder dimensions of the sexual, whereas "perversion" implies transgression and reflects the interdigitation of pain, pleasure, and anguish.

Perverse sexual encounters are transgressive, interembodied processes that can earn their psychic density over time and with repeated contacts. Rather than impulsive and thoughtless, as they are usually stereotyped to be, they take time and require revisiting to build their traction. While the buildup to overwhelm manifests itself in a singular scene/moment, overwhelm is not episodic in nature. Long interpersonal processes are sometimes required for iterative encounters to build the trust and momentum required to permit the move into limit consent and to court overwhelm. The repetition required for the buildup to overwhelm can make such sexual encounters liable to being misconstrued as compulsive iterations—especially when they congregate around trauma (as will be the focus of chapters 3 and 4). But compulsivity is not necessarily at work, and indeed this was the case with Isabela. She and Raven engaged regularly in elaborately planned and carefully scripted sexual scenarios. The move toward pushing Raven's (and Isabela's own) boundaries happened over a period of time and after the two women had come to know each other quite well.

A few years into our work, Isabela reported a sexual encounter that had occurred long before her treatment. Because of its significance, I will describe it in detail: Isabela led Raven into a dimly lit room. She had Raven remove her clothing. Placing leather restraints on Raven's wrists, she tied Raven's hands behind her back. She then blindfolded Raven, positioning her with her back against the wall. Isabela proceeded to carefully thread a hypodermic needle through Raven's skin below the collarbone. She continued symmetrically with more needles all the way down to Raven's thigh, on both sides of her body. Isabela then removed her own clothing. Standing naked across Raven, she similarly pierced her own skin. After she was done, Isabela threaded an elastic thread through the corresponding needles in their bodies. Upon completing this elaborate ritual, she removed Raven's blindfold. Raven looked down to take in the intricate bondage connecting their bodies. Isabela ordered Raven to hold her gaze. With their eyes locked, Isabela took a gentle step back, causing the strings to become taut. Stretched, the strings pulled on their skins, bringing about a painful sensation.

Isabela's skin hurt. She knew the same was true of Raven's. She stayed alert to her lover's body, wanting the intensity to mount but not to get out of hand. Knowing well the contours of Raven's emotional life, Isabela felt confident that she would be able to discern the limits of what Raven's body could bear: her focus was on the tightrope between what would have been too little and what might cause harm. Slowly moving her body farther away from Raven's, Isabela began intensifying the pull on the strings. The amplification of the experience, combined with the intense eye contact, was intoxicating to Isabela. Awash in this dysregulating experiential oversaturation, she felt that she was coming undone, that she was being ripped apart, "broken open" by experience.[21]

Isabela told me that she had intended this scene as an offering to Raven, whose body had been subjected to physical violence as a child. The aftereffects of Raven's traumatic childhood tormented Raven and strained the couple's romantic relationship. Raven's relationship to her body was also fraught on account of her being trans, something to which Isabela was sensitively attuned. Isabela shared with me that the threading of her body to her lover's was meant as an interembodied recognition of what Raven had suffered and of the ways in which Raven's body remained a contested site. A statement of Isabela's commitment to remaining tied to Raven despite their struggles, Isabela's engagement was not with a circumscribed body part but with Raven's skin surface— that is, it was diffuse in the way that infantile sexuality is. Since trauma had entered Raven through her body, Isabela told me, her offering to Raven required a somatic communication unmediated by language.

Despite this elaborate accounting of what this scene was meant to do vis-à-vis Raven, Isabela had notably little to say about what the sexual encounter might have meant for her. What she did describe in depth was the surge of high-voltage sensations it delivered. Almost in passing, Isabela mentioned that when she had felt broken open, she had a strong, albeit fleeting, sensation. I asked about it. She said that it felt visceral, incommunicable, embodied. She was concerned about forcing it into words for my sake, when no words would adequately describe it. She settled on it having felt like "a smell and a taste, a burning bitterness, like a burning." Adam came to my mind.

In the hour before I was to see Isabela again, I found myself unexpectedly craving Greek coffee, and I prepared a cup. This craving is familiar to me, but it was oddly timed; it usually occurs after my return to New York from my annual summer trip to Greece, a time when my nostalgia for my country, my language, and my people reverberates most acutely. But we were now way past summer. Still, I barely gave it a thought. Half an hour later, Isabela entered my office. Her demeanor immediately changed. Following an unusually long pause on the couch, she asked about the lingering smell she detected in the room. She could not identify it. Her struggling for words reminded me of how difficult it had been for her in our last session to describe the fleeting sensory experience when she had felt "broken open." Then, as she was reaching for language, it was like a hole opened up between us. It was unexpected. Isabela became distressed. She began to cry, at first quietly. Then things started to accelerate. Quickly, vertiginously, Isabela was now weeping. This was unfolding fast, too fast. I did not know what exactly was happening or what to think or do. Isabela, usually measured in her expressions of affect and never before tearful, now tipped into the void. I could not keep up. She was now sobbing, obviously pained. Her breathing became labored, syncopated. I was at a loss, unsteadied. Her distress upset me; in our several years working together, I had never seen her in such a state. I wanted to ground myself by understanding what just happened, to offer her some grounding. It is very hard to convey how startling and how difficult such moments can feel for the analyst. But this was not a moment for "understanding." Why? I can only formulate this retrospectively: trying to understand would have been to take us both out of the moment, to try to treat it as if representations were already formed, when Isabela's experience was emergent, not yet inserted in time. This, in other words, was not symbolic or signified experience, and to try to grasp it would have been about trying to slow down what was occurring for *my* benefit. Speaking, I felt, would interrupt something, though I had no idea what. I wondered if she could bear my silence. Or if I could, since I, too, was on the carrier wave of whatever was unfolding. I remained quiet. Slowly, Isabela stopped sobbing. She calmed. We sat quietly, immersed in shared speechlessness trying to absorb what had happened. The session ended. She left upset, not looking at me, the surge of the experience still crackling in the room. I was not sure she would be coming back.

Before the session I just described, I had heard much about my patient's sexual practices, which entailed varying degrees of physical risk. Spontaneously, Isabela would assure me about Raven's and her own physical safety. I had not felt that I needed those reassurances; my sense of Isabela was that she was a careful, responsible top. But I was also aware that these encounters involved physical and, importantly, uncharted emotional risks. While I felt confident that Isabela was not self-destructive or reckless, an accident could easily occur: Isabela was playing with fire, at times literally so. Something could get out of hand, on the physical or the emotional plane. I sometimes felt tempted to try to engage her toward learning more about what these interests symbolized, what was being enacted or repeated. I felt the pull to ask questions, to understand, to explain, to make links. But I did not think that this would be a good path. My questions would invite her to order her material before it had a chance to fully form. I had learned enough from my work with Adam to be able to appreciate that in this domain, it is not meaning per se that matters most but the rendering of the enigmatic into something apprehensible, something that can appear in the clinical room, which is another way of saying that asking after meaning would require Isabella to translate her experience for *my* sake and at *my* timing. Thus, I purposely did not ask Isabela about the possible meanings of her sexual interests. This is not to say that I did not think that there was represented material to which we could turn or that there were no links to be made with her past: not only did they exist, but some of these connections almost begged to be interpreted while others Isabela brought up herself. I felt strongly, though, that such interventions, however insightful or reasonable, would foreground more formed psychic elements, interrupting an unfolding process of more elusive psychic material, as if I were impatiently fishing out of the water an oyster that is still organizing its process around a grain of sand. Howard Levine cautions analysts not to "search for or await the emergence of something organized but hidden in the minds of our patients," highlighting that what may be occurring "may not have yet achieved the level of specificity and organization so as to be discernible and hidden; [it] may not [yet] be embedded in a network of associated meanings; may not yet have achieved a specific form and may only 'exist' as a spectrum of possibilities that have yet to come into existence" (2012, p. 608).

The analyst's task, Laplanche insists, is not to interpret, synthesize, or make meaning on the patient's behalf. This may sound surprising to nonanalysts and is actually hard for most analysts to digest, too. For Laplanche, it is the analysand who should be the hermeneut, who makes meaning, and it is in the interest of the analytic work that the analyst not hasten to bind the material for the patient (i.e., through interpretation). Narrativizing, Laurence Kahn highlights, risks producing a binding that is only mimetic (2018). To take this a step further, I would add that what this may mean at times is that the analyst may have to do some internal work of her own to avoid disrupting the patient's move toward her own unbinding, which can, in turn, fracture encrusted meanings (old translations). What this suggests is that the analyst must guard against the anxiety that arises in her as the patient's unbinding gathers momentum toward a state of overwhelm (Saketopoulou, 2017a). Too often attention is paid to a patient going too far and becoming overwhelmed, when it might sometimes be better placed on the *analyst's* resistances to the patient's overwhelm, to the analyst, that is, interfering with the patient going far enough for the possibility of overwhelm to arise at all. We may be reminded here of Imani's hesitation to follow Lumi's command, which speaks to how predominant the concern with safety can become. Safety, in that sense, becomes dangerous, a danger the costs of which are incalculable: one can measure what went wrong, but one cannot measure what never became, what one never got to experience.

A stance that is hospitable to overwhelm is obviously not without risk. With Isabela, I could not be certain that her risk-taking—especially in its emotional dimensions—would turn out well. This challenge reached its zenith when it infiltrated the transference/countertransference in the session I just described. Sitting with Isabela in the room while she was coming undone, both of us accosted by the charge and inexplicability of what was inchoate and beyond our reach, I worried that this would be too much for her, that she might end the analysis. And I hope that I have conveyed that the experience was quite unsteadying and too much for me as well.

Isabela started our next session with a memory that we had discussed before, albeit superficially. Her mother, whom she idealized and revered, had raised Isabela and her sister with considerable anxiety that poverty, immigration, and racial otherness would substantially constrain their lives, an anxiety that was not unwarranted given the reign of White supremacy, prejudicial views against immigrants, and the limits to dignified access to resources. Her mother worked diligently to impart to her children the skills they would need to navigate life in the United States, and Isabela was keenly aware of, and grateful for, these efforts. It seemed that, indeed, a combination of the mother's attentiveness and her pride in her heritage had equipped Isabela well, as Isabela was managing to navigate with strength and grace the many structural obstacles in her life. Her mother's hopes for a good life for her daughters took many forms. One of them became encapsulated in the fantasy that learning how to play the piano, an instrument the mother loved dearly, might place her girls in the right circles. To pay for private lessons, she took a second job involving arduous, painful manual labor that left her body aching and sore.

Isabela remembered the piano lessons in bright detail. Upon walking into the teacher's home, she and her sister would be presented with a cup of coffee, a tradition common in their culture. Isabela experienced the freshly prepared, scalding-hot coffee not as an offering but as a demand: the lesson would not start until she finished it. Her sister would set the coffee aside until it cooled down. But my patient agonized: every minute of delay wasted time paid for by her mother's arduous labor. Under the teacher's commanding gaze, she would hastily gulp the coffee down. The sensation would make her eyes tear up with pain. I thought of her description during the ego breach produced by her sexual experience: "a smell and a taste, a kind of burning bitterness, like a burning."

Throughout our work, Isabela had always spoken with idealizing admiration about her mother's work ethic and devotion. Closely behind trailed feelings of guilt and fears of being undeserving of her mother's suffering: the struggles of poverty, the losses incurred through immigration, the parents' ecstatic and insurmountable nostalgia, all in the service of a better life for their daughters. These sacrifices accrued a debt that could not be repaid. Isabela (felt that she) would never be good enough: she would never be worthy of being given so much, of so much having been given up for her sake. Further complicating things, her complex gender, her queer sexuality, her passion for intellectual work—none of these were readily legible to her mother. And as a queer woman, Isabela would never be able to produce the "good life" that her mother labored for, adding an agonizing layer of failure and insufficiency to her anguish.

But now we were able to go beyond Isabela's feelings of guilt about not making good on her mother's sacrifice. Thinking through the coffee ritual, Isabela came to wonder whether her mother's sacrifice was perhaps not as straightforward as she had always thought. Was the mother's own history and her commitment to her exhaustive labor more fraught than Isabela had imagined? Did her mother's pained relationship to class arise only upon moving to the United States? These questions did not rush in to replace Isabela's sense of her parents' difficulties in immigrating to the States as people of color who had limited resources and little formal education; they only further nuanced her understanding of it, adding more depth and dimensionality to Isabela's sense of her mother's relationship to immigration. Slowly, Isabela began to share memories of the way her mother would speak to her; Isabela now located impatience, even exasperation, in her tone. The mother's way of disciplining her looked harsher, even condescending at times. Large discrepancies between the way Isabela and her older sister were regarded by their mother also appeared in my patient's recollections. For the first time, Isabela began to contemplate her mother's relationship to her own mother and how her mother's differential treatment of her sister would sometimes play out in Isabela's romantic relationships. More new thoughts emerged. We explored these not as discovered truths or as recovered memories but as novel translations made by Isabela, as new ways of understanding her life. With time, Isabela started to regard her race, ethnic background, and queer identity more on her own terms. Increasingly, her relationship to her race, her heritage, her gender, and her sexuality came to feel like they belonged to her rather than being measured by their deviation from others' wishes for her.

In Isabela's sexual encounter with Raven, the mounting of extreme stimulation incited a state of overwhelm. Her description of feeling "broken open by experience" may thus be seen as the experiential correlate of ego shattering. The ineffable sensation she described (neither smell nor taste) arose in the crevasses opened up by that shattering. To me, this nearly incommunicable sensory morsel was a weakly represented enigmatic bit released through the shattering of her ego and through the unbinding of old translations. But it was only in the après-coup of my inadvertent introduction of the smell of the Greek coffee that this sensory bit acted to selectively activate her memory of the piano lessons and the traumatizing coffee ritual.

Some further explanation of this process may help clarify. We have seen how enigma cannot be veridically decoded, how it is either translated or repressed. Isabela's sensation ("a smell and a taste, a burning bitterness, like a burning") may be seen as an underdeveloped, rudimentary form that enigma took during the rupture of her ego, that is, during the detranslation of the enigmatic. For these freed-up bits to become further elaborated, however, they had to borrow a transient form from elsewhere. Where did this form come from? I would say that it came from me and from my own psychic process. Isabela's recounting of her sexual experience, of her coming undone, and of the vague bitter/hot sensation seems to have agitated something related to my own infantile sexuality, to have produced a "generative turbulence" (Civitarese, 2013) in me that connects to my oddly timed making of the coffee. For me, Greek coffee has an excess of meaning. It is a signifier of a country that I have partly lost through immigration—a feature I shared with Isabela's parents. At the time of my work with Isabela, this loss was especially inflamed for me, and the pain of being an immigrant was throbbing: the Greek economic crisis was full throttle and was precipitously unraveling my country's social fabric in unprecedented ways. The financial collapse caused a true humanitarian crisis: children were fainting in schools from hunger, people were losing their homes and livelihoods, and there was a surge in suicide rates. A disturbing skyrocketing of virulent, nationalist sentiment elected a neo-Nazi party in parliament. The party, Golden Dawn, targeted, tortured, and murdered immigrants, setting up blood banks and soup kitchens that exclusively served Greek citizens. I was brokenhearted by this unfolding disaster and pained by being in the United States when so much was going on in my homeland. Suffice it to say, I was transfixed by news reporting about it. All of this manifestly alarming but highly represented material was subtended by less represented, enigmatic matter—which is beyond my scope here.

So to return to the Greek coffee, I do not think that my urge to make it arose through some form of unconscious communication from Isabela, whereby her memory of the teacher's coffee-making somehow triggered an analogous response in me. Rather, the signifier of Greek coffee is something that I brought to the analytic exchange, it is a production of my own process that arose in the context of what Isabela's material evoked *for me*. It reflects, that is, my own serendipitous yet meaningful response to the patient's material, which, in turn, provided a medium through which the proto-form of the enigmatic in Isabela's experience (the burning, bitter/hot sensation) became elaborated, activating her own memory of the coffee offering and the piano lessons. The Greek coffee that I made, that is, derived its meaning from its retroactive effect on my patient's memory.

In my clinical writings, I have encouraged analysts to be mindful about interrupting the gathering of momentum toward a state of overwhelm. This, I have suggested to my colleagues, can be especially difficult to do when working with perverse sexual material, because of the evocation of the analyst's own infantile sexuality. In the presence of such material, the analyst may become excited, captivated, fearful, or defensively transfixed by the descriptive poignancy of the sexual scenarios discussed, thus wanting to slow down the patient or turn to the more highly represented, more energetically bound, dimensions. This is not to say that the scenarios that analysands enact do not have elements that can be mined for meaning. It is only to say that a hypertrophied focus on symbolic meanings can only reach symbolized experience; it can only access translations, but stays away from what is not psychically ordered. Orienting the clinical work toward uncovering meaning disrupts the ego's radical unbinding. A patient's overwhelm can be incredibly hard to sit with because it agitates the analyst's infantile sexuality; with Isabela, I was stirred, which excited the patient's earlier mnemic traces in the après-coup. Exploring those memories in the analysis led to Isabela rebinding freed-up enigma in new ways, giving it room to

become retranslated *by her*. Isabela's fresh translations made more degrees of psychic freedom possible for her, as these new translations were
less tightly coiled around the other's desire, coming more into her own
possession. A self with greater agency and freedom, one that answered
less to parental and generational phantoms or to cultural mandates, thus
became possible through the work of overwhelm.

To be clear, in referencing "more degrees of freedom," I do not mean
to imply that an emancipation from the social order or from history is
possible, nor am I referring to some newfound access to a "true" self or
"reality." Speaking of access or truth makes little sense because enigma is
not about recuperating some primal memory or even an unconsciously
transmitted intergenerational past that is finally recovered.[22] What
becomes available to the patient through this process is always—and
only—a new translation. New translations are no more definitive or accurate than the earlier unraveled ones; they, too, are subject to being
broken down and to being stitched together just like the ones previously
disbanded. What is at stake, in other words, is not a "final destination"
as far as translation is concerned, but how well a translation works at
a particular point in the patient's life. In that sense, we should assume
that the potential for mobility and shape-shifting exists in all translations: no one translation has the final word, as "the unconscious [is] an
endless generator of interpretations" (Cimatti, 2016, p. 208). To put it
differently, the promise of overwhelm is not an authoritative new translation, neither does it offer repair or "liberation." What materialized in
and through Isabela's ego shattering, my enactment, the recollection that
it brought forth, and the retranslations that arose in our work does not
capture anything with historical accuracy. Isabela did not "discover" the
mother's ambivalence, racial trauma, or class injury—though these may
well be there. What Isabela was able to do was arguably more urgent
than that: it helped her craft *a personal, subjective relationship* to her
class, to her race, and to her queerness, with them becoming more *hers*,
less answerable to the meanings and anxieties they generated in her family or in the ethnic and racial group she identified herself with, bringing
them more into her own possession.[23]

In the session with Isabela, overwhelm and the ego shattering that it
produced manifested themselves in the void that opened up between
the two of us: therein, I would say, we encountered something strange,

something impossible to articulate, something opaque. When overwhelm enters a space, we should expect dysregulation and discomfort. But, as I have been arguing, this disruption, however difficult, is not always or necessarily an indication that something is going wrong *but that something is going on*. At moments of such turbulence, it is only human to want to understand, to want to make meaning, to want to organize ourselves (to bind for ourselves), to want to help the other (to bind for the other). I have been exploring in this chapter how urgent these moments can feel, how much may (feel to) be at stake, how much it can look like the organization that meaning can offer us is the ethical and compassionate thing to offer. And I have also been suggesting that taking that path works to disrupt the gathering of momentum that leads to the unbinding of the ego—and will do so, in some instances, for our own comfort and to settle ourselves. Resisting this "compassionate" impulse (to bind for the other's comfort and relief) is not easy: to resist it, one has to side with doing what is necessary and required for unbinding to be a possibility. It is for this reason that Laplanche broke with most psychoanalytic traditions, which see the analyst as working toward a purposive goal. For him, by contrast, the analyst's role is to be an "artisan of unbinding" (1996/2015b, p. 200). To me, such a stance informs a deeply ethical form of sadism, a sadism that is driven by the exigency of doing what is necessary, what is required to intervene against the other's effort to master their unconscious through binding.

In offering this clinical case and in elaborating the importance of resisting the impulse to bind and offer meaning *to* the other, I am not advocating for a method of being in everyday relations. This stance is to be reserved for very particular forms of relations and contexts, and it needs time to cultivate and unfold. Further, as we will see in our extended discussion of exigent sadism, not everyone has the preference or appetite for these kinds of experiences, and not everyone is willing to subject themselves to the rigorous demands that exigent sadism makes *of the sadist*. Last, Isabela is my patient, which means that, at least to some degree ("some" because of limit consent), she has signed up for this process. Nor am I offering a how-to of overwhelm: overwhelm is not something to "achieve" or a "goal" one sets out to accomplish but an experience that arrives unbidden. Accordingly, I have wanted to show what *may* come out of making ourselves possible to experience, if we allow ourselves to be disrupted and to have the terms by which we understand ourselves contested, if we let ourselves travel into territories that make us profoundly uncomfortable without reaching to bind and, thus, to master the unintelligible that opens up in the encounter with opacity. Most importantly, I want to convey that such experiences do not necessarily culminate in traumatization, as is often the fear.

Chapter 3 takes up how some of these mechanisms are put in motion by subjecting oneself to "inciting traumatisms," small-scale painful events that reopen the implantative dimension of trauma. To linger in the interstitial space between unbinding and rebinding is a particular kind of aesthetic experience, which is why the ideas so far explored can open up such important vistas for thinking about how we relate to some performance, whether we give ourselves over to it to permit it to act on us, and that is more likely to happen with art and performance that crackle with the force of the infantile sexual.

3

Risking Sexuality Beyond Consent

Overwhelm and Inciting Traumatisms

"I was female-assigned at birth," writes the queer theorist Kathryn Bond Stockton:

> Though [my own sense was that] I was a boy . . . mistaken for a girl. And though I was, to my mind, the ultimate straight man seeking normally feminine women, I turned out a "lesbian," against my will—though in accord with my desires. As for my girlfriend she grew up, to her mind, normally feminine, as a rural Mormon raised in rural Utah. In her twenties, after her male fiancé died, after she didn't go on a mission, after she walked across the US for nuclear disarmament, she met lesbians and wished she could be one, so cool did they seem to her. But, she figured, she wasn't a lesbian. Long story short: I didn't want the sign ["lesbian"] but was pierced by it; she quite wanted it but didn't think she'd gain it. We have [both] been dildoed by th[at] sign. We've been pleasured by it, as it's come inside us—I've had to try to take it like a man. (2015)

Stockton's surprising, albeit sideways, treatment of consent is easy to miss.[1] Her delectable phrase ("against my will—though in accord with my desire") is followed by a provocative, queer claim: that she has been "dildoed" by the word "lesbian." The word "dildoed" does some heavy lifting here: being described as a lesbian interpellated Stockton as a woman; because she had thought herself to be a boy, this "screwed" her; this screwing is something she has tried to take "like a man." Is this wordplay meant to convey the stoicism with which men, as the story goes, are expected to endure hardship? Or is Stockton gesturing to a queer masculinity of anal pleasures? Whatever the case may be, Stockton's relationship to being screwed is unusual: it is against her will but in accord with her desires.

Taking Stockton's lead, I explore in this chapter what, other than being "screwed"—by discourse, by history, or through the intervention of the other—can come from being subjected to something to which we did not entirely, or even at all, consent. In previous chapters, I called consent that lives on the border of what we have authorized "limit consent." Limit consent does not concern itself with road maps specifying what the other is or is not allowed to do but pertains, instead, to what we open ourselves up to when we surrender to an other and to the otherness in ourselves. Limit consent involves the bending of one's will, though not to (re)stage an experience of satisfaction, as in affirmative consent. Rather, limit consent is about inviting surprise that opens ups space for fresh experience. This invitation is risky through and through; one steps into this space at the risk of being injured or assuming the risk of injuring the other. If such injury occurs, however, it is inadvertent, issuing from sexual urges that have gone too far, as opposed to a careless disregard of the other as is the case in sexual harassment and sexual assault.

In this chapter, we will continue to probe why one might court experiences that chafe against the limit. Such courting travels on the carrier wave of repetition to create states of overwhelm that may, in turn, catalyze psychic transformations by wounding one's ideas about oneself. In chapter 2, we discussed the processes by which enigma gets churned into representations and into identity. In this chapter, I focus on the violence that subtends the ego's formation and discuss the mechanisms by which the ego comes to staunchly refuse encounters with novelty. Because new experiences are resisted, anything that is new occurs at the border of the ego's consent, which means that for something novel to take place, the ego's resistances have to be countered. Repetitive traumatisms, that is, irruptions that are painful but do not reach traumatic intensity, can counter the ego's resistances—a key element in traumatophilia. After laying this conceptual groundwork, I then turn to Jeremy O. Harris's painfully beautiful theatrical work *Slave Play* to illustrate some of these ideas. Watching this play several times, across four productions, and attending ongoing conversations about it over several months helped me clarify the workings of overwhelm, limit consent, and exigent sadism.[2] I use *Slave Play* as a case study to ferret out the specific mechanisms through which erotic humiliation and racialized sexual abjection, which, on appearance, merely repeat ghastly historical crimes, may, in fact, work to help individuals bring more into their possession the way history "screwed" them. The concept of overwhelm helps us understand how such psychic work may be accomplished and shows its possible yield: not utopian reparation but expanded psychic freedoms. Even as such expansions are only partial solutions, they may work better for some subjects, which leads me to the main argument of this chapter: because traumatized subjects can never return to a pretraumatic state, I propose that we become less preoccupied with what can be done about trauma, an approach I call "traumatophobic," and that we become more curious about what subjects do *with* their trauma, an approach I describe as "traumatophilic."

To Be Dildoed by the Signifier: Aulagnier and Primary Violence, Laplanche and the Mythosymbolic

Let us return to Stockton's having been dildoed by the sign. To reflect on her ideas, I draw on Piera Aulagnier, a French psychoanalyst whose work uniquely addresses how the psychic process of coming into being tangles from the get-go the nonconsensual with pleasure.

The signs or, to migrate to psychoanalytic terminology, the signifiers by which the infant's early psychic life can be churned into experience precede us and are not of our choosing. Embedded in a network of other signifiers, they are linked with each other through the connective tissue of discourse. For Aulagnier, discourse does not refer to language per se but to the aggregate effects of the way the social is structured and to the way, in turn, it structures us (1975). Discourse inflects the adult's ongoing stream of gestures, facial expressions, affect, acts, and words, thus infiltrating the adult's responses to the child. When the adult responds, verbally or nonverbally, to the infant, they organize experience *for* the infant. In so doing, the adult inadvertently formats the amorphousness of the infant's experience, giving it a shape. That shape does not issue from the infant herself; it is introduced by the parent, and it is by means of that discourse that the primal, that is, the raw material of the infant's early life before the "I" becomes organized into a self, gets forged into units of experience.[3]

The shape given to the primal is, in part, influenced by the parent's own sexual unconscious and also by their early history and psychic conflicts. But Aulagnier's point is that caretakers are not independent or sovereign agents; they are themselves subject—and answerable—to external regimes of organized meanings, which will furnish them with their meaning-making templates. The infant's ego, in effect, draws on these parental templates for its constitutive, meaning-making efforts. We may think of discourse, then, as procuring the much-needed midwifing tools that the psyche needs to come into being. By implication, the ego develops as an assemblage of psychic representations that are made up of meanings largely delimited by what is already socially intelligible. Consequently, the only translational tools at the child's disposal come from what is already socially intelligible. Aulagnier is especially sensitive to the implications of this process for the infant's meaning-making endeavors. Although forming representations (binding) is a pleasurable activity, she also sees this process as exerting on the infant a form of violence that she calls "primary violence."

Considered through the prism of Laplanche, what Aulagnier's intervention argues is that the process of translation is violent and, to some degree, constricting.[4] The word "violence" may feel troubling and can be misleading, so let me clarify that Aulagnier is not referring to physical violence, nor is she referring to a caretaker's intention to prohibit, control, or oppress the infant's meaning-making efforts.[5] Rather, the concept of primary violence draws attention to the fact that the array of raw materials available to the infant for the crafting of their psychic representations, and thus their ego, is by nature restricted and, thus, restrictive. We can think of this restricted array of translational tools, which are provided by the parent's psychic imbrication with the social world and which temporally precede the infant's arrival in the world, as creating a translational funnel of sorts through which the infant's psychic world can then take shape. Primary violence delimits from before the beginning, then, how something will become psychically represented. And since primary violence is akin to translation, we see that translation and binding are also subtended by the violent restriction of meaning. Conversely, ways of being that have not yet entered the social and/or those that are not yet solidified in the wider cultural imaginary are less likely to become possible translational avenues. The subject compresses all meaning into already-existing shapes, and if you are thinking that this is limiting, it is because it is.[6] A culture's most dominant meaning-making templates will more readily lend themselves to becoming translational vessels. For instance, because procreative heterogenitality and binary gender are the most intelligible, socially sanctioned, and institutionally supported forms of sex and gender in Western culture, it should come as no surprise that they are the translational frameworks most plainly on offer for the formatting of the infantile sexual.

And yet, even as primary violence places constraints on the most elemental level of human becoming, its mediation is also indispensable for the infant to generate meaning at all.[7] A world without discourse, myths, or symbols is unimaginable. If, as a thought experiment, we imagined such a society, it would not be freeing but catastrophic: not only would it not provide greater translational freedom but, on the contrary, it would deprive the psyche of the much-needed tools for meaning-making. This is the psychic landscape of limit consent; even before the "I" is inaugurated, a lot has already happened without one's agreement but that, nevertheless, yields pleasure and possibility.

Aulagnier's ideas are highly compatible with Laplanche's. For him, as we have seen, an indecipherable surcharge (enigma) is implanted like an irritant on the infant's psychophysiological skin (primal seduction). The infant is compelled to interpret these enigmatic implantations but they can't be accurately decoded. The ego is composed by the meanings ascribed to enigma through fantasy (Scarfone, 2016). Importantly, translations are encoded as memory; that is, we remember them as something that happened to us, rather than as something we concocted (Scarfone, 2015a). In some ways, I would say, this is not a distortion: the translational tools on which we *have* to rely to translate enigma do, in fact, "happen" to us as they come to us from the outside, from the adults in our lives and their immersion in social life. Translation, therefore, evades the problem of binary reality—"did x actually happen, or did it not?"—making memory always a complex tangle between the real meaning-making tools of how we make sense of the world (the mythosymbolic) and the singular ways in which we use them (our own, personal translations). The enigmatic remnants that have not become meaning-full become repressed, forming the sexual unconscious, where they persist as question marks without answers—but which press for answers anyway (the sexual drive). Like Aulagnier, Laplanche also believes that translation occurs through interpretative codes used to represent the press of the sexual drive. For the infant's translational endeavors, the infant will resort to a cultural reservoir of "objets trouvés" (Saketopoulou, 2017b), namely, the socius and its "rules, myths, ideologies and ideals" (mythosymbolic) (Laplanche, 1987, p. 87). But no one accepts the plague of the other's sexual unconscious willingly; a certain degree of force, not a physical force but the force of primal seduction (Laplanche, 1987), is necessary.

It is this press, we might say, that Stockton so successfully navigates. In a world of binary gender, she is able to inventively concoct an idiosyncratic relationship to the binary signifier that dildoed her. She devises, that is, a way of being in relation to her sexuality and to her embodiment that singularly works for *her*. The point I am raising here is, obviously, not about Stockton per se but through her, rather, about the very complex matter of how improvisational possibilities (new translations) can be contrived even amid conditions of considerable constraint. We will soon return to an accounting of signifiers, to their dildoing effects, and to the overtures they make to enlarged psychic freedoms. But, for now, let us stay with the sexual dimensions of what it means to be screwed against one's wishes but in accord with one's desire. Enter the queer theorist Tim Dean, whom we will follow to a gay men's sex club to hear about his experience with piss play, the erotic practice of urination for sexual pleasure (2015).

Piss Play

In Dean's prior experiments with piss play, he describes having been "happy to give but unwilling to receive" (2015, p. 122). Things changed one night, however, after following a leather-capped stranger into the shadows of a sex club.

> [The stranger] pushed me to my knees . . . encouraging me to work his soft cock through the mesh of his jockstrap. My mouth registered that the jockstrap was already damp . . . When I became aware that he was gently pissing through the jock, the tasteless warm fluid flooding my lips, I spontaneously ejaculated. Both his piss and my body's response *took me completely by surprise*. I did not consent—and *would not have consented*—to being pissed on; yet I loved it. That night the man in the

leather cap, whose face I never saw, gave me the gift of *erotic astonishment*. (2015, p. 125; emphases added)

How do we understand Dean's experience of "erotic astonishment," and why should we care about it? Is his erotic astonishment, which I argue amounts to more than just physical pleasure, related to the absence of his consent?[8] I think that it is. Of course, even intimating that a sexuality beyond consent is worth theorizing—let alone having—will raise eyebrows. Affirmative consent, we are told, is key to ethical sexual relations; it ensures that power differentials are well tended and sees to it that ongoing and enthusiastic agreement is secured. It also promises mutual sexual pleasure and a protection from trauma, not to mention legal liability. Established as the sole acceptable ethical rudder, the discourse on consent has utterly "magnetized us" (Fischel, 2019, p. 176). Today, writes the analyst Anne Dufourmantelle, "the principle of precaution has become the norm" (2019, p. 1). Not just the lawman but the actuary now also oversees our sexual encounters.

But while the absence or violation of consent is a meaningful and important analytic for psychic and political life, affirmative consent is conceptually thin—and, to me, not very useful. In short, affirmative consent fails to deliver on its promises of mutual pleasure and safety or to adjudicate desire (Fischel, 2016, 2019). From a psychoanalytic angle, it is easy to see why: the affirmative consent model presumes a fully conscious subject even though desire is often unconsciously conflicted; traumatic irruptions complicate agency and incite repetitions; psychic time, especially the temporality of psychic trauma, is nonlinear and this can introduce perilous asynchronies between the time when consent is negotiated and the experience that ensues. Most importantly for my project, though, affirmative consent seeks to reproduce known pleasures or, at least, pleasures that can be hoped for or envisioned (meaning already psychically represented ones), whereas the sexual courts the strange (Davies & Dean, 2022) and the ineffable (Dimen, 2017; Stein, 2008).

These critiques notwithstanding, speaking about consent that congregates to the limit is scary territory. Limit consent may have animated the encounter that generated Dean's erotic astonishment, but someone less able to give themselves over to this startling experience might have felt injured by the novelty or even experienced it as a form of rape—and we could easily understand why. Obviously, in veering away from the contractualized reciprocity demanded by affirmative consent, my point is not to endorse violation but to explore the psychic processes set in motion when one lets oneself become passible to another, coming up against the limits of their own ego. I take this term "passibility" (*passibilité*) from Lyotard (1988/1991) and will have more to say about it shortly. For now, I want to note that passibility is a border concept, hovering in the interstices between activity and passivity. It involves giving oneself over to the other, not in capitulation or in masochistic surrender but in a state of susceptible receptivity to one's own and to the other's opacity (Lyotard, 1988/1991; see also Scarfone, 2019).

To go forward from here, let us turn back the clock by a hundred years.

A Hundred Years Ago

In *Beyond the Pleasure Principle*, Freud described

> as "traumatic" any excitations from outside . . . powerful enough to break through the protective shield. . . The concept of trauma necessarily implies a connection of this kind with a breach in an otherwise efficacious barrier against stimuli. Such an event as an external trauma is bound to provoke a disturbance on a large scale in the functioning of the organism's energy. . . . There is no longer any possibility of preventing the mental apparatus from being flooded with large amounts of stimulus, and another problem arises . . . mastering the amounts of stimulus which have broken in and of binding them, in the psychical sense, so that they can then be disposed of. (1920, p. 102)

In this account, trauma arises when external stimuli (excitation) breach the protective shield, leaving the overwhelmed ego scurrying to try to bind, that is, to repair the breach.

But the problem of how the psychic apparatus manages the influx of energy preoccupied Freud from much earlier. In *Project for a Scientific Psychology* (1895), Freud first proposed the following model of the ego: outside energy excites neurons whose job it is to conduct and discharge it.[9] Impermeable neurons are unable to let energy course through them; if the amount of energy reaching them is substantial enough, their contact barrier is broken. Repeated breaches establish a path through which stimuli have previously passed. Neurons that have been broken through together now begin to fire in unison, creating pathways that direct the free flow of energy into what we might think of as a trough. The ego is the aggregate of these neuronal facilitations, a permanently cathected ensemble that ensures that discharge does not proceed chaotically. The ego, we might thus say, is the product of repetition and habit. When new stimulations occur, the ego protects the organism from the unpleasure of freely circulating energy by attracting newly excited neurons, which simply means that the ego assimilates these new stimuli into its structure. By directing the commerce of new psychic energy along established grooves (binding) so as to preserve the organism from an influx of energy spikes (unbound energy), the well-functioning ego works to appropriate unto itself everything that is new and foreign. The ego, that is, is "hegemonic: it lays claim to being the whole and is potentially the whole" (Laplanche, 1994/2015a, p. 116). In the introduction, I used Glissant to highlight how the ego's appropriative tendency rhymes with colonial logics. I now want to pinpoint the psychic processes that underlie this link.

As we have seen, binding spares the organism from damage: the ego diminishes any "excess of reality" (Scarfone, 2015a, p. 30) by preventing excitation from spreading in unforeseeable and unregulated ways. This grants the psyche a sense of stability and an ongoingness of being free from constant threat. But the fact that the ego works to assimilate new experience into its preexisting structure means that encounters with the new will be resisted and inhibited. In that respect, the ego is not just a stabilizing agent but also a conservative and inhibiting force that never fully relinquishes its resistance to novelty (Laplanche, 1995; Scarfone, 2015a). As such, we should expect that nothing new happens with the ego's consent. (The ego, of course, does not offer or withhold consent. But I hope that the reader will permit me this anthropomorphizing locution for reasons that will become clear later.) The ego contorts the alien and the unfamiliar into what is already known, and this gobbling up of freshness and surprise can calcify it. Of course, the ego's resistance, its refusal to consent to novelty, if you will, does not mean that nothing new occurs. But it is incumbent on us to outline the mechanisms by which change—newness—happens, given that the ego is so formidably staked on its own preservation.

Our thinking may be helped along by turning to a largely overlooked point made by Freud (1895, 1920). In discussing breaches of unlimited degree (trauma), Freud mentions others, of lower intensity, that are not incapacitating. These produce "a breach in continuity" (1895, p. 307), causing physical and, probably, psychic pain. This intermediary state lies between the steady, well-regulated space of the ego and the disabling effects of trauma. I introduced the term "overwhelm" in chapter 2 to describe states in which the ego's concerted investment to keep things stable/knowable/bound is overrun. In overwhelm, we saw, the ego surrenders its overly tight hold over its translations (binding), resulting in a process of unbinding in which the links between enigma and its representational coatings dissolve. This disaggregation of previously bound enigma from its psychic coatings is pleasurable, but it is also anguishing. And it is a transient condition—something that flashes *into* experience but that cannot be sustained for long. A radical state of unbinding will urgently seek stability through fresh bindings (new translations) or will kindle repression. When neither occurs, we are in the domain of what we understand as psychotic phenomena—or what is more colloquially referred to as a "breakdown." We see that unbinding is a very serious matter. Overwhelm's transiently dysregulated states may be pleasurable, but they are also crisis points that offer no reassurances: we cannot know in advance "whether the unbinding, which creates the uncertainty, will lead to restoration of previous binding or to a new binding or to neither" (House, 2019, p. 181).

In that sense, unbinding is a door that can lead to many different directions, including possibly problematic and dangerous ones. Even when new bindings do occur, we cannot be certain that they will be preferable or good ones. For example, in the introduction, when discussing Moten's call to us to "listen" to Emmett Till's photograph, I emphasized that there is no way of securing ahead of time that new listening will produce something oriented toward what is ethical or just. Such listening could conceivably also give way to translations that may be evil, ugly, even fascist. The risk in such unbinding, then, is that we cannot know ahead of time how freed-up enigma (unbound energy) will become translated or to what uses those translations will be later put. That risk is ever present and cannot be eliminated. At the same time, new translations can also be expansively transformative—not because they uncover what "really" happened in infancy or because they help "regain contact with . . . our essence" (Foucault, 1997, p. 282), because enigma is always a question mark without an answer. But through detranslation, the breakdown of old structures, one may emerge reconfigured. In that sense, the unbinding accompanying overwhelm offers something far more consequential than "the truth" of what happened; it can put something new in motion.

This considerable potential notwithstanding, overwhelm should not be romanticized. Even though pleasurable, the ego's breach is an intense state that may be experienced as painful, disorganizing, even dangerous.[10] This, by the way, is also the critical difference between overwhelm and Bersani's notion of self-shattering. The latter is unquestioningly optimistic as to the possibilities of new bindings and underplays the not-insubstantial dangers and costs of unbinding. Still, overwhelm does not destroy the psyche; it only liquidates the ego's obdurate links. Unbound states do, and should, worry us: because of the risk for mental health crises, severe acting out, and so on and also because we sense that their pleasures can have magnetic effects—sometimes with detrimental impact. But the distinction between trauma and overwhelm is an important one because it allows us to be less panicked about individuals who have a propensity to pursue experiences that can breach the ego's barrier and who search for trauma-like experiences.

Traumatophilia

In a text that has not yet had wide circulation, Laplanche (1980) makes passing reference to traumatophilia, a term I unearth to develop into a full-blown concept.[11] The term was first explored by Karl Lowenfeld, who observed that some of his patients "hunger for experiences and excitement, [showing] a 'greed for impressions,'" and "provok[ing] situations which . . . become traumatic" (1941, pp. 117–118, 121). The "traumatic" situations Lowenfeld alluded to, though, did not behave as trauma ordinarily does: they were neither ruinous nor detrimental. Instead, they produced generative crises akin to overwhelm. An appreciable difference exists, then, between trauma and intense trauma-like excitations that may incite growth-inducing work. To uphold this distinction, we will henceforth use Laplanche's phrase "inciting traumatism" (*traumatisme incitateur*; 1980, p. 195) to describe behaviors that repeat with a seemingly unstoppable fervor, drawing the subject to a previously traumatic site, building up to overwhelm. Laplanche likened overly tight binding to a "death by the ego" (1987, p. 171) and cautioned that an ego that does its inhibiting job *too* well can create a suffocating inertia, as when one is too certain of who one is, overly confident one knows with certainty that one knows oneself, or convinced one knows with certainty how something works. Traumatisms can disrupt such structures that have become too stale. Offering possibilities for revivifying internal experience, traumatisms can thus help generate aliveness and inspiration.

This process is akin to description of the workings of the anarchic drive proposed by the French psychoanalyst Nathalie Zaltzman. For her, excessive binding can make reality too banal, rousing cravings for an encounter with novelty "to create new drive movements" (1979, p. 57). She, too, described patients who, smothered by too much binding, would expose themselves to risky and extreme situations. Zaltzman, more than any other analyst, brought attention to the generative possibilities of unbinding and to the enlivening properties of the drive's anarchy.[12] For her, the need to put one's life at risk or to go to extremes may salvage psychological processes from stalemate or stagnation. Despite appearances to the contrary, this puts the anarchic drive in the service of life—or, to be more precise, in the service of a fullness in living, making it into a force that kindles "a taste for change" (Zaltzman, 1979, p. 77). Such "taste for change" should not be confused with neoliberal ruses and capitalist plugs that advertise the consumption of new experiences sold to us as expansive and life-changing. Rather, Zaltzman refers to something much more nuanced than that: to changes that may take us to places we did not anticipate, animating new energies. These changes are not accretive and supportive of what we already think we know about ourselves, nor are they of the sort promoted by campaigns that seek to buttress our narcissism (e.g., "be your best self" and so on). They refer, rather, to experiences that open us up, exposing us to the surprising and to the strange in ourselves.

The processes described by Laplanche and Zaltzman share an emphasis on the transformational heft of moving past sluggish, inert ego structures.[13] We are now beginning to see from a somewhat different angle that the limit that is overrun in limit experience is the surface of the organized ego. This surface is our sense of ourselves, which is constituted through primary violence and thus the mythosymbolic, and it is this, our ideas about ourselves, that can get wounded when we come undone.[14] Since self-understandings are, to begin with, crafted through the mythosymbolic—and the prejudices swirled in it (e.g., White-supremacist ideas, sexism, and so on, as we saw in chapter 1)—the ego's unbinding has personal but also political ramifications. In chapter 2, for example, we saw how Isabela's relationship to her race, her ethnicity, and her sexuality shifted through her experience of overwhelm in the sexual encounter with her lover and in the consulting room with me.

Limit Experience

Let us return to Bataille's and Foucault's work on limit experience, introduced in chapter 1. Limit experience, as discussed, may be arrived at through various means, such as ascetic practices, art, meditation, erotic experience, BDSM, extreme sports (Lyng, 2004; Martin, Gutman, & Hutton, 1988; Newmahr, 2011), and we may now think of those activities as producing generative traumatisms. What nominates such practices to become inciting traumatisms is not their particular complexion (what they are) but their economic charge (their intensities). Put differently, the behaviors/acts in question need to have been commandeered by the sexual drive, to run on an economy of escalating excitations. Why? Because, from the perspective of Laplanchean metapsychology, it will take a force that large to come up against the limits of the ego's fortifications, to successfully contest the ego's investment in its stability and to override its resistance to novelty (that is, to go against its consent). Contesting the ego without letting up when it mounts resistance and without becoming appropriated into the ego's acquisitive operations requires considerable psychic energy.

Not all experiences can meet this economic criterion. Those that readily match the economy of the sexual drive are more likely candidates for such work. We saw in chapter 1 that sexuality is especially likely to be thus enrolled by the sexual drive because it involves the excitable body, rousing a renewed circulation of unbound energy. The erotic, in

Bataille's words, "attains a wild intensity, an insanity," that opens "directly out upon a certain vista of anguish, upon a certain lacerating consciousness of distress" (1956, pp. 137, 139). This may be amplified in sexualities that are behaviorally perverse, because they are exquisitely porous to the rogue, deviant, and savage properties of the infantile sexual. Also, traumatic repetitions have the potential to generate iterative movements that may innervate inciting traumatisms. Why is trauma especially well suited for this? Because of its economic affinity with the sexual drive: the economy of traumatic repetition is "more primitive, more elementary, more instinctual than the pleasure principle," as if watching "some 'daemonic' force at work" (Freud, 1920, pp. 23, 35; also 1914b, 1933). Traumatophilic repetitions, in other words, exert a force that can challenge the ego's complacency. To be clear, traumatophilic repetitions do not escalate out of compulsive frenzy but, rather, out of an acquired taste for the "more and more" of experience. That is, this is not repetition driven to rote iteration (as in "repetition compulsion") but for the sake of pleasure, and it is that which rescues traumatophilic repetitions from the hopeless hamster wheel of recursion (Nyong'o, 2010). Animated by a taste for more (for more excitement, for more curiosity, etc.), such iterative behaviors can be pleasurable, and when inserted into an interpersonal scene of address (Reis, 2009; Scarfone, 2011, 2019a), they may even become "vehicle[s] of [their] own transcendence" (Reis, 2020, p. 101). The daemonic force of such repetitions is also at work in some performance, as the discussion of *Slave Play* will explore, delivering traumatisms that can incite the characters' psychic transformations, as well as the actors' and some theatergoers'.

Blanchot (1980) was especially interested in the contestation of the ego produced by limit experience, where things cannot be regulated or foreseen, where one's very existence may be felt to be at stake (see also Bataille, 1928, 1954; Foucault, 1991). He cautioned, however, against exaggerating our ability to narrate what happens in these psychic spaces. A principled stance would require us to admit that these states cannot be precisely languaged, which is another way of saying that to discuss them we will have to forgo the gratification offered by precise description (binding). Too great an enthusiasm for clarity can distort; we need, instead, to make ourselves receptive to the opaque sexual force running through them. Such a stance requires that we become passible as well, possible to the opaqueness in ourselves. "Our efforts," wrote Foucault, who experimented with limit experience himself (J. Miller, 1993; Wade, 2019), "are undoubtedly better spent in trying" to make this experience "speak from the depths of where language fails, . . . where the subject who speaks has just vanished" (1963/1977, p. 40). If we permit ourselves the imprecision of speaking in approximations, we might say that in limit experience/overwhelm, one finds oneself in the presence of the sexual drive. Divested of its representational coating—a vesting created through the primary violence exerted by the mythosymbolic (translation)—this is as bare and unmediated as the drive can be. This stripping of the drive's coating stands to relieve us from how the violence of discourse has shaped our subjectivation, breaking up existing translations to open up room for new possibilities of being.

Such experiences, however, cannot not be planned or orchestrated. They become accessible "through excess, not through want" (Bataille, 1954, p. 22), which means that the situation has to carry one over. To be carried over entails letting oneself become possible to the other (Lyotard, 1988/1991) and to the unknown. This, again, emphasizes that limit consent is not about inviting violation but about a loosening of one's defenses so that one can be transported to an elsewhere. This loosening "is the opposite of action" (Bataille, 1954, p. 46) and it entails the bending of one's will, the lowering of an internal resistive barrier. One enters such experiences without knowing where they will lead but nevertheless involving oneself as a full participant, taking responsibility for oneself and for what the experience will rouse. What will ensue cannot be anticipated: that is the condition of possibility for overwhelm, and it is also this risk that accompanies it.

Let us now return to Dean and to his leather-capped stranger, whose intentions we never learn and Dean probably did not either. Their unscripted piss-play scene did not go off the rails to become traumatic. Dean does not tell us what followed this scene, so it may look like we cannot know if his erotic astonishment developed the density of overwhelm. But we do know something of consequence. In "an arena of experimentation in which I was exclusively top," Dean writes, this stranger "made me his piss bottom" (2015, p. 125). Dean is not someone who commits himself to identitarian projects (that is, he does not "identify" as a "piss top" or a "piss bottom"); what this experience breaks down for him, in fact, in him, is how he had thus far engaged in piss play, and therein inheres his experience of the erotically astonishing. His readiness to surrender himself to this stranger, the stranger who without his consent pissed in his mouth, is subtended by Dean's capacity to give himself over not only to the stranger but also, and most significantly, to the strange in himself. "I did not and would not have consented" to being pissed on this way, he emphasizes, and it is precisely what occurred beyond, though not against, his consent that animates his erotic astonishment. In being made into a "piss bottom," what matters most is not identity (i.e., that he bottomed as opposed to topped) but the quality of transitiveness in his eroticism. In polymorphous perversity, pleasure "countermands the claims of identity" (Dean, 2012, p. 480); the key is not perversity but polymorphousness (Scarfone, 2014).

The polymorphously perverse seems also to reign in Stockton, who was able to pluck a queer pleasure from the signifier that dildoed her by inventively trying to take it "like a man." Stockton may have felt the pain of being screwed, but she related to it not through masochistic submission or rageful grievance but by crafting her own, singular relationship to the signifier "lesbian," by crafting, that is, a new translation. What is significant about Stockton's new translation is that her use of the word "lesbian" is not organized according to the symbolic order that usually trails the term: the symbolic order, as we have seen, can serve as the primary bulwark against unbinding, which is the domain of the sexual. Rather, Stockton was able to lift the signifier out of the conventional gendered frameworks in which it had been given to her, establishing her own, polysemic meanings around it. We may go so far as to say that Stockton took the signifier more into her possession—even as the signifier will never fully belong to her, any more than any signifier ever fully belongs to any of us (2019).

Stockton's and Dean's vignettes are too brief for us to trace overwhelm in its full excitement, impetus, or duress. While we know something about Dean's erotic astonishment, we are not privy to whether his or Stockton's experiences came "as close as possible to . . . that which can't be lived through" (Foucault, 1997, p. 241). For that, we will have to turn to *Slave Play* and to the brilliant mind of Jeremy O. Harris.

Slave Play

You should not work to make the audience comfortable with
what they are witnessing at all.
—Jeremy O. Harris, "Notes on Style," in *Slave Play*

So they fucked up and gave us a Broadway theater.
—Robert O'Hara, *Slave Play* director, on closing night

Slave Play landed on the New York theater scene with a thunderclap, igniting a panegyric round of reviews and a tide of celebratory appreciation for Jeremy O. Harris, its gifted thirty-year-old, queer, Black playwright. Deemed "one of the best and most provocative" new plays (J. Green, 2019), it delivered a "shot across the bow of the Great White Way" (*New York Daily News*, 2019). The extensive commentary (Holdren, 2019) focused on its artful portrayal of how White supremacy grates in the everyday (Marks, 2019). But the play is not addressing White people; it speaks to *the relation between* Black and White people in the shadow of chattel slavery.[15] *Slave Play* engaged consent at its most gnarled site, at the especially difficult junction between sexuality and the traumas of the antebellum past. Strikingly, critics left mostly untouched the most controversial aspect of the play: the erotics of interracial desire and the play's implication that racism carries an erotic charge.[16]

Unfolding on a southern plantation, the opening act stuns the audience with three interracial, psychosexual encounters involving nudity and vigorously simulated sex. In the first encounter, Kaneisha, a dark-skinned Black enslaved woman, is subjected to an erotically tinged scene of racial denigration by Jim, the White plantation overseer. Jim humiliates her, calling her a "useless hefer [*sic*]"; makes her eat off the floor "like a dog"; describes her twerking as "jigabooing"; and refers to her as a "negress" (Harris, 2018, pp. 21, 23, 27, 51).[17] Kaneisha obeys his orders while also softly challenging his authority with questions like, "you actually want an answer to that?" (2018, p. 22), making pronouncements like, "it ain't dirty in my estimation" (2018, p. 23), and dissing him for being unable to tell a watermelon apart from a cantaloupe. The use of the watermelon as a signifier distended with humiliating racial tropes is intentional: "race's eroticism is often linked to its hyperbolic absurdity," writes

Jennifer Nash, and as such "racial fictions can be both comical and alluring" (2014, p. 127). For the audience, indeed, these exchanges dart all
too quickly between the horrid and the hilarious. Jim and Kaneisha's
exchange also toggles between debasement and soft acts of irreverence.
Tension, sexual and otherwise, escalates, culminating in Jim's seeming to
force himself on her sexually. As the sex becomes vigorous, we transition
to the second couple.

Alana, a White, dim-witted, and funny southern mistress, is commanding her handsome, mixed-race slave, Philip, to play on "his little
fiddle" some of that "mulatto magic" that makes the female slaves "hoot
and holla . . . waiting to run on ya later" (Harris, 2018, pp. 30, 31, 34). The
word "fiddle," and Alana's intonation of it, imply that the real instrument
of Philip's magic is his penis. This marks the complex space that Harris
wants his audience in: eroticism and depersonalizing violence do not
belong to competing registers but to synergistic ones.[18] Philip dutifully
complies, and before long, he finds himself face down on her bed. Alana
proceeds to forcibly sodomize him with a sizable black dildo, an heir-
loom given to her on her wedding night by her mother, who correctly
predicted that her White husband would be unable to please her—and
we are led to imagine here her White husband's small penis size.

In the third encounter, a Black plantation overseer, Gary, orders
around Dustin, the White-passing indentured servant. Gary oddly insists that he be referred to as "Nigger Gary"[19] (Harris, 2018, p. 41). Dustin
complies yet mocks him, citing Gary's "White" comportment and man-
ners. The insinuation that Gary is not Black enough leads to a physical altercation. High on indignation and arousal, the two men begin to
wrestle. Sexually inflamed, they strip each other down to their underwear. When Gary bites Dustin under the gleam of excitement, Dustin's
already-thin servility falls off: "[I could] have you lynched for deigning
to touch me like that," he threatens. "You can talk to me anyway you
please. But when it comes to touch . . . I am Dustin The White" (Harris, 2018, p. 44). From "lynching" to "calling the police" on "suspicious"
Black people, Dustin's threat unmistakably parallels the present, referencing how easily White and White-passing people can endanger Black
people's lives by involving law enforcement.[20] Dustin is well aware of this
and willing to weaponize it: the stage momentarily swarms with danger.
In response to this, Gary flexes his authority as overseer: he climbs atop

a cotton cart, and from there, towering over Dustin, he orders him to get on his knees and lick his (Gary's) boot. Sexually intoxicated by this switch, Dustin readily gets on all fours to deliver an unabashedly lustful, sensuous boot-licking that drives Gary to a spectacular orgasm. His pleasurable convulsions quickly give way to a frightening, involuntary shaking. To Dustin's—and the audience's—confusion, Gary collapses into a tearful, hyperventilating puddle.

Briefly, we return to Kaneisha and Jim, who is "behind her thrusting wildly" (Harris, 2018, p. 50). As the thrusts intensify, Kaneisha is nearing climax. In a way both insistent and peculiar, she asks him to call her a "Negress! Mista Jim, please Negress!" (2018, p. 51), leading to Jim muttering that he cannot go on and losing his erection. Interrupting her momentum, he calls out "Starbucks"—first tentatively, then loudly. We, the characters and the audience, hear a loud horn blast. Everything stops, ending the first act.

Racial trauma and colorism pulsate through *Slave Play*'s first act under the heavy burden of history and to the garish, clamorous accompaniment of guttural sexual moans. There is no question that the first act is pornographic (there is nudity, there is simulated sex, there are sex toys, there is orgasm), but naming it as such has been difficult for many audiences. This difficulty is not entirely surprising. "Far too often," Nash writes, "the word *black* in front of the word *pornography* is treated as an intensifier, as something that produces political anxiety rather than as something that [can] engender[] theoretical energy and analytical sophistication" (2014, p. 146). It is no wonder that the play's director, Robert O'Hara, decided to manage the audience's anxiety by withholding an intermission, rightly anticipating that anyone made uncomfortable by the demanding horrors of the first act (that is, anyone with a pulse) would be tempted to walk away.

The lack of an intermission did not, of course, prevent this from happening: offended theatergoers still got up and left during the first act, broadcasting their displeasure by passive-aggressively gathering their belongings as if in slow motion before heading for the exit (Daniels, 2019; Harris, 2019b).[21] Audience members who walked away were mostly Black, as were the majority of those who voiced their upset on social media, podcasts, and online reviews. The gist of these protests was similar to Alice Walker's 1971 commentary on an interracial lesbian couple involving a White mistress and a Black self-identified slave: "I was incensed to think of the hard struggle of my students to rid themselves of stereotype, to combat prejudice, to put themselves into enslaved women's skins, and then to see their struggle mocked, and the actual enslaved condition of literally millions of our mothers trivialized—because two ignorant women insisted on their right to act out publicly a 'fantasy' that still strikes terror in Black women's hearts" (1971, p. 121).

The combination of sex, trauma, and degradation played out through racial tropes is not easy to bear. But, O'Hara explains, if you go to see a play that calls itself *Slave Play*, "it should cost [you] something to watch it and to experience it" (Kai, 2019). What exactly the price to be paid is he does not tell us. But the lack of intermission suggests that it may have something to do with subjecting the audience to an intensification that one is not allowed to escape. The audience has consented to watching *Slave Play* without knowing how relentless it is, and the play's demand tracks differently across theatergoers depending on their psychic makeup, personal history, and intersecting positionalities. Built into the force of this performance is the particular kind of sadism I call exigent: the audience is given neither a rest nor the time to recover from the first act's intensities, and while there is not intent to inflict harm, some theatergoers did feel injured. The play unfolds such that the audience is prevented from easily rationalizing its enjoyment. We might say—and this gets revisited in chapter 5—that the play exerts an ethical kind of sadism that is exigent in that it issues a necessary and imperative call to the audience to endure something difficult, something that will challenge them through its intensity and *by means of what it repeats*. Theatergoers who are able to bend their will (to stay in the theater and to give themselves over to the play rather than trying to "control" their reactions, or inhibit their pleasure, or leave) might then be able to endure an aesthetic experience that both strains and excites, calling something forth in them, something that can be perverse and overwhelming.

In the second act, we find the three couples sitting in the plantation home with two therapists.[22] The audience now discovers that what we just watched was day four of a therapy dubbed "Antebellum Sexual Performance Therapy." The second act has an immediate retroactive effect on our understanding of the first act, leading us to reshuffle its meaning. We now learn that these were consensual sexual encounters intended to heal the Black partners' sexual anhedonia—Kaneisha has lost sexual interest in Jim, Philip suffers from erectile dysfunction, and Gary has not orgasmed in months—and required the couples to act as if one were a master and the other a slave. Scripted by the Black partners, the sexual acts were meant for their pleasure—not that of the White partners, who spend the remainder of the play protesting having been made to do racist things against their will (but, as we will see, in accord with their desire). To those who are familiar with kink communities, the devised sexual scenes (the "slave play" in *Slave Play*) are also a reference to race play, a controversial, albeit well-established, BDSM practice (Cruz, 2016; M. Weiss, 2011; Woolfe, 2016)—though not everyone in the audience is aware of this citation. In kink communities, race play belongs to a subgenre called "edgeplay," a term used to denote sexualities that are risky and that court forces of sexuality and of memory, the intensities and impact of which cannot be anticipated ahead of time. For the second act's remainder, the therapists help the couples plumb the racialized dynamics in their erotic relationships.

The transition from the first act's pornodrama to the second act's jargon-filled metalevel—psychoanalysis, queer theory, and queer of color critique seesaw from insightful to hilariously caricatured—calms the agitation roused in the first act. The move from the erotics of racist iconography to the language of psychotherapy and the interrogation of race relations is an economic downshift: from less bound energy to a more bound state. Even as thinking about race is absolutely critical in the United States today, this resituating of the conversation in the sphere of racial identity transports us to more familiar territory, a territory with more precise coordinates and with clearer rules of engagement.[23] The reveal that the slave play was part of "therapy" allays the anxiety that someone has been violated against their will; but the second act is also where we come to recognize, through the multiple microaggressions and racial enactments still unfolding despite the role-play being officially over, the tangle of past and present. While in the first act the slave play had been offered to us *as an intentional re-creation of the past*, it is in the second act that we see it wrinkled into the present, where we have to confront that the ancestors and "the dead are living everywhere" (Schneider, 2011, p. 26), including in us, the audience.

The second act illustrates how the not-me quality (Sullivan, 1953) of desirous disavowal rhymes with the logics of White supremacy. Despite the protestations of the White and White-passing partners, the second act reveals that they were not simply acting or "in role." Anyone paying attention notices that Jim, Alana, and Dustin were excited by the racialized/racist feelings they were asked to "perform." Indeed, Alana was so excited that she took over her scene with Philip, rather than let her Black partner direct their sexual engagement—as had been the instructions for each of the couples. The White members of the audience are implicated in this dynamic too. "No one has forced anyone to see a play called *Slave Play*," O'Hara stresses; "[it is] your own interest, your own curiosity, other things bring you through the door" (Kai, 2019). Being told "you, after all, came to watch" is a searing indictment. And with the back wall of the proscenium being a set of giant mirrors, we, the audience, are not exempted from the racial crises unfolding on the stage. Watching ourselves watch and with our faces reflected back to us, we have to wrestle with the fact that we, too, are implicated: we, too, are part of this slave play. The play's set design thus refuses us a stable vantage point from which we can repudiate our sexual voyeurism, a complication that the play's scenic designer, Clint Ramos, has purposefully invited into this make-believe plantation (*Slave Play* Sunday discussions, January 5, 2020).

An effigy of colonial white manhood, Jim keeps announcing that he did not find the role-play arousing at all. He protests being "made to call [his wife] a negress" (Harris, 2018, p. 70), not once contending with the complexities of the erection he visibly sported through some of the first act. However incontrovertible the evidence of his embodied participation in this sexual encounter, his conscious relation to it is one of denial. Of course, Jim's disavowing his arousal is also why he could not fully get into the erotic play: his passionate thrusts became more inhibited after his racial slur (calling Kaneisha a "Negress" [Harris, 2018, p. 51]) sent Kaneisha into a psychosexual intoxication.[24] Losing his erection, he eventually safeworded, halting the sexual encounter just as Kaneisha was about to climax. In contrast, Alana announces that (play)raping Philip, "was just hot to me, really hot," adding that her role-play character, "unlocked some doors, let me tell ya" (2018, pp. 62, 63). Unlike Jim, she owns her arousal—but not that race was at play, hence her subsequent operatic outburst when Philip recalls that they met on FetLife, "like Tinder for fetish fiends" (2018, p. 104), to role-play a cucking fantasy in which Alana's White husband would "get off watching a black man fucking his white wife" (2018, p. 105). "It wasn't racial, I swear" (2018, p. 106), Alana wails, her histrionics escalating as she tries to draw a firm line between the FetLife role-play and that of the therapy. The former, she claims, "had NOTHING to do with race, it was just what got *him* off" (2018, p. 105; emphases in original). Dustin, too, strenuously protests post facto "what [Gary] made me do today" (2018, p. 72), even as he clearly enjoyed the sex that partly drew its titillating charge from Gary's being asked to be addressed as "Nigger Gary." The racial epithet, the threat of lynching, and the boot-licking of "this big black thing" (2018, p. 47) quickened Dustin's arousal.

The Slave Play in *Slave Play*

That racism has an erotic charge for White people is not really new news. One need only reflect on the sexual undercurrents subtending the US history of lynching (Dray, 2003). It is precisely this not-me quality of rapturous racist desire that enabled lynch mobs to virtuously participate in sexualized-crimes-turned-into-spectacles. In *Slave Play*, the erotic excitement of anti-Blackness resounds in the libidinal body: we see it in Jim's erection, in Alana's flushed glow as she eyes Philip's "fiddle," in Dustin's delirious stripping of his overseer's clothing and in his ravenous licking of Gary's boot. These erotics, *Slave Play* insists, are not erotics of the past; they are erotics of the present. Offering up this difficult but known fact is also Harris's theatrical feint; it is what allows him to move to what he is also after, which is something much more incandescent than calling Whiteness to task: these erotic indignations and the racial fetishization were solicited *by the Black partners*. The most difficult claim mounted by *Slave Play* is that what Sharon Holland calls the "erotic life of racism" (2012) inflects not just the oppressors' psychosexuality but also the oppresseds' (see also Lindsey & Johnson, 2014; Musser, 2016; Stockton, 2006). These Black partners do not want to be respected, at least not in the conventional sense of the word. Kaneisha, Philip, and Gary are seeking experiences that mimic the atrocious history of chattel slavery in the past, to fuel spectacularly complicated intimacies in the present, sexual pleasures that do not readily line up with the logic of recognition, equivalence, and value (Muñoz, 2019).

It is not difficult to see why Harris's detour via Whiteness is an expedient and necessary tactic: it is painful, if not explosive, to discuss a desire for sexual abjection, especially in the inflammable territory of race. In this regard, *Slave Play* uses race as the proverbial Trojan horse through which charged, queer forms of desire are surreptitiously imported into dignified discursive spaces that would otherwise negate them. Here is queerness at its most complex, not as identity but as affect and as aesthetic; this is queerness as pertaining not only to lust or intimacy but also to sexual desiring that conducts shame, injury, contempt, defiance, despair, and hate (Reid-Pharr, 2001). Relevant here is de Lauretis's description of the queerness of the sexual drive as a "perverse, non-reproductive, anarchic sexuality that does not depend on gender or sex, [that does not] impose conditions to genital sexuality, [that does not] attach strings of love" (2017, p. 1926).

In *Slave Play*, however, the perverse is working not just with its usual materials (enigma) but also with the temporal dimension of generational trauma's afterlife. Trauma in this case does not immobilize the infantile sexual: it commandeers it. The result is a combustible example of how the sexual drive's polymorphous perversity may annex traumatic history. The darker set of desires volitionally enacted, and actually *needed*, by the Black partners marks how the "then" of the historical past is conducted into the "now" of the sexual body. It is on this very thin strip between past and present that the slave play in *Slave Play* ricochets. Harris thus offers an extended visitation, if not a vertiginous descent, into taboo and forbidden sexual appetites, into perversity that is "capable of stressing nearly every boundary required for the order of 'civilized society' to hold" (English, 2010, p. 73). Kaneisha, Gary, and Philip are not hoping to be recognized or to be offered empathic witnessing; they want something else entirely, something that has more to do with pleasure and with the more and more of experience.

Gary Fisher: Fucking with History

Jeremy O. Harris does not explicitly link Gary's character in *Slave Play* to the actual person of Gary Fisher, but the connection is too obvious to

ignore.[25] Gary Fisher, a Black gay man who died of AIDS-related com-
plications, authored a set of diary-form notebooks that were published
posthumously, and at his request, by his teacher, the queer theorist Eve
Sedgwick (1996). This strange compendium included extensive narra-
tions of erotic fantasies/experiences revolving around his wish to be
sexually dominated by a White master. His writings were received with
unease, shock, and consternation. Statements such as "racial humiliation
is a huge turn-on. I enjoy being your nigger, your property and worship-
ping not just you, but your whiteness" (Fisher, 1996, p. 231) confused and
puzzled his readers. The strangeness of such desires has operated like an
enigmatic message, spurring many critics to theorize how the folding
of the haunting traumas of slavery into someone's sexual complexion
might extend beyond stalled repetition (Muñoz, 2019; Musser, 2017;
Nyong'o, 2010; D. Scott, 2010; Sinfield, 2004; Stallings, 2015; Woodard,
2014). "The very structures we critique and seek to dismantle," Nash
writes, "can also thrill" (2014, p. 150). Fisher, Amber Musser highlights,
is well aware that he "is part of a historical structure," even as it is one
that he has not consented to be born into (2017, p. 230). Is Fisher trying
to find a way out of that history, to repair the trauma of slavery? Is he
trying to heal from this intergenerational trauma? To me, it seems more
accurate to say that he may be trying *to find a way to be with that history.*
If we approach Fisher's notes through the framework of traumatophilia,
the analytic of what one may do *with* trauma as opposed to what one
may do *about* trauma (i.e., resolve, heal, overcome, cure), we may be able
to ask a different set of questions, questions that engage Robert Reid-
Pharr's description of "Fisher's genius" (2001, p. 141).

"The shock of Gary Fisher," Reid-Pharr writes, "turns squarely on his
fierce articulation of what lies just beneath the surface of polite, 'civil'
American race talk. The life of the nigger is so caught up in the debauchery of the white master that even when 'nigger' is translated to 'black' it
is still possible to sense the faintest hint of the raw milk smell of cum
on the breath" (2001, p. 148). Fisher, he reflects, "allows none of us to
remain innocent" (Reid-Pharr, 2001, p. 149)—a characterization that applies as much to Fisher as it does to Harris, who wants his audience amid
a plantation scene and on a collision course with its own enjoyment. It
is hard to convey exactly how startling Fisher is. His notebooks are filled
with passages like this: "so, yous dead, nigger, with your dick cut off

and hanging out of your mouth, so yous dead with someone elses dick *in* your mouth, so yous *alive* with someone elses dick in your mouth, nigger" (Fisher, 1996, p. 70). Amid the swirl of cum, fear, defiance, desperation, arousal, and abjection, Fisher strangely muses, "I haven't read Hegel yet. Why haven't I read Hegel when I am somewhat in love with this? I'm afraid to know. Half of this is the wandering, the obscurity, the possibility of surprise. . . . When I get there I'll be able to say I've always known this would happen to me" (1996, p. 203). Perhaps, José Muñoz comments, Fisher's avoidance of Hegel is about Fisher having come up against the limits of the "anticipatable calculus of equivalence ending in some recognition of the self in the other. Instead, it is about the incommensurable" (2019, p. 199). Muñoz gives us a reading of Fisher's passing comment on Hegel that steps off the dialectics of recognition into the space of contradiction, into an erotic domain that is seething with irreconcilable tensions.

Reid-Pharr is also compelled by Fisher's reference to Hegel, which he reads to imply that "the black is not inculpable, that she is as much perpetrator as victim . . . Fisher's constant return to the erotics of slavery and his insistence that the black is always an active and potent agent within these erotics not only places him among the most perverse of Black American authors but suggests a model of black subjectivity and black expression that at once masters *and deforms* some of the most cherished idioms of Black American vernacular tradition" (2001, p. 139; emphasis added). "Fisher's genius," he continues, "turns on his ability to spoil all our expectations, to *deform* our most cherished models of human subjectivity" (2001, p. 141; emphasis added). The word "deform" appears twice in these quotes. What is it to "deform"? Might deforming be a synonym for delinking, for the kind of disaggregating processes that dissolve the self and the encrusted meanings that subtend it? Because, as we have seen through Aulagnier and Laplanche, the self is threaded through the primary violence of the mythosymbolic, deforming the self would also stand to break down how we think about dignity and respect, to wound our very ideas about consent and sexuality, even to put pressure on some of our most cherished modes of what it means for someone to be humanized.[26]

In Alexandre Kojève's reading of Hegel (1947), two self-consciousnesses are caught in a death stare. Without recognizing their interdependence on each other, neither of their subjectivities can be sustained, and death imperils both.[27] Confronted with the possibility of their negation, both relinquish their claims to sovereignty. Recognition thus becomes the synthetic both/and solution to the problem of either/or, lifting both the master and the slave out of the deadlock. Recognition thus closes (that is, it "repairs") the gap between them. But Bataille, who is also preoccupied with Hegel (1954), counters that such a retreat from the confrontation with one's own negation, that is, with one's own death, amounts to a refusal to come into a confrontation with nonbeing. When the confrontation with nonbeing is taken off the table (in order to protect being), he argues, we are left with a somewhat impoverished notion of what being can encompass. Psychoanalytically, this would be tantamount to a refusal to come into contact with enigma, that is, with our constitutive wound. What would be refused in thus turning away from one's negation is the possibility of encountering one's own opacity. To avoid facing one's nonbeing is, for Bataille, to miss out on the extravagance of life. "The death of not dying," he writes, "is precisely not death; it is the ultimate stage of life" (1957, p. 240). What is at stake is losing one's footing in the self, an unsteadying that causes one "to live more violently, so violently that [one may be] on the threshold of dying" (Bataille, 1957, p. 240). And while Bataille did not concern himself with the history of slavery, it may be that Fisher does have something to say about that: Fisher's confrontation with his own negation is inscribed in his racialized, libidinal body. Instead of turning away from his negation, as we have been taught to expect subjects to do—especially Black subjects, for fear that they will be then seen as "deserving" their suffering—Fisher dares to stare it in the eye. It is arguably this very confrontation with his own negation that makes Fisher's writings so difficult but also so frightfully important. Fisher finds a way to revel in the open wound of slavery, which is throbbing on his sexual body, which is another way of saying that he is not oriented toward (Hegelian) transcendence and repair but toward enduring the experience of his nonbeing.

Such endurance has an aesthetic dimension. These, however, are not aesthetics of the beautiful or of the harmonious as given to us by the tradition of Western philosophy; they are aesthetics of the terribly beautiful (Moten, 2003). If, as readers, we are able to shift from reading Fisher to glean his motives or to understanding his text, if we can refuse the temptation of looking to him for mere confirmation of what we (think we)

know about the way trauma conjugates sexuality, and if we stay attentive, instead, to the way his perversity appears in the text, his notebooks
may become aesthetic objects. This is, in fact, what happens for Muñoz
when he shifts from the "how *do we understand* Gary Fisher?"—a question that rummages for answers in how the erotic is embroiled in racial
relations—to "how *can we read* Gary Fisher?" If we read this question
as a provocation about what we may encounter in ourselves if we give
ourselves over to the disturbance of his text, we may be able to avoid the
perennial "why" (as in, Why would an educated, Black, gay man be erotically compelled by racial debasement?) to ask "how" these erotic currents course through him and to what effects. Such asking is not without
cost. "I UNDERSTAND! this self-slaughter," Fisher writes in an entry on
Christmas Eve 1985, "but it scares me. I am trying to *decreate*. Trying to
go back; not to an easier time, but to a more honest one. Shit, slave, nigger, cocksucker; like the wind, and darkness, the Auroras of Autumn. *I'm
doing it with sex and society, bludgeoning myself with misconceptuous facts,
or the fictive facts that were 'in fact' bludgeons then*" (1996, pp. 188–189;
emphases added). What Fisher is doing "with sex and society" is a very
serious matter: perversity becomes here a series of traumatisms that, with
escalation, may feel akin to a self-slaughter, a bludgeoning of his ego, that
brings him to the limit, to decreate (his own word) and to deform (Reid-
Pharr's). Is this, perhaps, another way of talking about detranslating, of
dissolving links? And if so, what links would these be? The links, I would
propose, are chiseled from these "misconceptuous facts" (Fisher, 1996, p.
189), the "facts" through which Black subjectivation has always already
been bludgeoned, translated through a mythosymbolic order awash in
anti-Blackness. It is those fictive facts that were "bludgeons then" (Fisher,
1996, p. 189) that make it impossible, as Reid-Pharr notes, "to say 'black'
without hearing 'nigger' as its echo" (2001, p. 149).

To see Fisher as doing more than merely returning to, and being
trapped in, the past, we, too, have to come into contact with something
in ourselves that reaches beyond recognition, to make ourselves passible to his text. To do so, we have to bend our will, to look at it again
and again, though not with a "looking [that] comes before [and that]
holds, replicates, reproduces what is looked at" (Moten, 2003, p. 72) but
to look at it so that it may act on us, so that we may travel beyond the
horror in Fisher and toward the horrific in ourselves. Fisher's project is

about how to rearticulate the terms that he has been given by the socius, a socius that is constructed by and through White supremacy and anti-Blackness and, as we saw in chapter 1, may well be swirled into Fisher's very *ego*; *indeed, it may have been part of his very subjectivation*. This is why no less than a bludgeoning and a self-slaughter are required for something to be reassembled, albeit differently. This is another way of saying that Fisher cannot go *around* history or get away *from* history— that what he is doing here may very well be fucking *with* history. This is not something one has conscious control over. That is, Fisher's desire "to give in to a system that wants to (has to) oppress" him (1996, p. 187) is not of his deliberate choosing. Erotic desire comes to us unbidden. We do not choose it, it chooses us. At work, in Laplanche's words, is an "agency cast in the nominal mode," which is "'perched' on a mount that it does not command" (1994/2015d, pp. 126, 128). At play are the forces of the unconscious and of the uncanny, which is where resistance to power proceeds from: not from the ego, which seeks to conserve itself, but from the unconscious, which is unconcerned with being depleted or spent. Whatever is taken over by the infantile sexual's polymorphous perversity can afford the extravagance of risk and the squandering of itself without concern for safety, dignity, or respect. It is this that makes it so powerful and dangerous and, therefore, so incommensurate, even at odds, with the logics of safety or self-preservation or "good" politics.

Toward Singularity

But, one may wonder, is it fair to read Gary Fisher, or *Slave Play*, for "evidence of experience," as Joan Scott (1991) put it? Might Fisher's transgressive writing be, rather, a textual strategy—"Fisher"—that thematizes its own textuality? Similarly, might *Slave Play* be best read as staging a certain operation of irony, preserving the doubleness and ambiguity of speech and address, in its multitiered recursive structure and self-deconstruction, as opposed to also presenting the "real" desires of a "real" person? It seems to me that reading Fisher's text and engaging with *Slave Play* for what Fisher and Harris teach us about some forms of queer, Black desire is not only fair but *necessary and politically urgent*. Fisher's desires for White sexual domination are not unique to him; they are desires that scholars writing on queer desire have been exploring for some time (Musser, 2014; Reid-Pharr, 2001; Rodríguez, 2014; D. Scott, 2010; M. Weiss, 2011) and about which BIPOC race-play activists have been quite vocal (see Cruz, 2016, for an extended discussion). To treat Gary Fisher's notebooks as literary works only runs the risk or, to put it more bluntly, does the work of obscuring erotic desires that are inscrutable to many people.

Of course, none of this line of thinking is to suggest that Fisher's desires for racial debasement are universal to all, or even many, Black people or that the characters of Kaneisha, Phillip, and Gary are meant to represent all Black people. *Slave Play* makes no such homogenizing move, and neither does Gary Fisher. Race play, insists the prominent BDSM race-play activist mike bond, "is not a message about all of black kind" (Hernandez, 2004). In an interview with me, bond used the "unvarnished" phrase "n* slave" to refer to a particular subset of race play wherein the Black person wants to be racially humiliated by a White partner, rather than the more generic way in which "race play" may refer to varied ways in which racial identification or racial fantasy can organize a BDSM scene, without the Black person being necessarily the bottom, and that may involve a range of other racial pairings and identities (including non-Black partners). The argument that not everyone is into n* play, is, he insists, a "non sequitur": "I never said that everyone likes what I do . . . I am being made to, like, you know, counterargue something that I've never said and, really, never alluded to" (interview, October 20, 2021). In insisting that he is asked to defend an argument he has never made, bond points to the ecstatic anxieties that the existence of n* play desires generate. Indeed, in a social milieu teeming with anti-Blackness, the thread separating consensual race play from an easy slippage to racialized sexual violence may feel very narrow.[28] One way to deal with this anxiety, bond explains, is to invalidate it *as a sexual desire*, by diagnosing it as racial self-hatred or pathologizing it. "How much weight could a nigger slave ever put on a scale to make [our existence] convincing?" he asks rhetorically. "Unlike with bigfoot tales, race-play theories," he says, "come with living bodies" (email communication, October 26, 2021). The fact that these desires exist among real people (Cruz, 2016; V. Johnson, 1994; M. Weiss, 2011; Woolfe, 2016), including in our consulting rooms (Saketopoulou, 2011b, 2018a), merely speaks to the fact that they are not just literary devices or theatrical characters—and that they very much draw on the materiality of the crimes of slavery and anti-Black racism.

Said differently, to reduce Fisher's work to mere textual method—or *Slave Play*'s characters to mere theatrical fantasies—may be a way of turning away from how his notebooks act on us. Might that be, for example, the ego's way of appropriating the turmoil that the imbrication of the erotic with the racially traumatic can rouse in us? Might relocating such erotics from the field of sexual desire to that of literary criticism or ideology critique be a way to master the fact that it disturbs the protocols by which we are used to think about race and trauma? My interest, in other words, is not in Fisher as a psychological entity (i.e., I do not use his text to psychoanalyze *him* as a subject): it is we, his readers, who are the psychological entities I want to put under scrutiny, and it is what we permit ourselves to consider and to be subjected to that I want to put under pressure in this discussion.

Such sexual appetites, *Slave Play* insists, do not leave "the historical bitterness of the past" on "the other side of the leather door" (V. Johnson, 1994). Harris shows, instead, that erotic excitement can become painfully and pleasurably interdigitated with the signifiers of slavery's traumas, kindling strange experimentations vis-à-vis what tastes, other than, or, in addition to bitterness, such histories may produce. "Racial hating is so old," writes the psychoanalyst Kathy White, "that it has come to define us, and maybe not only in awful ways . . . contribut[ing] to depth and complexity in our relatedness to one another, and to our individual and cultural identities. I can see possibilities here, but my awareness is shadowy. I sense that I have only barely caught onto the edges of a richer, deeper reality" (2002, p. 421). Dwelling in these shadows can feel dangerous, even treasonous: the more bound domains of identity, of rights, and of social justice are much more appealing even as they are also upsetting, because they appeal to the ego's organizing functions.

"It is to our detriment," Dean writes, "that we remain skeptical about pleasures that we regard as contaminated by power, as if . . . there are pleasures that are not contaminated by power" (2012, p. 481). These contaminations are not equitably distributed among different subjects, and that may be one reason why *Slave Play*'s move—to enmesh erotic excitement with the signifiers of slavery's traumas—can be so difficult. Said differently, while the racial fetishism in *Slave Play* draws its erotic heft from the materiality of antebellum scars, it does not belong to the genre of Blaxploitation. Still, it is important to ask: When Gary asks Dustin to address him as "Nigger Gary" or when Kaneisha goes into sexual convulsions upon being told, "You feel so good Negress" (Harris, 2018, p. 51), are we in the deadness of strict, stale repetition? Or, might these be traumatophilic repetitions, inciting traumatisms that may build density toward a state of overwhelm? For the latter to occur, such scenarios need to escalate even to the point of the monstrously extreme, if they are to develop enough energetic momentum to rupture the ego. This, as we shall see, is what happens in the third act.

For some audience members—those who petitioned the play to be shut down, who vociferously voiced their upset on social media (Tariq Radio, 2018), or who openly flirted with the notion of suing the playwright (Cobb, 2022)—the play felt offensive (Vestal, 2018), if not traumatic. Others felt untouched by it. For some, it functioned as an inciting traumatism that put theatergoers in an especially demanding position, as we, too, are subjected to the repetition simply by observing it (to be discussed in chapter 4). This is akin to the position analysts sometimes find ourselves in in the consulting room—not just observing the patient's repetitions but being subjected to them and, thus, to some degree participating in them. At moments like this, disengagement might be a way to spare oneself from the demands that iterative engagement makes on us. This would be one way to understand what occurs when Jim safewords, hurting and angering Kaneisha: on the conscious level, Jim halted the play because he saw (only) the woundedness in Kaneisha's desire; he was unable to appreciate that her wound had also acquired a taste for pleasure. His inability to see her excitement as anything but historical injury detracted from her creative endeavor to do racial pleasure differently; this inability constituted its own violence. "I am feeling a bit betrayed," explains Kaneisha, "because . . . the minute I express what I need from him, how I need it. He shut down . . . I made a damn fool of myself, a fool . . . for me, for us, and he . . . and he couldn't even . . . he stayed in control" (Harris, 2019a, pp. 74, 86).

Why would we trust, though, that in *Slave Play* we may be in the domain of a potential inciting traumatism and not of rote, mechanical repetition? Undeterred, Harris turns the heat higher: the Black partners not only have requested these racial denigrations, they have been deeply and uniquely pleasured by them. Philip, who suffered from erectile dysfunction, was able to get an erection during the "forced" sodomy slave scene: "Not with a pill but with . . . our improv" (Harris, 2018, p. 64). And he will later connect this to other times in his life when he was brought to experience himself as Black: "I could feel his eyes seeing me as a nigger, a big ol' nigger on top of his white wife" (2018, p. 107), he adds, reflecting on the cucking scene with Alana's then-husband: "Maybe my dick likes, LIKED, that I'd been finally been forced into some kind of space where it knew how it was being desired" (2018, p. 106). An earlier memory emerges. A White classmate sees Philip naked in the shower. "Look at donkey dick over there," the classmate says, "I always forget Philip is a nigger till I see that thing swinging" (2018, p. 93). This memory of racial objectification, of reducing a person to a body part, is trailed by a long racist history, and it is painful. And yet, insofar as it simultaneously gestures to a corporeal sexuality overbrimming with potency and virility, these denigrations also feed into Philip's sense of sexual superiority, his experience of himself as "a hot guy" (2018, p. 93). This is the both/and of sexualized racial humiliation. For Philip, the role-play thus seems to have acted like a traumatism that, in the après-coup, renders Alana's husband's gaze traumatic for him, and it is newly experienced as racialized in a way that it was not before. This spawns Philip's transformation, a radical change in his relationship to his racialization: whereas he previously had described himself by saying, "I'm not black I'm not white, I'm just Phillip," as "this super human dude who's beyond, like, black and white" (2018, pp. 93–94), Phillip now begins to see how he has stood at a distance from his Blackness. "How," he howls in despair, "am I just hearing myself say this?" (2018, p. 106).

Overwhelm and transformation also swarm Gary's encounter with Dustin, which permitted him to climax for the first time in months. Following Dustin's threat to have Gary lynched, Gary orders Dustin to get on his knees and to lick his boot—which Dustin greedily does. Gary thus reaches an astonishing orgasm that quickly mutates into a sobbing, hyperventilating collapse. When Dustin later asks Gary if he was hurt in the way he wanted to be hurt, Gary says several times that he did and that he enjoyed the experience. The phrase "Gary came" is the laugh line on a loop throughout act two, as if Harris wants to ensure that we do not lose sight of the sexual play's yield. Like Dean's experience of erotic astonishment, Gary's orgasm is gorged with pleasure; his hyperventilating collapse is more an overwhelm state. And it galvanizes the psychic work we watch Gary go through in the second act: "for almost a decade I've given myself over to you," he tells Dustin, "who acts like he is the prize and I am the lucky recipient. No motherfucker, I am the prize" (Harris, 2018, p. 113). In this powerful speech, we witness a hard-earned self-transformation that required the suffering of pleasure. One of the most quoted lines of the play, it stands out as an especially triumphant moment that leaves Gary in searing pain but which also marks his reconfigured sense of his self and his new relationship to his Blackness.[29]

Sites of Woundedness as Sexual Sites

For traumatized subjects, there is no return to a pretraumatic state, no restoration to the innocence of some prelapsarian moment, nor will agency ever be unconstrained by the past's wounding effects.[30] Projects of restored freedom and of complete psychic emancipation are fantastical constructions existing only in the minds of those who are unwilling to concede that trauma has irremediable scarring effects, hence my urging for us to become less preoccupied with what to do about trauma (to become less traumatophobic) and to consider what subjects do *with* their trauma (to become more traumatophilic). What traumatized subjects may hope for are not liberatory outcomes but enlarged *degrees* of freedom: these issue from redrafting one's relationship to the terms by which one has been laminated by the socius.

For Black subjects, new self-definitions come in many forms. These include not conforming to White people's narratives about Black subjectivity and/or bypassing White people's charitable—and thus condescending—concerns about what is really agentic, especially since agency is differently drafted for subjects formed through histories of enslavement (Hartman, 1997; Musser, 2016). In *Slave Play*, we see how such protectionism is fueled by White liberalism, which is nothing more than the White ego's investment in how it is perceived—that is, as the good White person. Jim, for example, interrupts the racially humiliating scenario that Kaneisha wanted and, more precisely, needed, protesting having been made to "call her a negress," whereas, he emphasizes, "she is my queen" (Harris, 2018, p. 70)—thereby stumbling

against another problematic racial stereotype. Jim sees himself as de-
fending her dignity (and their relationship), but in appointing himself
as her defender, she remains the object of his desire (as *his* queen),
rather than a desiring subject who has voiced, time and again, what she
needs. In that sense, Jim is steadfastly holding onto the power of being
the one who determines the precise coordinates of what is and is not
dignifying to her as a Black woman.

His stance is, no doubt, also a repetition: Jim's insistence that
Kaneisha's desires were "insane" follows on a long history of Black
people being refused the prerogative, and the pleasure, of their own self-
understandings, and it is, in large part, how enslaved Black people were
bludgeoned, to return to Fisher's language, with "fictive and misconceptuous facts," about Black bodies as too unruly, Black music as devilish,
and Black life as overall requiring White people's civilizing influence.
Consequently, although it may be hard to see race play as anything but
capitulation to anti-Blackness, Fisher, Harris, and bond show us how
signifiers as loaded as a racial slur can paradoxically become a site of enlarged freedom-work. The sexual, unwilled and overbrimming, pushes
beyond identity categories and past the ego's binding at the border of
consent (limit consent), engaging desires that do not yield to the Or-
wellian censorship of good politics.

Enlarged freedoms also involve not having to carry the burden of representing all Black people, not to succumb, that is, to the pressures exerted on any one Black person (or any one Black character in a play, for
that matter) to speak for or to carry the burden of uplift for their entire
race. For someone to say about their sexuality, "I want what I want" or
"I belong to a group, but I am not answerable to it" is a frightening step,
especially when the group shares a collective past of exploitation and
oppression that stretches to the present. In reading Gary Fisher, Dwight
McBride reports, that what most made him cringe were not Fisher's desires in themselves but "the public nature of these declarations, the fact
that they were out there in the world . . . [Fisher's notebooks] did not
ascribe to the 'positive' representation of black life, or of black gay life,
that we have been so thoroughly programmed to respect, revere, and . . .
produce" (2005, p. 98).

"When walking into a BDSM club," bond says, "black people are
always black first . . . Our behavior is always measured against those

definitions of what a black person is supposed to do" (email communication, September 14, 2021). In regard to race play, bond explains,

> For example, there's the Black rebel, you know, the guy who is fed up with Massa, and he's gonna burn down the plantation, or whatever. So you are supposed to be some kind of strong Black man . . . You have to come to the [BDSM] scene and . . . play[] out your civil rights role . . . But you are not allowed to flip on the other side . . . When I outed myself, someone actually said to me, 'What would Malcolm say about what you are doing?' . . . So my sexuality is supposed to conform with, you know, revolutionary politics . . . I am supposed to play these roles. I am not supposed to be on my knees in front of White people. (interview, October 20, 2021)

But his sexual predilections, bond emphasizes, do not follow racial justice lines. Arguing that they should, he argues, is "like trying to talk [someone] out of homosexuality. I don't care what your arguments are. If I'm gay, I'm gay. Period. When I say I am a nigger slave, I don't care what you think . . . We can talk all day, and it's just not going to change" (interview, October 20, 2021). Sometimes, the objections to bond's race play took the form of "protecting" him from his desires. Yet he highlights that protectionism is not actually protective. Insofar as it amounts to "creat[ing] special censorship rules for blacks" (quoted in Cruz, 2016, p. 110), it, in fact, mimics the logics of White supremacy, animating a kind of racism that looks antiracist—what we may think of as antiracist racism. "From what I understand from the stats," he continues,

> one out of four women get raped, but no one [in the BDSM scene] says we shouldn't do rape play . . . I went to a dungeon and this woman takes off all her clothes and her top writes on her body every filthy misogynist slur you can imagine . . . and no one, I mean no one, runs in to save her from herself and to tell her about feminism, and to ask her if this is ok with her mom or if her ancestors would be ok with this. No one goes up to her top to ask him if he has anger issues, if he has cleared this with his psychiatrist, or his Rabbi, or his priest . . . But black people don't really have the same kind of freedom with race play, it's well, do you have a note from your tribal leader? From your community? From your pastor? Did you speak to a historian?

Do *I* get to come in here and say, here, destroy my identity, just like this woman had hers destroyed? People come up with these rules for me as a black nigger slave, that didn't apply to anyone else . . . [The idea that] someone else's social justice is going to protect you from yourself, . . . that's what I mean by racial inequality. Because for other people that [kink] faucet is wide open and [for me] for years it's just dripping. (email communication, January 24, 2022)

Some people might say that we should not be doing rape play either, and, as we have seen, debates about the proper boundaries of good feminist sex are ongoing. And many analysts would say that both rape play and race play are symptoms of unresolved trauma. As should be clear by now, I do not agree with these positions. But what I want to highlight about bond's argument is that even in a community that understands itself to have well-structured protocols for consent and to be open to a diverse range of sexual fantasies and practices, such as the kink community, race play in which the person of color in on the bottom is not only beyond the pale but, ipso facto, also beyond consent.

Racialization and Different Paradigms of the Unconscious

The points raised by *Slave Play*, Gary Fisher, and mike bond raise important questions about which version of the unconscious we think with when it comes to Black subjects or, to say it differently, which versions of the unconscious Black subjects are seen as deserving. Black people are frequently saddled with an impoverished version of the unconscious: not one that can be translated anew, giving rise to a range of possible desires, symbolizations, and interests, but a sedimented one that is filled, if not fixed, in the intergenerationally transmitted trauma of slavery, ongoing racial abuse, and police brutality. This notion of a filled-in, repressed content is what Laplanche called the "pseudo-unconscious" to mark that it is not a dynamic, malleable force but a static and listless reservoir of translated content (see chapter 1). Of course, the intergenerational legacy of slavery and anti-Black racism are critical components in Black psychic life, but a liberal insistence that Black subjects (or traumatized subjects more generally) need to be understood on the level of the pseudo-unconscious alone that is, only in relation to their trauma, refuses them the humanity of an unconscious that might become retranslated in the après-coup. Reserving for Black Americans an unconscious that is only expected to produce a fixed relationship to trauma treats the historical past as if it has a timeless, immutable quality in the psyche. To say, for instance, that Gary Fisher could only be replaying the past, as opposed to playing *with* his generational past, effectively nails Black persons to the history of slavery. I use the word "nail" purposefully to mark that such insistence is an epistemic violence that freezes the Black subject as only and always the product of the past. We do not have to settle for such concessions in thinking Blackness. "It's not blasphemy," says Mollena Williams, a Black woman and prominent race-play educator, "to want to touch that wound"—the wound of slavery's generational history and the open wound of racism. "That wound HAS to be touched," she presses; otherwise it will "remain in its original state of pain" (2009b). This touching of wounds relates to traumatophilia, the return to the site of the traumatic.

Engaging such complex dynamics, however, is no small ask. It can be a roaring success or a crushing failure, sometimes both at once. In the third act of *Slave Play*, we find ourselves in Kaneisha and Jim's hotel room, with Kaneisha packing her bags about to leave (him?). His refusal to listen to her and to her body, she says, has made the relationship untenable. On the level of affirmative consent, her charge is unacceptable; Jim should not have to do something he does not want or that conflicts with his values. But that is not where we are at; we are not in the domain of affirmative consent but "in the wake" of trauma (Sharpe, 2016), in the terrain of risk and in the weeds of crafting something new—in other words, in the territory of limit consent. Jim's unwillingness to become passible to Kaneisha, to let himself be taken over by his own racialized sadomasochism and to be carried by the situation, will no longer do. To be clear, Jim is not asked to "help" Kaneisha with processing *her* trauma. Antebellum (and colonial) history is not the history of the trauma of Black people (or people of color) alone; it is the shared history of the traumatic relationship between White people (and/or colonizers) and Black people (and/or the colonized). To "listen" this way, Jim will have to bend his will, so that he may listen with his libidinal, racialized body, thus risking an encounter with something opaque in himself. This commerce between his opacity and hers is ethically important: a preoccupation or even the exaltation of the other's otherness, or her need, that does not embroil one's own vulnerability is exoticizing. And in that sense, it is also a turning away from the ethics of alterity that condition the form of eroticism under discussion in this volume.

Increasingly despondent, Kaneisha is recounting to Jim how he failed her when he suddenly shouts at her in the thick southern accent of the first act, "Shut up, you dirty negress" (Harris, 2018, p. 130). The offensive command pierces the theatrical space, startling her—and us. The gravity of what is occurring astounds the audience: Jim is no longer just playing along, something internal and voracious has leaped forth. "You are a nasty little bed wench who's been asking for this all day, ain'tcha?" (2018, p. 130), he says, pulling out a whip. Jim has finally bent his will, ceding his identity staked on being the good White partner. Grabbing her violently, he climbs on top of her, spreads her legs, pulls off her underwear, and plunges forward. Kaneisha softly signals her agreement but what happens next is delivered to the pitch of an actual violation. Shockingly disinhibited, Jim grabs her throat as he thrusts into her while racially debasing her. Is this what Kaneisha really wanted? Kaneisha starts resisting, tapping him, scratching him, eventually forcefully pushing him off her, "her body shivering from groin to skull" (2018, p. 132). She lets out a harrowing sound, part shriek, part howling, and calls out, "Starbucks, Starbucks." He stops. She gets out from under him. She is wrecked, her entire body convulsing in tears. And then, suddenly, a guttural laughter. Kaneisha, the script describes, "is overcome" (2018, p. 132). And so is Jim, who looks absolutely gutted. He turns around and, encountering himself in the mirror, vomits.

The encounter is extraordinarily intense, disturbing, and confusing to watch. The dynamics of overwhelm, the not not-rape (Schechner, 1985) scene suggests, do not reward Jim, Kaneisha, or the audience with clarity or cathartic release. Jim looks destroyed. Kaneisha strangely composes herself. She sits at the edge of the bed with her back to him. Looking at the audience, she utters the closing line, "Thank you, baby, thank you for listening" (Harris, 2018, p. 132).

"Thank You for Listening"

The play's ending leaves the audience unsure as to what Kaneisha means and whom, if anyone, she is addressing. Is her tone grateful? Ironic? Enraged? In the most obvious way, Jim listened to her need to be racially humiliated, delivering the sexual scene she had been requesting from the very start. But on another level, following our earlier discussion on Moten and the idea of listening not to grasp the other but as a form of dispossession, Jim's listening may have more to do with tuning into the aesthetics of the terribly beautiful *in him*. Perhaps what Jim has finally been able to do is eavesdrop on himself, to listen toward his own disruption, to encounter something in him which he had so far resisted, something that made him vomit.

There are not many stage directions in the script of *Slave Play*. But regarding this closing line, Harris instructs, "The actress playing Kaneisha does *whatever she feels is right* before looking at him [Jim]" (2018, p. 132; emphasis added). Built into the script is the awareness that the Black actress playing Kaneisha needs a way out of being crushed by the exacting difficulties of the scene. The actress, Harris also recognizes, is not pretending; she needs to let forces be roused in her that are difficult and demonic, forces that are actual rather than simulated or mimetic. "I ask a black actress to get on her knees and twerk while eating a cantaloupe," Harris says, and "that's an insane thing to ask someone—not to pretend to do, but to actually do" (Tang, 2019). The instruction to deliver the closing line, thus, doing whatever the actress feels is right *for her* empowers her to translate the script's last line in the way she needs to, bringing it into her own emotional idiom. "I wanted to give an opportunity to an actress," explains Harris, "to have the sort of versatility inside of a character that I've only ever seen white actresses given the opportunity to have" (Kai, 2019).[31] In inciting the crisis but authorizing the actress to translate freely, Harris grants his protagonist the full spectrum of her humanity. Antoinette Crowe-Legacy, the actress playing Kaneisha in the August Wilson production, describes the closing line as "the one part of the play where I don't feel responsible to *anyone*; I don't feel responsible to the audience, I don't feel responsible to the story, it's just me and Kaneisha and we are going to have our moment . . . It's the one moment that's just for us, it's just for us" (Sunday discussions, December 19, 2021). What Crowe-Legacy describes, that moment that feels hers and that is relieved from the burdens of responding to, or thinking about, others, is a moment of self-sovereignty—and chapter 4 discusses this concept in depth.

A large body of Black feminist scholarship (Chude-Sokei et al., 2016; Musser, 2017; Nash, 2019; Stallings, 2015) has been delinking Black female sexuality from the melancholic tug of histories of violence, rape, and exploitation and has done so without minimizing the reach of that history. Through Harris's engagement of the anarchic dimension of the infantile sexual in his characters and by routing it through history, he shows how new libidinal movements, movements that are irreverent and disturbing, may contest the inert hold that a long history of sexual violation has had on Black people, especially Black women.[32] Inscrutable pleasures and tense excesses proceed from complex subjects, not from those who are affixed to the past in singular ways or who have to be constantly explicating their desires on others' terms.

The third act of *Slave Play* brings the audience to a state of overwhelm from which we, too, have to recover. One leaves the theater confused as to what one has just watched, disturbed by the intensity of the affect, and unclear as to what message the ending is supposed to convey. Did we witness a redemptive victory over historical trauma? A pathetic re-enactment of something ultimately fucked up? The closing act refuses to soothe us. The play comes to a screeching halt at the place of maximum tension, that of the audience's unbinding. Having already seduced us into lowering our defenses, the play exacts from the audience a strange kind of participation, working on us at the limits of our consent, pressing us into discomfort while also having transfixed us through its humor and its aggression, an aggression that has been specifically sexual. For those who are not too inhibited to enjoy it, the laughter that the play provokes disrupts our ego from retreating into the known and the familiar, cutting through pretense and propriety.

The idea that the woundedness of the flesh (Spillers, 1987) can recruit the spasms of desire to move someone toward opacity and to expose them to the fullness of their humanity may feel counterintuitive.[33] So, too, might the proposition that a desire for intimate subjugation may open up transformative possibilities. The pairing of the erotic with historical atrocity manifests a series of interlocked contradictions: humiliating but dignifying, selfish but generous, explicit but veiled, daring but cowardly, tender but cruel. The matter of how traumatized bodies can make bids to soften the grasp of histories to which they did not consent but to which they are nevertheless subject is that complex. And it is that urgent. It is in response to this urgency that Jeremy O. Harris has offered us the open wound that is *Slave Play*.

4

Toward a Theory of Traumatophilia

La Negresse
Term for rear-entry intercourse in Alex Comfort's *Joy of Sex*
(1972)

Coined for the curved mountain of our backsides,
front legs table top collapsed,

the term is French because we're foreign
(women's desires impolite English),

the term pejorative because I want
my crêpe-paper, lily-white-secretion maker

trifled with. Worse than *doggy-style*,
the conflation of animals and deep penetration,

la negresse implies only black women like it
-my ass in tuned vibrato-

or are the only ones willing to admit it.
Mostly, though, I want to know

if that's how you liked it, Sally,
if Paris made you

in its manner of blackness.
—Chet'la Sebree, *Mistress*

In this chapter, I pick up where I left off at the end of chapter 3 so that I may reflect more deeply on the concept of traumatophilia. I have been exploring the somewhat counterintuitive proposition that we may be overly focused on what can be done *about* trauma, suggesting instead that we slacken our grip on the therapeutics of trauma to allow ourselves to become more interested in what subjects do *with* their trauma.

I introduced the term "traumato*phobic*" to capture the former approach and the term "traumato*philic*" for the latter, purposefully choosing the suffixes "-phobic" and "-philic" to pack into these terms a shorthand that respectively conveys the repellent effects of fear and the attractive forces of affinity.

Deepening our exploration of traumatophilia will involve developing greater conceptual elasticity for thinking about repetition: what it is, what it does, what it looks like, and how it can feel. As we saw in chapter 3, repetition is not necessarily destructive but, when laced with pleasure, can be transformative, even conducive to expanded psychic freedoms. In this chapter, I offer further conceptual tools from psychoanalysis to convey what such repetitions look like (extravagant and superfluous) and what they can feel like (anguishing and magnetizing). My hope is to demonstrate that repetition deserves our trust and, also, our commitment. To flesh out these ideas, I return to *Slave Play* but now from the angle of my own repeated viewings of the play, to discuss what my bizarre and perversely iterative relationship to the play did to, and for, me. I take myself as a case study to probe how traumatisms may come to repeat toward sovereign experience. Focusing in particular on the play's third act and the various controversies the play generated, I offer reflections on how giving oneself over to repetition, though arduous and anguishing, is related to undergoing aesthetic experience. In this chapter, it is not just ideas about repetition but also the *action* of repetition that is at work. Put more strongly, repetition is not only the theme but also the method of this chapter.

The chapter concludes with an examination of the documentary *The Artist and the Pervert*, which narrates the relationship between Mollena Williams-Haas, the Black woman we encountered earlier as Williams (her pre-married name), a prominent sex educator and an artist, and her husband, Georg Friedrich Haas, an Austrian-born, White man and prominent composer. To be clear, I am not analyzing their individual psychologies; rather, I offer the example to stretch our thinking about what being drawn to the touching of wounds can look like. The example of Williams-Haas and Haas shows what may arise when two individuals step into the fray of traumatophilia together. This exploration fortifies the bid I make in this book: for us to orient the resources of our critical attention toward the permutations in which trauma re-appears (traumatophilia) rather than remaining focused on trauma's repair, that is,

on how to make trauma dis-appear (traumatophobia).[1] Traumatophilia
does not dismiss the negative effects suffered by traumatized persons.
Rather, recognizing that trauma both disrupts *and* shapes us (Saketopoulou, 2014), traumatophilia puts pressure on the all-too-human impulse to overpromise the reversing of injury and moves us away from
the instrumentality of cure. "Cure cannot be taken as the aim of psychoanalysis," writes Laplanche, "'cure' is no more relevant an aim than
divorce. Both imply the social adaptation of the profession. . . . Psychoanalysis has to put all socially-adaptive aims—that is, the whole notion
of self-preservation—in brackets" (1992a, p. 6). The task of psychoanalysis is "to keep the injury of the other open" (Laplanche, 1999, p. 241), to
"reopen[] the wound of the unexpected" (p. 280).

My concern about "cure" is not just that it can easily be routed toward
supporting the existing social order, turning the consulting room into a
Procrustean bed of normative adaptation. Even more importantly, I believe healing is unrealistically overpromised, sending us and the patients
we treat on a wild goose chase. As a practicing psychoanalyst, I would
say that trauma is never cured and that no one has ever been delivered
back to an intact, pretraumatic state, no matter how motivated they are
or how good their access to care or their resources. This is a statement
that many clinicians would agree with in theory. But when the rubber
hits the road, that is, when we sit with patients who need help, many of
us, just like many of our patients, get caught in the quicksand of imagining that psychoanalysis or therapy can restore mental health, that it can
help repair and, in some way, undo wounds. This belief prevails outside
the clinic as well: both popular culture and academic discourse like to
imagine subjects whose injuries (personal or structural) may be worked
through, ridding the subject of their imprint. At best, though, we learn
to live in trauma's afterlife, and I say this not to imply that political struggles for betterment should be therefore abdicated or that we should give
in to social injustices, but because I am concerned about the burgeoning
neoliberal economies that promise impossible healing and worry about
the seductive assurances of contemporary medicine-men who tell us we
can overcome pain.[2] I am equally concerned with the renaissance of in-
dividualism that is insidiously smuggled even into social movements
that seek liberation, enticing us with alluring fantasies of mastering pain
and of a resolutive draining of the traumatic past.

But wounds never fully close. They leave behind marks and scabs that can reopen and that *we are strangely drawn to touch*. To touch them, we must first reopen them, which involves cracking open their encasements that, as discussed in chapter 3, are crafted through the primary violence of the mythosymbolic. This touching of wounds involves the revisitation of trauma. It is through repetition that the touching of wounds can acquire the psychic density of traumatisms that, escalating to overwhelm, can invigorate new translational activity. Part of what makes a traumatophilic touching of wounds so impactful is that it can enable immobilized trauma to be put back into circulation. By "immobilized trauma," I refer to trauma that has been fully narrativized, whose meanings are rigidly affixed, making it impervious to fugitive possibilities. Fugitivity, for Moten, "is a desire for and a spirit of escape and transgression of the proper and the proposed . . . a desire for the . . . outlaw edge proper to the now" (2018, p. 131). Moten is describing openings to uncharted forms of newness. Psychoanalytically speaking, newness involves *re*newing, the calling forth of something old that may be revised. Such revivification, Laplanche writes, "is not trauma but seduction" (1994/2014, p. 31), which is another way of saying that traumatophilia may look like retraumatization—in fact, it often does—but what it stands to do is reopen enigma. Such reopening kindles the psychic irritant of untranslated enigmatic remnants, turning the irritant into a muse that can inspire new translational movements. Said differently, the disquiet of enigma has ties to inspiration and to enlivenment but only as long as the "subject can stay open to the trauma *by means of the trauma*" (1994/2014, p. 33). Instead of repair, a traumatophilic lens is interested in the way trauma is not purged but lived through, though on different terms from those that originally inflicted the injury. Through this reanimating, the visitation of trauma may become an ever-renewable source of inspiration, acting on us in potentially transforming ways.

Importantly, because we become subjectivized through implantative trauma, there is no intactness in our being to begin with to which we may ever be restored, which is another way of saying that we can never be cured of our unconscious. If we start out always already compromised by the intervention of the other's sexual unconscious into us, trauma is constitutive of our very ontology, not a piece of shrapnel to be removed. Important lineages of thought, starting with Fanon (1952, 1961), running through Spillers's work on flesh (1987), Hartman's thinking on racial subjection (1997), Patterson's ideas around social death (1982), Sexton's interventions on Black negativity (Barber, 2017), and more recent interventions made by Afropessimism (Wilderson, 2020), point to the way violence and trauma are foundational to the subjectivation of the Black subject in particular. The idea that implantative trauma is constitutive and part of the human condition overall, that it cuts through all humans independently of their racialization, does not deny the specificity of Black suffering and the particular historical conditions that have traumatized, and continue to traumatize, Black people en masse. Nor does it overlook that neo–Jim Crow continues to shape Black subjectivation to this day. Rather, what it highlights is that the argument that these violences have inscribed Blackness outside the category of the human is premised on a very particular understanding of the category of the human. Said differently, ontological negation is not the particular province of Black subjects.

The version of psychoanalysis I am working with is premised on the idea that ontological negation is, *part of our very humanity*. And yet the social order provides all sorts of sutures to White subjects such that White people may not have to confront their always already traumatic ontological status. This allows most White people to proceed with life as if their subjecthood is intact, obscuring that the social privileges of Whiteness expeditiously patch over fissures and gaps, permitting them to experience themselves as unbroken and as deserving to remain unbreak*able*. White dominance ensures that compensations are always on hand to support this fiction, amounting to a mythology of Whiteness that is so robustly subtended by the formidable structures of White supremacy that it comes to appear natural to all subjects independent of their racialization. This is another way of saying that Whiteness's ideological function is to naturalize the suturing of the traumatically constitutive condition that befalls all humans, projecting it onto Blackness, where it appears as ontological negation. The refusal to acknowledge that opacity lies at the heart of what it means to be human and the resistance to accepting that not everything can be mastered (Laplanche, 2003b; Scarfone, 2021) or grasped (Glissant, 1990; León, 2020a) is what gives Whiteness its density. Part of the rage that some White people experience when faced with enlarged social freedoms and equities for people of color may be understood from this angle: when inequality gaps narrow, there is a chipping away at some of these social compensations, in turn unveiling the stitchings that the social has installed to support the ideology of Whiteness's ostensible intactness.

Breathless Excitement

Two years ago, I was ravished by Jeremy O. Harris's theatrical work *Slave Play*.

Describing my experience this way may sound melodramatic. But my language is intentional, meant to do more than amplify how much I liked this play or felt changed by it—though both are also true. What took me over was far wilder and infinitely more bizarre: it felt absolutely exigent. The first time I saw this play I felt my whole being called to attention, rousing my senses in a way that no work of art ever has. From there on out, I was overcome with a fiery desire: to experience the play again and again. All I knew was that I wanted more. Interests that normally held my attention were overshadowed, everything else simply felt dampened. What followed was a long period that I can only describe as a possession, as if I had been taken over by a strange force. Repeatedly attending performances felt more like a path I had to follow than a decision. Only in retrospect did I connect this feeling of being possessed to Freud's description of repetition as a demonic force, or link it to the play's third act, which is titled "Exorcism." What exactly the "it" to be exorcised is—and whether that "it" can be exorcised (which, I will argue, is a traumatophobic approach) or merely brought into presence so that one may make contact with it (which I see as traumatophilic) is the main theme explored in this chapter.

Strangely, the experience also felt liberating, though what I was feeling liberated from I could not tell you. I became preoccupied with reading and rereading the script, with thinking and rethinking the dialogue. Week after week I attended Sunday discussions organized by the play's production. I went enthusiastically and enjoyed them immensely. But I was soon also quite chagrined to realize that I could not *not* go. Even as professional obligations and deadlines pressed for my time, I nonetheless found myself regularly heading out for these Sunday salons, eager yet also helpless to resist them.

I was fascinated but also scared by this play *and by my own reactions to it*. In retrospect, I was drawn to it like one who, standing over a cliff, looks down and, feeling an inexplicable draw, steps back. Only I did not take a step back: I stepped into the vertigo. For a year and a half, I watched the play again and again and again. I watched it alone, and I watched it with others. I went at planned times and I also went impulsively, as if seized by a grotesque longing. I once headed to the matinee right after the Sunday salon because the discussion stirred in me a need to experience the play right away. Over time and one repetition after another, I started observing small differences in the way the actors enunciated their lines, the way their bodies' affective charge shifted across performances, the way different audiences laughed (or did not) at certain lines. I talked about the play incessantly to anyone who was willing to listen. I followed Jeremy O. Harris around New York City to hear him talk about the play. Friends forwarded me announcements about talks, interviews, and podcasts about the play, enabling my preoccupation.

Becoming so infatuated with a work of art is not an experience I had had before. It was dazzlingly intense: I felt fiercely alive and throbbingly present. And it was also dizzyingly burdensome: I found the "demands" of my interest confusing, exhausting, and, at times, even terrifying. That only further drew me in. In retrospect, I would say I followed the play the way one follows around a lover before one's first heartbreak, before, that is, one learns to hold some things back. This particular response was, of course, specific to me. I have given much thought to what kept me so engaged, though I should say that I am far from being the only person whose involvement with this play grew unusually intense. *Slave Play* went on to earn a record number of twelve Tony nominations. It received rave reviews as well as unusually lacerating critique, including petitions to shut it down.[3] More than its reception though, it is the impassioned way in which theatergoers loved or hated it that I want to emphasize. At the Sunday salons, I met several others of varied racial backgrounds who were also attending the play frequently. Since then, friends, colleagues, and Twitter have made me aware of many others also magnetically drawn to it, returning to the performances again and again. From the perspective of fan studies, it might look like we were constituting a nascent (and irrationally intense) fandom (Booth, 2018; Hills, 2015), but the word "fandom" trivializes the urgency and zeal that swept over me. The difference is in the quality of the repetition: the return of the "fan" may not be the same as the return of a person who is having the kind of aesthetic experience I am describing, where one revisits not to affirm what one already knows but to be exposed to something at the limits of her understanding.

My dramatic experience with *Slave Play* continues to intrigue me. And it has led to much introspection that, early on, took a form I now see as somewhat naïve and that focused on how my own positionality—as a White, queer, immigrant woman who partly grew up in the former British colony of Cyprus—relates to how engrossing I found it and why. It took me some time to be able to distinguish between my experience of the play and my process of thinking and talking about it, the latter being more about how the play took residence inside me and how that manifested itself outwardly. Thinking and writing *about* the play have involved the conversion of the aesthetic experience I had, which decentered me, into a recentered one that can be tracked and narrated. What was most precious to me about *Slave Play* is failed by words (though, in this chapter, I will try): it was about wonderment and a rousing of an energy in me that is beyond my reach—not a yet-unreached understanding but an unreach*able* one.

When the play's first Broadway run was ending, I attended the closing performance to bid the play farewell. Leaving the theater that night, I felt bereft. I eagerly awaited a future production. When the pandemic hit, making travel unsafe and closing theaters across the country, it became clear that I would be unable to attend a forthcoming production that was scheduled to open in Los Angeles in the spring of 2020. I felt the cost of this loss acutely—and that itself felt bizarre. To the time of this writing, I continue to think about the play regularly, which is another way of saying that I have established a thinking relation with it in its absence that permits me the luxury of ongoing contact. Turning *Slave Play* into an object of contemplation has transformed it into something that I can hold onto and recall. Of course, the gap between the memory and the experience itself is unbridgeable, and that is itself an experience that I have learned to savor.

Strangely and despite the compulsively iterative and, at times, torturous quality of my relationship to *Slave Play*, this irresistible press did not impair me—and that still surprises me. I developed a strange, meditative curiosity about my experience and was able to continue seeing my patients, teach, supervise clinical work, run my study groups, and publish. Unsurprisingly, my torrential affair with *Slave Play* imprints itself on my writing and teaching: for example, the script now appears in my syllabi for courses on psychosexuality that I teach to psychoanalytic trainees. I am not mentioning this productivity to extol the play's fruitful impact on me—as you will see, I am moving in a very different direction than simply professing the play's "usefulness"—but because I am genuinely surprised that my taxing need to experience the play again and again did not compromise me.

When I was under the play's spell, *I had an experience*—not an experience *of* something but what I can only, and inexactly, describe as pure experience. There were moments when I was singularly focused, acutely present. And despite the general disorienting state I just described, I felt overflowing with life. I am often asked why I kept going back. The question is usually asked of me as a White person—and not, for example, as a Cypriot postcolonial subject who is kept revisiting a play depicting a British man encountering himself in the mirror, and vomiting; or as a queer woman who returned to luscious depictions of queer desire; or, as a woman who went back to watch a rape/not-rape scene again and again. I do not know how to answer that question on the level it is asked without recycling tropes about what we (already think we) understand about racialization. What feels most honest of an answer, though, is that what I was so fervently chasing after in my iterative viewings of *Slave Play* was precisely this state that I described earlier as pure experience—an experience that went far beyond my various positionalities.

I mention in detail my intensely consuming preoccupation with this theatrical piece so that I may query the mechanisms and processes by which this play in particular, and aesthetic experience and performance more generally, may illuminate the workings of repetition and the subject's undoing. Where I thematize my changed relationship to my racialization, I do it not because my personal change per se is relevant to my arguments but because *the fact* that something changed in me is central to my analysis of the way performance can have the transformational impact claimed on its behalf. In other words, my personal growth comes into this chapter only as a way of concretely illustrating the force with which some performance can act *on* us, how it can evoke states of overwhelm, what performance has to do with the sexual drive, and with the kind of sadism *Slave Play* inflicts on its audience. This sadism, as Gary Fisher's work introduced in chapter 3 and my discussion of *The Night Porter* in chapter 5 will also suggest, courses through varied works of art that may, if we give ourselves over to them, transform us.

Tracking how cultural objects, especially art and performance, make their imprint on us, my interest is in theorizing the mechanics of aesthetic experience. I want to probe the territory that lies beyond meaning, to offer a psychoanalytic inflection as to how theater and other forms of art develop the density of their affective contagion (Pellegrini, 2007) to produce transformative aesthetic experience. I am not reaching for hermeneutic interpretations, I am after the pulsations of experience and the mesmerizing effects we undergo in some performance. For this reason, I refuse the usual call to probe *what* is stimulated in us on the level of meaning when we are beckoned by a work of art and pay more attention to the movements magnetized in us in the encounter with an artistic event. My self-observations may, I hope, serve as a departure point for theorizing not *from* experience toward hermeneutics but *about* experience for the sake of experience alone.

In chapter 3, I discussed *Slave Play* at length and will briefly summarize it again here with a slightly different emphasis. This repetition is not only to refresh the memory of readers who have not seen the play but because, as already mentioned, repetition is both the focus *and the method* of this chapter. In other words, this repetition, much like my iterative relationship to the viewing of the play, is not just a repetition *with* a difference (Deleuze, 1968); it is a repetition *toward* a difference. I try to lay bare the mechanisms of how theater can conduct the force of "affective immersion and communal event" (Pellegrini, 2007, p. 926) and how repetition courts the reappearance of trauma by re-presenting (rather than representing) that which exists outside "lived experience" and which cannot be thought or culled into language.

Re-Presenting Slavery

All comparatively intense affective processes, including even
terrifying ones, trench upon sexuality.
—Sigmund Freud, *Three Essays on the Theory of Sexuality*
(1905b)

On the surface, *Slave Play* appears to be concerned with the atrocious
history of slavery in the antebellum South and its continued afterlife in
the present. But *Slave Play* is after something quite different than inciting our horror at the institution. *Slave Play* does indeed push White
audience members to discern their ongoing immersion in anti-Black
racism and asks theatergoers to consider their relationship to colorism.
But the edge on which *Slave Play* really vibrates is the revivification of
slavery in the embodied theatrical space, bringing theatergoers into contact with how slavery's history is inscribed not only in intergenerational
memory but also, and especially, in the excitable, libidinal body. *Slave
Play* does not play *with* race; it demonstrates the play *of* race, "how we
play race and even how race plays us" (Cruz, 2016, p. 60).

Slave Play opens with three interracial couples in a southern plantation. The White and White-passing partners subject their Black partners
to different varieties of erotically tinged, racially offensive humiliations
involving onstage nudity and simulated sex. These lavish, all-out assaults
on dignity are rousing in the many senses of the term, an effect dexter-
ously achieved by the playwright's capacity to harness the energy of the
obscene and by his masterful use of humor, which lowers the audience's
defenses. Indeed, the play is incredibly funny for those who are not too
inhibited to enjoy it. These effects are further amplified by the director Robert O' Hara's calculated decision to refuse the theatergoer any
reprieve from the first act's intensities by having the play run without
an intermission. The first act thus operates on the psychic economy of
the sexual drive: ever-intensifying excitations that escalate toward "more
and more."

In the second act, we learn that the first act's erotic debasements were
staged by the Black partners, who engineered them as part of an un-
orthodox couples' treatment. The slave play in *Slave Play*, we thus discover, follows on the heels of a rigorous three-day prep during which

the White and White-passing partners were rigorously immersed in the materials (flashcards, vocabulary words, and movies) that they would need to enact their roles persuasively and with historical exactitude.[4] But it is not those who were debased who most struggled: it is the White and White-passing partners who most vociferously protest. The slave play is abruptly halted by Jim, a White British man, who initially gets turned on by it but ultimately safewords, disappointing and angering his wife, who has made herself vulnerable by finally asking for what she wants.

Resolutely desexualized, the second act presents a caricatured, theory-filled exegesis that "explains" to the characters and to the audience what occurred in the preceding act. Despite its being, or perhaps because it is hyperintellectualized, this code-switching has a containing and calming effect, delivering the play's most memorable monologues (Gary's "I am the prize" and Kaneisha's "You are the virus" speech). The insights are emotionally laden and difficult, but, unlike the first act, they do not leave the audience feeling disoriented or shaken up—in fact, at times, the audience applauds or otherwise expresses its approval. These lines, therefore, offer orienting moorings for understanding the first act and extend illuminating insights that theatergoers who were themselves in interracial relationships seem to have appreciated.[5]

The third act delivers a most forceful blow. Jim, who in the first act had only halfheartedly participated in the racialized sexual debasement that Kaneisha requested, belatedly gets on board. Jim now demeans Kaneisha, treating her like a slave and addressing her with racial slurs. But is his participation *real* (is he now "getting off" in racially denigrating her?), or is it *make-believe* (is he still play-acting, inflicting the racial abjection on her command)? As for Kaneisha, it is similarly unclear if she is getting what she (thought she) wanted or if she is finding herself in a hauntingly messed-up replay of her historical past (the character's ancestors were slaves). The final scene appears to mimic a rape—and I say that it "appears to mimic a rape" because what unfolds between Kaneisha and Jim is purposefully ambiguous. On the one hand, it has many of the signifiers indexing sexual violation: there are ripped clothes, physical force, protest, resistance, anguish, and evident distress. On the other, it is portrayed in a way typical of BDSM encounters: the scene has been requested, negotiated, and orchestrated in detail. But does Kaneisha still want now what she had requested earlier?

Importantly, the rape/not-rape scene is preceded by a subtle onstage negotiation: Jim offers his whip to Kaneisha and she leans into it tentatively, biting down on it such that it becomes a gag. Later on, when Jim threatens to beat her, he strangely pauses to add, "You can nod your head" (Harris, 2018, p. 131). The stage directions for this exchange read, "Kaneisha and Jim stare at each other in a weighted silence. She slowly nods her head in the affirmative. He nods as well. She nods again" (Harris, 2018, p. 131). This nonverbal exchange may be easy to miss, but anyone acquainted with the way such communications proceed in BDSM encounters will recognize a standard method by which some tops ensure, without breaking character, that the bottom still wants what they had previously authorized. Across numerous interviews and talk-backs, Harris routinely took pains to remind the audience of this often-overlooked nuance.[6] But if it is easy to miss, that is also because the delivery of this moment varies: even when the same actors are onstage, the nod is more or less discernible across different performances—sometimes more, sometimes less emphatic. Does this variability itself index something about the ambivalence of this interaction, as if the character, but also the actor playing Kaneisha, is herself unsure of her relationship to these repetitions? In discussing this, Antoinette Crowe-Legacy, one of the actresses who have played Kaneisha, notes that the nod is as if Kaneisha were saying, "I am not completely sure, but I think I have to do this, I need this. And I think," Crowe-Legacy continues, "that living in that place is hard. It's hard to live in an 'I don't know'. . . It's hard to press forward when you feel that there is possibly something that could go very right or very wrong" (Sunday discussions, January 23, 2022).

This nonverbal aspect of her exchange with Jim (the nod, the biting of the whip) is where we see the bending of Kaneisha's will. What Kaneisha takes a chance on, the kind of erotic experience and interpersonal engagement she is risking escapes affirmative consent, even as it shares its signifiers. What we see unfold on the stage is not a nonverbally expressed "yes" but a movement inside the self not based on reason but animated by the drive (limit consent)—what Crowe-Legacy describes as Kaneisha having to do this, needing this. (Here let us also remember Carmen, from the introduction, for whom consent was an interior affair.) Limit consent, we see in Kaneisha, proliferates in the body, which affirmative consent sees only as unreliable or dangerous. Kaneisha's nonverbal vocabulary of actions (the nodding of the head, the biting of the whip) index what cannot be spoken, what cannot make it into words, and it is here, to return to Moten, that we may listen for something that is not there and yet could be made audible. Some audiences interpreted the last act as a rape, but saying with certainty that Kaneisha was raped may be the audience's own attempt to bind and thus to master the undecidability of the closing scene, which confronts us with something at the limits of what we can grasp. To assume the kind of risk Kaneisha takes requires a sense of self-sovereignty: one has to have a will before one can bend it. Her form of eroticism allows her to engage with something that may produce overwhelm, not only violation; and in that sense, self-destructiveness at such moments does not reside in taking a risk *but in failing to take it.*

Before long, however, the scene becomes too tangled even for those who are familiar with BDSM signifiers and the nuances of consent. Jim forcefully pins Kaneisha down, entering her violently. She mildly fights back. He keeps going. She pushes Jim, and when he still keeps going, she scratches him.[7] Finally scrambling out from underneath him, she pierces the audience's stunned silence with a harrowing wail. She begins to sob. What is unfolding is tipping into the abyss. Are we watching Jim rape his wife, or is he taking her against her protests as per the scripted sexual play? The indeterminacy of this scene becomes a particle accelerator, sending questions about consent into a tailspin. Even as Kaneisha had nodded her head, she no longer wants this—though we cannot know if it is because it comes too late, or because she did not quite realize what she was opening herself to, or something else entirely. "The risk of emotional damage can be great," warns Mollena Williams (2010, p. 56), to whom we will loop back later in this chapter.

What does it mean for a Black woman to ask to be play-raped by her White husband against an ancestral background in which female slaves were stripped of the right to withhold their consent (Hartman, 1997; Musser, 2016, 2018; Spillers, 1987)? What to make of the play's ending, where Kaneisha thanks Jim for listening, is the subject of much postplay conjecture. The play ends with the force of shock and at the site of rekindled enigma, refusing to tell us what we are to make of this jolting mess. The playwright has us leave the theater rattled and without consolation, disturbed about what we have just watched and confused about what he and the play itself want from us.

Harris's refusal to tell the viewer what to do with or about the blazing intensities of the third act is its own enigmatic surplus. In interviews and talk-backs, he routinely declines to comment on what the takeaway is supposed to be. For Antoinette Crowe-Legacy, "there is debate inside of myself about how much [Kaneisha] is hurt by the end of the play and by what specifically, as she gets closer to what she asks for" (Sunday discussions, December 19, 2021). The play's argument, if one can be attributed to it, is that the history of slavery remains nested in the bodies of both White and Black subjects, in a state that Scarfone has called the "unpast" (2015b). It is unpast because the past is not yet past but, instead, resurfaces and reappears in the present where it agitates us through the libidinal body. In *Slave Play*, this reappearance materializes at the margin of our (the audience's) consent. Harris re-presents this unpast, not in the sense of representing it but in the sense of presenting it again (Scarfone, 2015b), calling it forth in the theatrical space by means of its outlandish erotic charge (Holland, 2012).[8] This re-presentation of White America's foundational crime is, to borrow Schneider's expression, a masterful slashing of the imaginary membrane that separates the past from the present (2011). "The time of slavery persists," writes Hartman, in the interminable "longing for a way of undoing the past" (1997, p. 6)—but in *Slave Play*, the longings are infinitely more grotesque, hoping not to undo the past but to dramatize it in real time.

These dramatizations do not seem to me to be rote repetitions but inciting traumatisms. Midway through the third act, Kaneisha explains that her enslaved elders have been watching her and Jim: "[They have been] watching me lay in bed every night with a demon who thinks he is a saint. And the elders don't care that you are a demon, they lay with them too. . . . They just want you to know it. And me to know it. So I can lie with grace. So I can lie with their blessing" (Harris, 2018, p. 129).[9] Rihanna's "Work" plays in the background—"I mean who am I to hold your past against you? I just hope that it gets to you. I hope that you see this through. I hope that you see this true"—which helps frame Kaneisha's ask: this is not just her history, it is Jim's too.

In a classic essay on the historical palimpsest of Black female sexual exploitation that moves from slavery to the present, Hortense Spillers writes, "Whether or not the captive female and/or her sexual oppressor derived 'pleasure' from their seductions and couplings is not a question we can politely ask. Whether or not 'pleasure' is possible at all under conditions that I would aver as non-freedom . . . has not been settled" (1987, p. 76). For Musser, settling this question is a sheer impossibility "because our understandings of pleasure rely on contemporary notions of individuality and personhood, which cannot be grafted onto the historical reality of slavery" (2014, p. 165).[10] What can we do with questions that are impolite, questions that cannot be settled because the terms that organize them are historically inapposite to the time of our query? We can, I propose, give ourselves over to the force of their action on us. To explain what I mean by that, let us turn to the use of humor in the play, which gives Harris a way to tackle the questions that Spillers frames as impolite without addressing them head-on, which would be nothing less than inflammatory. To take them on directly, Harris elaborates, would be "almost like punching you in the face. But if you laugh. . . all of a sudden you've opened yourself up and are consenting to, like, more. . . You want more of that, because it's so funny. . . Your mouth gets wider and wider and wider, and then I just throw ideas down it" (Smith, 2019). *Slave Play*'s jokes do not secure the audience's informed consent; they act, rather, as (Laplanchean) seductions, thereby implicating limit consent in the lowering of our defenses, which means that the jokes strewn through the play exact a strange form of participation from the audience, working on us at the limits of our assent, pressing us into discomfort while also transfixing us through their aggression, an aggression that is also, specifically, sexual.

The laughter the play coaxes is thus part of its strategic approach, a way for Harris to engage the questions Spillers describes as impolite.[11] Seduction, as we have seen, happens not with or against our consent but at its limit—and we may remember here how Mia felt seduced and, thus, "screwed" by me after I told her my fee. Many theatergoers attend a play expecting something to unfold onstage, not expecting something bewildering and strange to unfold in themselves. There are expectations as to what we think we are agreeing to when we enter the theatrical space, what we believe we are stepping into and are prepared for, and we may not even know we have such expectations. It is only in retrospect, when these expectations are broken or dashed, as was the case with some *Slave Play* audiences, that we become aware of them. But this is also precisely what makes some performances so potent: what is stirred up cannot possibly be negotiated through any kind of ordinary or affirmative consent. These kind of aesthetic experiences are in the province of limit consent; they do not give us closure but reveal the teeming of contradiction. By lifting established meanings from their everyday coercions, such aesthetic experiences stand to rattle the ego. Such rattling takes something familiar and puts it into a foreign context so that we can be slowed down, wrested away from our habituated thinking (Adorno, 1970).

The question of whether one can consent to being rattled is, in many ways, one of the themes that is threaded throughout this volume. Many theatergoers ruminate on the third act in the hope of some clarification, to get a better grasp of whether Jim genuinely listened to Kaneisha. What this may miss is that the closing act is not conjugated according to our usual ways of assessing whether someone was "heard" but breaks down, instead, the very terms by which we measure whether "listening" has happened. What all subjects need, and what Black subjects in general and Black women in particular are often denied, is listening for "interiority, difference, and relational standing" (Chambers-Letson, 2020, p. 279). Many theatergoers understood *Slave Play* as giving White audiences a way to reckon with how their own racialization materializes in the flickering shadow of histories of domination.[12] To me, what the closing act more radically offers is not racial education but a reordering of the terms by which we are accustomed to thinking about sexuality, racial difference, intimacy, and agency. This is not a reordering that happens through instruction, and it has no determinate end; it has to be risked by the audience's willingness to undergo aesthetic experience. My guess is that some "repeaters," those theatergoers who went back time and again to see *Slave Play*, may have also returned to experience something summoned in themselves. That certainly was the case for me.

The Driving Force of Repetition

In psychoanalysis, repetition has a bad reputation because it is mostly regarded as a degraded form of remembering. Necessitated by the absence of other, higher-quality mnemic inscription, repetition is considered problematic in that it requires the action of, rather than the symbolization of, what is repressed. A truncated overview of these ideas follows to help contextualize my intervention.

In 1914, Freud posited repetition compulsion as a form of remembering through action. Repetition is how the repressed returns: the patient repeats "without . . . knowing that he is repeating" (1914b, p. 150). Repetition was thus "a present-day force" (1914b, p. 151) that encysted mnemic traces. This encystment permitted them to be conducted into the present, but it also muted them, making repetition an obstacle to recollection. Freud's advice to analysts about this problem was to give repetition unencumbered latitude in the circumscribed space of the transference, so that the patient's relationship with the analyst would become a playground "in which [repetition] is allowed to expand in almost complete freedom" (1914b, p. 154). This opened a path for the unremembered events of the past to come alive, to be dramatized in the transferential space. Analysis of these repetitions would then help the patient remember and narratively symbolize the past, effectively rehousing anamnesis from the domain of action to the psychic sphere. Freud later formulated repetition compulsion as a relentless, unstoppable return to the site of trauma that is driven, as mentioned in earlier chapters, by a demonic force (1920). From this angle, repetition compulsion's hope is to master trauma, and it is always doomed to fail. Repetition, that is, botches the project it sets out to accomplish—to master the traumatic past. Between that and repetition's reliance on the re-presentation and the restaging of trauma rather than the higher-grade, symbolic form of remembering, psychoanalysis has thus regarded repetition as a necessary evil.

Psychoanalytic theorizing has since covered much ground regarding repetition. Epigrammatically here, the psychoanalyst Bruce Reis has described *creative* repetitions that do not repeat as fixation but that instead carry "a yield of pleasure" (2020, p. 104). By inviting pleasure rather that iterative suffering, creative repetitions open up paths to the possibilities of new experience. Other theorists are also nuancing our understanding of repetition, providing well-theorized and sensitively handled clinical material in which pleasure, the patient's and the analyst's, becomes critical to the patient's repetition being churned toward creative outcomes (Schwartz-Cooney, 2018; L. Levine, 2016).

I find this theorizing expansive and helpful in that it has lifted repetition out of its entrenched, previously devalued position. But, at the same time, this foregrounding of pleasure strips repetition of its more destabilizing dimensions, which means that a repetition that is rehabilitated through pleasure loses its footing in the demonic. This move relocates the problem of repetition to a taxonomical divide between pleasurable and, therefore, creative repetitions and those that are more demonic and, therefore, destructive. What about repetitions, however, like my own with *Slave Play*, which embroil pleasure with vertiginous difficulty? Engaging in them involves a bending of the will, a countering of the ego's tendency to repeat mechanically, and a resistance to being pulled into our customary understandings/translations. Chance also plays a role as to how such repetitions will proceed and whether they will come to constitute traumatisms, and this chance factor is also why this form of experience cannot be preplanned. Further, we oftentimes rely on the *effects* of repetition to adjudicate whether they are creative or destructive. The outcome of repetition, however, relies on many factors, including factors outside repetition itself.

If a clear distinction between creative and destructive repetitions can only be claimed retroactively, we may have to concede that the force of repetition may be agnostic, that it can go either way depending, each time, on the interplay of binding and unbinding. For example, I very much enjoyed *Slave Play*, and it, no doubt, spurred a creative process in me. But to say only that something generative came out of my enjoyment of a play that so graphically re-presents the sexual atrocities of slavery and that stirs the audience with intemperate displays of erotic abjection would be to leave out the baser and rawer elements that drew me, and so many others, to it. It is, in fact, this very perturbing enjoyment that this play in particular and difficult performance overall artfully stimulates in theatergoers. And here is the rub: since the sexual is agnostic as to ethics, that is, since it is not subordinated to moral reasoning, its evocation opens up to a range of possibilities—not just pleasure but also cruelty, not just creative potential but also barbarism. It is only in the après-coup, then, that we will be able to know what came of these forces and to what effects they were used, which is another way of saying that repetition is not a project with a determinate end. It is us, speaking always in its aftermath after knowing what repetition came to, who confound repetition's effects with its causes.

As for my own repetitive relationship to *Slave Play*, the aesthetic experience I had caused something in me to shift: at the moment, I could not capture in words what I was experiencing. I only knew that it was drawing me closer to my being, to something enigmatic and opaque that I still cannot put into words. To do so would be to defile the experience I had. In the proceeding months, as I continued to attend performances, the play was gradually transformed into an object of contemplation that made me think of consent and sadism in new ways. But that is only what happened *after* the experience: it is the set of translations that I forged in order to cope with the strain the play produced in me. In that sense, while I can tell you *what* I have done conceptually with this play (and the ideas in this book are partly derived from that process), I do not have access, nor can you, to the more enigmatic, opaque elements that drew me to it so feverishly.

What I do know is that in its aftermath, I was singularly changed: I came to this country as an immigrant from two home countries in my twenties, one with virtually no racial diversity or conversations about race (Greece) and the other (Cyprus) released only in the mid-twentieth century from the tight grip of British rule, with virtually no appreciation of its postcoloniality. Upon coming to the States, I worked hard to develop an understanding of my racialization and to appreciate the workings of racial dynamics in the United States. So nuanced thinking about race was not new to me when I came to *Slave Play*; I had done serious and dedicated intellectual work, and my social and personal life had been far from monochromatic. Still, *Slave Play* gave me an experience of overwhelm that tore up my ego, and in that opening, something new was forged. No matter how much time I had previously spent thinking about race, the experience of *Slave Play* did something that could not have happened otherwise. But, for the purposes of this book, *how* the play acted on me is less important than *that* it did—though, again, it is impossible to talk about the latter without mentioning the former. What matters, in other words, is not my personal transformation per se: the fact that this transformation happened speaks to *how* some theater and performance exercise a force on us that can shatter and transform us.

What mattered most to me during the period of my iterative infatuation was not what I learned from *Slave Play* or how I was changed by it; these coagulated later, after the play had taken residence in me, and are merely its outward manifestations. What mattered most was the *aesthetic experience itself*, not what it touched in me or what it meant to me but the contact with something alien and foreign to me. Even as I was unable to articulate it to myself at the time, and even as I still stumble for words to recount it today, having that experience again and again is something that I valued and that I fiercely, despite some cost to myself, protected. Repetition of the kind I experienced with *Slave Play*, in other words, is about something much more sacred than even creativity: it can usher us into experiences that vibrate at the highest intensity of being.

Sovereign Experience

And sometimes working within me you open for me a door
into a state of feeling which is quite unlike anything to which
I am accustomed—a kind of sweet delight which, if I could
only remain permanently in that state, would be something
not of this world, not of this life.
—Augustine, *Confessions* 10.40 (qtd. in Miles, 2021, p. 3)

In chapters 2 and 3, we explored how repetition works to progressively wear down the binding of psychic energy, energetically overwhelming the ego's bindings, causing its shattering. Repetition escalates toward overwhelm by delivering traumatisms (not trauma but psychic and/or physical pain) that work at the limit of our consent. For example, I gave myself over to the play, thus permitting it to "work on" me: it "worked on" me by rousing certain forces and appetites that I came into contact with obliquely through attending the play and at the Sunday discussions that, as I mentioned, I also felt unable to resist. Repeating traumatisms operate like a persistent microdosing of pain. With enough buildup, this microdosing can bring about a state of overwhelm, inciting a crisis in the organized ego, dissipating its boundaries.[13] Overwhelm unravels the connective tissue between translations and enigma/the sexual unconscious, which is another way of saying that existing translations become unbound. Unbinding releases psychic energy that is too much for the psyche to bear. The ego will, therefore, quickly go into overdrive to suture up the open wound; as it assembles anew, new selves become possible.

Indeed, let us now examine at a higher resolution what happens *within* the domain of overwhelm, in the interstitial space after the ego has come into contact with the drive but before it repairs itself by creating a new structure.[14] The space between de-subjectivation and re-subjectivation opens up a contact zone with the drive and is the domain of pure experience—as opposed to an experience *of* something. In this interstitial space, one may undergo a very fleeting divestment from the burdens of subjectivity (the unbinding of the ego), to luxuriate in what Bataille called "sovereign experience" (1954, p. 113)—a transitory burst of intense liveliness during which "attention passes from 'projects,'" that is, teleologically oriented actions, to deliver a "startled jump of our entire being" (1954, p. 113).

To prevent any misunderstandings of the loaded term "sovereignty," I want to clarify that I am not referring to a process by which one attains a durable sense of self-possession that is vacated of personal history, historical events, or social forces. Nor am I unaware of the complex political lineages around indigeneity, tribal land claims, and anticolonial movements that trail the term "sovereignty." Sovereign experience is also not meant to codify an autonomous self as fantasized, promised, and sold to us by neoliberalism, a self, that is, that wills choices and selects experience as if from a smorgasbord of consumerist options. Sovereign experience, in the sense I am discussing it, is also not about the acquisition and consolidation of institutional power as when used in political theory (i.e., in the sense of political sovereignty). Sovereign experience, as I use the term, is a burst of self-divestment that arises in the confrontation of being with nonbeing, when everything is put on the line (Blanchot, 1969). Bataille's "idiosyncratic concept" of sovereignty, Martin Jay writes, "meant the loss of willed control by a homogeneous agent [aka the subject] and submission to the heterogeneous forces that exploded its integrity" (1993, p. 67). Therein, an immeasurably brief escape from the pummeling effects of political projects, discourse, and organized meanings becomes possible (Bataille, 1957).

This very fleeting separation from identitarian projects and from the demands of the political realm can make sovereign experience feel immensely freeing. Because it offers a (short-lived) span outside subjectivity, it makes a powerful claim on the present, an ephemeral psychic space where—contra Hegel—we do not rely on the other to recognize our existence or to affirm our self-consciousness but we can luxuriate, instead, in the formlessness of being. This is as intimate an experience as one can undergo *with oneself*. We may think of it as an encounter with our opacity, a meaningful encounter with the limit of what we can know or access about ourselves.

Sovereign experience is a most private and personal space, although here words fail me. When I say "personal," I do not mean it from the perspective of the ego or from an "I" that speaks for itself or from the standpoint of an organized self. The experiential domain I am describing is the opposite of notions of "lived experience" in the sense of first-hand accounts or in the way the term "experience" is used nowadays to describe the conscious reporting of living as a member of a particular group. None of this relieves us from the ways in which we are dependent on one another or ethically responsible for the other, but it does offer a furtive relief from the lacerating demands of relationality. Transiently stripped from the workings of power, discourse, and self-narrativization, sovereign experience can feel like a boundless sense of freedom—though I want to stress that by "freedom," I am not referring to an emancipation from persons or structures. What we are momentarily freed from is the burden of identity-driven and/or hermeneutic understandings of the self. We are not liberated, that is, from anything other than our own selves, momentarily startled by the arbitrariness of our own translations—though even that is only immeasurably brief. Still, when it happens, we are momentarily exposed to the raw nerve of being.

What does it mean, though, for experience to "flash" before us? I do not mean that something previously bewildering becomes illuminated or comes into crisper focus. In sovereign experience, time comes to a heightened standstill, interrupting the flow of chronological time. A jolting reorientation to the present, it refuses the ability of future time to hold sway over us. Sovereign time is thus not a progressive onward march but an intensified "now," a hyperpixilated present in which time does not pass. The temporality of sovereign experience is akin to Scarfone's notion of "actual time," "a very specific kind of present, not [an] eternal but [an] atemporal [one]" (2015b, p. 77)—"atemporal" being the word by which Freud described the time of the unconscious (1915c). Scarfone distinguishes between time that is eternal, where one may be caught in an inescapable, ongoing loop, and time that is atemporal, time that vibrates with the intensity of *now*. This implies a vital difference between stalled time and still time, that is, between time that is "stuck" in the unpast and time that, in its stillness, may become coextensive with experience. In stilled time, we find ourselves in a pronounced now with no temporal unfolding, where we may be fully claimed by the present. Arising in the crevasses of the ego's dissolution, where our very being is at stake, sovereign experience stands to bring us into contact with the extravagance of life.

The high-energy psychic states arising during overwhelm are quickly transduced to new translations that, one hopes, will work better than the ones that have been broken down by the force of repetition. Whatever feels new, creative, or even clarifying issues from what the ego crafts *after the fact, as a way of patching up the hole opened up by overwhelm*. Creativity, if it occurs, is not about the opening up of the ego but what is left behind when it gets stitched together anew. Any amelioration, however, that arises through this process is by no means guaranteed—*nor is it the goal of repetition*. A "better translation" (e.g., my new relationship to my racialization) is not the telos but merely an epiphenomenon, a side effect, if you will, of the ego's expeditious work, which is to promptly restore itself to a more intact, enclosed state. Translations crafted in the wake of sovereign experience arise through the anguish and the toil of overwhelm and are hard-earned. Crucially, because they carry inside them a rudimentary trace that an experience of sovereignty was endured, they may feel especially valuable and, in some ways, more "ours."

The "It" That Repeats Has to Appear: The Actual and the Enigmatic

The intense clarity of the image failed to satisfy us, for it
seemed to hide as much as it revealed; and while it seemed
to invite us to pierce the veil and examine the mystery behind it, its luminous concreteness nevertheless held the eye
entranced and kept it from probing deeper.
—Nietzsche, *Birth of Tragedy*

In Freudian repetition compulsion, as we saw, the subject repeats (rather than remembers) something "forgotten" or something that, being unacceptable to the self, was repressed, that is, relocated to the unconscious. But Laplanche does not subscribe to Freud's "jigsaw puzzle model" (2006a, p. 127) of memory. Whereas for Freud repression marks something that has gone missing, for Laplanche, it is the inescapable fate of the enigmatic surfeit. So if, for Freud, repetition is the return of the repressed, in Laplanchean thought repetition would have to mean something different than the reappearance of a painful or unacceptable inscription. The "it" that galvanizes repetition, that is, would not be an obscured memory but would relate to what is at the origin of primal repression: the ontological trauma of enigma itself. But how, we would be justified to ask, can that trauma repeat when enigma is itself a hollow, devoid of content? It repeats, I would say, as experience, or, to be (slightly) more precise, as a contentless experience that puts us *in the presence* of the unknown. Repetition in this sense does not represent some thing: it re-presents, in the sense of presenting again *an originary experience*. How would we sense its recurrence? We sense it, Scarfone notes, by its propulsive force, where it has "the effect of presence," "convey[ing] something more and something other than the semantic order" (2015b, pp. 117–118).

To make this a bit less abstract, let us consider Scarfone's description of the fresco of the Annunciation in the Oratory of San Giorgio in Padua. "Lodged in the very middle of the classic scene," he writes, "between the annunciating angel and the Virgin. . . is an oculus, a sort of rose window through which, in the daytime, a blinding light usually shines" (2015b, p. 71). To enjoy the visual experience, visitors "must give time for their eyes to adjust to this luminous irruption" (2015b, p. 71). What first appears as an interference to being able to look at the fresco "turns out to be an extraordinary deepening of the aesthetic," as this particular placement is exploited by the artist not just to represent the scene of the Annunciation but to perform the action of "*annunciat[ing]*, *summoning* the spectator who soon feels seized by this light, without which nothing can be seen, but under whose spell one is but half-blinded" (2015b, p. 72; emphasis in original).

For Scarfone, the draw one feels to the oculus is akin to being exposed to a mysterious presence that is felt to almost personally address the visitor. By incorporating this oculus into the fresco, the artist has been able to conduct the sun's luminosity, which gives the artwork an intensity that draws one in but from which one also has to turn away. Together, the two give the visit its experiential depth, as this unmediated stream of light is responsible for the scene having become much more gripping than any Annunciation scene, however beautifully executed, ever could.

The oculus thus becomes a source of "a profundity going far beyond what is represented, endowing [the fresco] with a presence, granting it the status of a *presentation*" (Scarfone, 2015b, p. 73). This presentation is potent, but its potency does not inhere in its offering understanding (e.g., of the mystery of the Annunciation); it derives from the fact that "it marks the limits of representation, signal[ing] the existence of something beyond the representable, the intelligible, something beyond meaning, an ungraspable core, an opaque or empty nucleus dwelling at the heart of any representation" (2015b, p. 73). Scarfone relates the experience of the oculus to what lies at the core of our being, to the "foundational and insurmountable fact" of the opaque nucleus implanted by enigma. This nucleus, akin to the enigmatic core, obtains from the infant's failed efforts to translate the adult's sexual unconscious. Borrowing Freud's term "actual," Scarfone refers to it as the internal alienness that always remains inside us in unelaborated form, resistant to any and all of our efforts to understand or symbolize it. On the one hand, the actuality at the core of our being poses an obstacle to understanding; on the other, this enigmatic depth preserves inside us something mysterious that cannot be appropriated by discourse, that cannot be exhaustively understood through language, and that resists being organized in the sphere of identity.

The ego cannot eliminate the actual or fully "know" it; it can only shroud it in something else in an effort to dissipate its strangeness, into something more hermeneutically familiar. This does not obliterate its enigmatic power, but it does succeed in making it seem more graspable, which is another way of saying that it offers the actual a way of hiding in plain sight. Like the purloined letter, the actual is obvious yet also obstructed by the obviousness in which it is coated. Importantly, a goodness of fit has to exist between the actual and its coating. This "fit" is neither a complete correspondence nor a total strangeness but a matter of an energetic match (I am obviously referring here to psychic energy). Trauma, especially in its imbrication with the excitable body, is an opportune coating for this function, because it definitionally involves inassimilable psychic energy. Thus, events of our past that have wounded us, be they personal, generational, or cultural, are especially likely to draw us closer to experience, offering shroudings that may be "stickier" (Ahmed, 2004), more readily linking up with the excitation of enigma.

Slave Play, as we have come to see, is a double entendre: on the surface, it announces itself as being a play "about" slavery. But it is not—at least not exactly. The play is about how slavery's history pulsates through the present, but it is not about slavery per se (not in the way that, say, *Amistad* or *12 Years a Slave* is). Slavery, we might say, as a documented and known historical event, becomes the shrouding, the known element that the ego uses to scotomize the strangeness of a raw, racialized, sadomasochistic sexuality. One might justifiably ask: how can something as horrific as slavery be seen as a shrouding? It is worth remembering here that the shrouding is not slavery itself but the discourse around it. Trauma discourse, to say it differently, centers rather than decenters the ego; it organizes the way we see the world and offers translational tools with which to master the disquiet of enigma. It is the second meaning of "slave play" that the upper case of the title shrouds, and as such, the title *Slave Play* simultaneously points to and away from race play, to a raw, racialized, traumatophilic sexuality. Race play does, of course, draw on the sexual crimes of slavery, but it also enrolls the complex erotic syntax of the sexual drive's infantile sexuality: sadism, masochism, voyeurism, nongenital pleasures, part-object functioning, and degenitalized excitements, excitements that are distributed across "the entire cutaneous surface" (Freud, 1905b, p. 201).

If you are doubtful that something as horrific as slavery can become a coating, consider how even with the words "Slave Play" on the marquee, some theatergoers still felt tricked by the playwright, asserting that they did not know what they were walking into—and thereby implicitly invoking the metric of affirmative consent. They seemed to be saying, "We should have been told what we were getting into," a demand that overlaps with contemporary conversations and battles over trigger warnings. Introducing trigger warnings into a play imports into it the neoliberal demand that we be offered a detailed inventory of what emotional experiences are on offer before we decide if we will want to consume them. Let us leave aside, however, the sheer impossibility of such a "warning"—because who would be able to anticipate, and on what basis, how exactly a work of art will "hit" any one of us? Let us wonder instead why the title of the play was not seen (by those who protested) as having issued a warning that difficult materials would be addressed? Is the issue that the play does not tell us what it is "about," or is the problem that the "impolite" questions (Spillers) raised by the play (about the slave play in *Slave Play*) cannot be asked directly or seen head-on? What kind of warning could possibly prepare anyone for the feelings that this play might evoke, even if the artist were prepared to issue it? Much like the oculus, which cannot be looked at directly but which, nevertheless is responsible for the deepened experience, this topic is just too incandescent and the affective charge around it too intense to be bearable, sending the ego into overdrive in order to shroud it into something more familiar and respectable.[15]

It might seem odd for me to be suggesting that slavery is the respectable and less difficult shrouding. In so doing, I do not intend to minimize its horrors but to underscore that even known, hellish nightmares are preferable to the ego than to risk its own undoing. Affirmative consent here proves itself, once again, to be more allied with the conservative work of the ego (that is, the ego's work to conserve itself) rather than with the new self- and world-making possibilities of limit consent and the exigent sadism enabled by limit consent, to which we will turn shortly.

The Artist and the Pervert

In February 2016, the *New York Times* published a piece titled "A Composer and His Wife: Creativity through Kink" (Woolfe, 2016). The article focused on Mollena Williams-Haas, whom we encountered earlier in this chapter, and her husband, Georg Friedrich Haas, one of the world's leading microtonal composers. The couple live in a 24/7 kinky relationship. The article's author, Zachary Woolfe, refrains from stating explicitly that their particular type of dominant/submissive arrangement is organized around their racial difference. For example, it does not mention that Williams-Haas's life is dedicated to serving Haas, who, prior to meeting her, had considerable trouble accepting his desires as a sadistic sexual dominant, but it only hints at their kink's racialized character. For example, there is mention of Williams-Haas keeping a blog called *The Perverted Negress* but not of her advocacy around race play; it references her nicknaming Haas "Herr Meister" as if it is done in jest, when she regularly addresses him as "Master" and "Sir"; and the photo accompanying the article shows her wearing a collar around her neck but leaves out that it signifies his "ownership" of her (Woolfe, 2016).

Drawing our attention to while also prying it away from "the erotic life of racism" (Holland, 2012), the piece grinds up against the couple's perversity. Ultimately, however, it recoils, staying within the more dignified confines of their successful heterosexual marriage, which—and this is much emphasized—boosts the husband's productivity, something underlined in the article's title.[16] The article, we might say, masks what it also puts on display: by highlighting Haas's coming-out narrative as a sexual dominant, it evades the difficulties of sadomasochistic interracial desire that, sex positivity aside, syncs up all too well with the history of slavery—and Williams-Haas's ancestors, it should be noted, were slaves. While the article boasts that Haas's creative output has "roughly doubled," we are not told what this has to do with Williams-Haas having become what he calls his "muse."

I do not minimize that coming out can feel freeing, and I am in support of people having sex in whichever way and with whatever body parts or objects they desire. Nor do I dismiss the impact that this relationship has had on Haas's work. Rather, I am moving in a rather different direction, to explore what links perversity may have with trauma and inspiration.

I am not convinced that Haas's transformed relationship to his art straightforwardly proceeded from the affirmation of his identity as a sexual dominant alone. The idea that the affirmation of his identity is key is in itself part of the mythosymbolic realm (that discovering our true sexual desires will be liberating) and may well be Haas's own translation. In fact, I would insist that what deserves our attention in Haas's work is not his increased productivity per se—which reduces his art to the vulgarity of the assembly line—but the transformation of his aesthetic relationship to it. "When I'm writing [music now]," he explains, "I feel more concentrated, at ease, lighter than I used to. I no longer need composition as a form of psychotherapy. Instead, it's become a spiritual act; in exploring the world of sound, I venture into places . . . other people look for that feeling in religion" (Brown, 2016). Such remarkable transformations may not inhere in the reassurances of our being "seen" by the other (those reassurances do psychic work, too, though of a different kind) but may have more to do with the rousing of inspiration, the kindling, that is, of psychic energy—a process that falls under the aegis of primal seduction and that differs from sublimation, which consists of a utile, socially acceptable channeling of the drive. I draw out these arguments through materials around Williams-Haas and Haas's relationship—interviews, writings, and the documentary of their relationship, *The Artist and the Pervert*—using them as springboards for my thinking about traumatophilia. To be clear, these are not attempts to psychoanalyze them as individuals but, rather, to draw on them to further fine-tune the conceptual apparatus I am proposing.

As an experienced race-play activist and also as a Black submissive woman, Williams-Haas says in the documentary that she has often had to explain, if not defend, her sexuality against charges of false consciousness, or of dissociated collusions with Whiteness. In the documentary and elsewhere (Williams, 2009a, 2009b, 2009c, 2009d), Williams-Haas responds to the critique that her sexuality undermines gains made by feminist activism by arguing that what makes her submission agentic is the fact that she is willing the conditions of her domination. As to the charge that her racial submission disrespects the legacy of slavery, offering problematic representations of Black sexuality, she refuses to be interpellated into representing her entire race. Categorically rejecting the notion that her sexuality needs to be respectable *because* she is Black, she writes irreverently, "my vagina isn't really interested in uplifting the race" (Williams, 2009a). "To say I can't play my personal psychodrama out just because I'm black, *that's* racist" (Woolfe, 2016).

To think alongside Williams-Haas and Haas's relationship, let us turn to some further conceptual clarifications.

Implantation, Intromission, and the Touching of Wounds

We have already seen how the trauma of implantation involves the incursion of the adult's sexual otherness into the infant. The adult's psychic trespass into us never gets fully processed in the sense of being "resolved" or completely symbolized. Instead, as we have seen, it becomes partly appropriated into the ego, becoming shrouded in secondary meanings through the ego's fantasizing function (translation). But a remainder lingers, always present as an internal foreign body that eventually constitutes our sexual unconscious, sometimes agitating and at others traumatizing us from within when that wound is touched. Next, I want to explore the draw to touch—and our resistances to touching—these unfathomable implantative wounds, wounds to which we are inexplicably drawn by what Laplanche described as the sexual drive's "exigency." Exigency, he writes, "is the object that keeps knocking at the door, this intruder, this other within us which we still refer to . . . as the Unconscious" (Laplanche, 2006a, p. 278). The exigency of our alterity, of our own strangeness to ourselves, fascinates and compels us.

Implantation, I remind you, is a normatively traumatic process, as opposed to intromission, which is contingently traumatic in the sense that it may or not occur. Intromission *foists* meaning on the infant, it comes with an interdiction against the infant's independent fantasizing activity around a traumatic event. Consider, for instance, a little girl who goes to her mother to say that her uncle touched her "down there" and who is told, "You must be confused," or that "nothing happened" and that she should stop making trouble. This girl is now dealing not only with the impact of the sexual abuse itself but also with the mother's forbidding her to think about what happened and to make meaning of it. The mother's communication, "You must be confused" does not just inflict the harm of neglect and disbelief: it is also a demand that the girl *be and remain* confused. That demand is jammed into the child's mind to short-circuit the girl's autonomous meaning-making process. Or consider a Black family that petitions the state for justice following the death of a family member killed by a police officer, only to be told, in the form of a not-guilty verdict, that "nothing worthy of attention happened here." This prohibition against one's own separate meaning-making may be resisted (after all, Black communities know very well *what* happened), but that does not make it any less soul-killing or crazy-making.

For Laplanche and for Laplanchean scholars (Fletcher, 2007; House, 2017; Tessier, 2020), the distinction between implantation and intromission is critical. Implantation is normatively traumatic and thus developmentally inevitable, whereas intromission exceptionalizes trauma as something contingent and avoidable. Under intromission, one's translations are forced by external diktats, forced into translating this way or another. We may, thus, think of intromission as the trauma of a mind-fuck—a word I use intentionally to mark how the interdiction to translate freely is disrupted by the other's sexual unconscious.

I am not persuaded, however, that the distinction between the trauma of intromission and the trauma of implantation is as conceptually watertight as Laplanche has intimated. I would actually suggest that the opposite is true and that implantations are by far more difficult. This is because in intromission there is at least a possibility, even if in the après-coup, to identify what was done to us, to name, that is, the injury, to pinpoint its origin, or to mark its precise interpersonal location. This is not so with implantation, however, where the other's sexual unconscious pierces us enigmatically and without our distinct awareness from the get-go, leaving behind a deposit that sets in motion the process of our becoming. Further, intromission is also a message: the interdiction to translate freely is, actually, a message (of prohibition). As any other message, therefore, intromissions also carry an enigmatic charge. Intrommision, in other words, always has an implantative dimension. The mother who tells her daughter, "Your uncle didn't mean it that way," or a court that avers that the killing of a Black teenager was "self-defense" are not merely conveying "messages" (e.g., about which lives matter); they also introduce something inscrutably perplexing (e.g., Why do Black lives not matter and White lives do?).

The fact that intromissions are always laced with implantations is not a problem. In fact, it should give us hope because what that means is that all trauma, even the most heinous, has an enigmatic surcharge that can be retranslated. To say this differently, all trauma leaves behind a snag. This snag is akin to a loose thread in a sweater that, if pulled repeatedly and without interruption, can unweave the sweater (in this case, the narrative) completely. To flesh out the metaphor, traumatophilic revisitations of the implantative dimension of full-fledged trauma are equivalent to the action of pulling on the thread of the ego. What stands to come undone is nothing less than the subject's translations (not the fact of the traumatic event but how it's been narrativized). What this undoes is not trauma itself but the ego's relation to it. Because the implantative dimension is closely tied to the enigmatic and the infantile sexual, traumatophilic repetitions give us a way to understand what Freud means when he says that trauma makes sexuality active again (Laplanche, 1994/2014). Even the most explicitly horrifying and heinous crimes, or perhaps especially those, generate a remainder that can never be fully assimilated: these may be questions like, "What did that smug look on Derek Chauvin's face mean?" We can hypothesize, but the point is that even when the facts are incontestable—depicted on lynching postcards, recorded on body cams, caught on a passerby's cell phone—an enigmatic overflow endures. This traumatophilic pulling of the thread is easier said than done: as we have seen, the ego will mightily resist any contestation of its structural integrity, which is why repetition's demonic force is critical to traumatisms building the momentum to overcome the ego's defenses and overwhelm it.

Because traumatophilic repetitions lean on the sexual drive, they can look—and often are—perplexingly superfluous, even extravagant. What gives traumatophilia its perplexing character is its unusual economic coordinates: whereas the ego is organized around preserving itself and maintaining its homeostasis, traumatophilia involves processes that look, and are, wasteful rather than productive, use-less rather than use-full, and that flamboyantly pursue the "more and more" of experience without regard for conservation. Such pursuing does not follow the contractual obligations of affirmative consent but relies, rather, on limit consent. Limit consent does not involve an other who respects our limits but a surrender to an other whose opacity may besiege us and, also, a surrender to the opacity in ourselves. In the clinical setting and beyond, traumatophilia may appear destructive, senseless, or like unconstrained discharge—what de M'Uzan called "slaves of quantity" (2003, p. 711). But it is not. I owe to Bataille and to his theorizing of the notion of general economy and expenditure the possibility to formulate this: wasteful expenditure and useless squandering without a determinate end are not the same as acting out. Instead, they may open up to a different kind of possibility—of making contact with experience.

I just presented you with a lot of new conceptual material, so let me put it into contact with the race play between Williams-Haas and Haas. While much can, and has, been said about *Williams's* race vis-à-vis repetition (Cruz, 2016; Musser, 2014), Haas's Whiteness is treated as unremarkable—as if any White man, given the chance, would jump at the opportunity to sexually dominate a Black woman. In fact, finding White men who were willing to racially debase her had been quite difficult: "most 'white folks,'" she reports, "are MORE uncomfortable around this than you know" (2009a) think, here, of *Slave Play*'s Jim.[17] So here is a bit more about Haas's Whiteness from *The Artist and the Pervert*:

> GEORG HAAS: I grew up in a way that seems very idyllic if you look at it from the outside . . . [in a small town] in Austria, close to the

Swiss border. I had a very sheltered childhood, spent a lot time in nature. But this idyll was a lie.

We then hear from his mother, Rolanda Haas:

ROLANDA HAAS: My husband stood in front of me, a bouquet of dark red roses rested on my bosom, and he said, "You gave birth to a blond son." [*The film cuts to a photo of baby Georg with a lock of blond hair next to it.*] You can't imagine what a miracle that was. He grew up like any other boy. He was a sweet child. He was a good and smart boy. He was happy.

Then the film cuts to the adult Haas, who recounts,

GH: You have to imagine it like this: They had absolute power. The father is the Führer. The mother is the Führerin. My grandparents were Nazis. They were murderers. My parents were Nazis. My mother still is. They were perpetrators who, after the war, perceived themselves as a persecuted minority of "decent" people.

We return to the mother's interview:

RH: Not National Socialist. Because that was over. Of course, back then, we were. But . . . those were the times. We understood it was wrong. The Allied forces dissociated us from all that. But . . . well . . . how shall I say? . . . At home, Georg was brought up and taught in this way. I had no idea that he has a Black girlfriend. He knew about . . . my racial hatred. . . You should keep yourself, your race, pure—purity in the sense of keeping your being. . . Now I am getting myself into things I didn't want to say . . .

The fact that Haas comes from a family of unrepentant Nazis adds a whole other layer to the way we may view his position as "Master." And it also offers us an unusual opportunity to turn the lens on the White member of a race-play dyad. Haas is greatly ashamed of and anguished by this lineage, but it is one under the weight of which he has to live. We are "all at base always abject," Darieck Scott writes, "abject to histories we cannot unmake" (2021, p. 2). Haas's past puts a different stamp on the couple's Master/slave relationship: it helps us discern that it is not just Williams-Haas but also he who may be touching generational wounds. If, through race play, Williams-Haas is touching the wound of slavery and racism, for Haas, it may well be that the wound he is trying to touch is that of his family's Nazi and totalitarian history—and how that is reproduced in his upbringing. This makes the dynamics of their relationship more exigent for both of them. Rather than drained of its historical specificity, their relationship may work precisely *because* of their histories, which are distinct but, in some ways, also matched.

Such a couple, a White man, the descendant of Nazis, identifying as a "Master" and a Black woman, descended from slaves, identifying as his "slave," appears as a repetition of historical harms. But I would suggest that their coupling reveals race play as a medium that brings something into presence. As such—although there is no way to know this for sure—a partner who was not herself constellated by a comparable wound might not work as well for Haas any more than a non-White partner might work for Williams-Haas. Racialization thus proves substantive: desire, here, is not "color-blind," it does not transcend, but is rooted in racial difference.

Wanting us to imagine beyond "false consciousness [as] the only explanation for black subjects who garner pleasure from race," Nash urges us to read interracial couplings "'against the grain'—against prevailing conceptualizations of racialization— . . . to engender theoretical and political space" that explores what use can be made of "racialized fictions that have shaped . . . sexual imagination[s]" (2014, pp. 84, 87, 89). Daring to claim a different way into such pleasures, Nash opens up paths for us to think about interracial desire in a less constrained fashion, giving us access points to consider how racial difference may be critical to some erotic arrangements, without being exploitatively fetishistic. Haas, for example, as the documentary shows, is not merely a purveyor of Whiteness for Williams-Haas (which would correspond to a fetishistic flattening of his subjectivity), even as his Whiteness is anything but redundant to their erotic scripts. In other words, the fact that Williams-Haas needs her sadistic lover to be White does not have to mean that *any* White person would do, any more than any Black person would work for him. What his Whiteness may harvest for her could be the force of possibility for the touching of wounds. Similarly, Williams-Haas's racialization may also be key for Haas: in other words, neither is her race incidental (it is a meaningful feature of who she is), nor does it override her personhood to flatten her into a trope—and the documentary offers many and varied examples of that. Of course, their wounds are not the same, nor are they complementary; but they may nonetheless be a "good-enough fit" for their coupling, showing us how a pairing like Williams-Haas and Haas's, which at first glance appears to repeat horrific histories, both draws on and resists rote repetition.

We encountered earlier Williams-Haas's refusal to prioritize the up-lifting of her race over the singularity of her desire. Her refusal to be fully claimed by her identity (in this case, her racial identity) and her willingness to meet Haas outside the confines of what feels politically correct can generate extraordinary intimacies that reach into territories that have little to do with recognition or with feeling validated (both of these are the ego's project) but that may instead lean into emotionally risky, not to mention politically controversial, terrain.

A traumatophobic analysis of Williams-Haas and Haas's Master/slave relationship would be to see both as repeating their intergenerationally transmitted histories. But what would that offer us other than simply reinscribing what we think we already know about Black and White relations in slavery's aftermath or about totalitarian legacies? Further, such a framework does not necessarily grant Williams-Haas or Haas the possibility of new translational capacities: it affixes them, instead, to a filled-in traumatic past. In contrast, a traumatophilic lens can enable us to see their repetitions as a way of their stepping into the fray together, of bringing the past into presence by reopening its implantative dimen-sion. This is where the possibilities of overwhelm and for the new reside, because the only way that filled-in trauma can be wrested from its tight semiotic encasements is if the implantative dimension can be reinvig-orated. It does not help that our current discourse sacralizes filled-in trauma, especially when it can be pinpointed as a factual or historical event. Psychoanalysis may well need to be dragged out of its fixation on trauma's repair, and so may queer of color critique.

Let me now return briefly to my earlier criticism of how the *New York Times* leveraged Haas's productivity as the alibi for the relationship. Traumatophilia, we saw, stands to reopen the implantative dimension that undergirds full-fledged trauma. By agitating the "internal foreign body" (Laplanche, 2003b, p. 208), that is, untranslated enigma, a state of overwhelm may arise, followed by the kindling of new translational activity. It is in this sense that traumatophilic repetition can become a muse, stirring new drive movements, and it is such renewed drive movements that may be related to Haas's changed relationship to his art. For Laplanche, sublimation is the domain of inspiration, which he saw as a component of sublimation. The problem with sublimation, however, is that it has been psychoanalysis's covert way of dispensing with the problem of the drive's insatiable press and its perverse appetites. Sublimation gives us a way of imagining a routing of the sexual's anarchic elements to outcomes that command respect—in this case, Haas's increased productivity. Sublimation, in other words, is productive. This warrants caution: because sublimation seeks to quell the sexual drive by directing it toward socially acceptable end products, it is more likely to enroll it into goals that are more about adaptations to the existing social order and that implicate the subject into the capitalist production—and productivity—machine. By idealizing sublimation and championing creativity, psychoanalysis tends to reify the logics of productivity. For this reason, because sublimation seeks to organize psychic energy and thus to quell its intensities, I would disagree with Laplanche's idea that inspiration and sublimation are of kin. Rather, I see sublimation as belonging to the order of translation, that is, as trying to master and tame the unconscious. Also importantly, the transformation of the libido into "socially useful" achievements is acceptable when it comes to artistic and cultural productions (like Haas's) or professional pursuits (as in an aggressive man who becomes a successful surgeon), but we hit a wall when it comes to sex and perversity, which will have a harder time being seen as respectable. The idea that one can sublimate rage or trauma into something productive (e.g., good poetry or beautiful art) reinforces capitalist logics—and is traumatophobic.

Inspiration, however, belongs to a different economic sphere. As the "creation of sexual energy" (Laplanche, 1980, p. 249), it is a libidinal neosurgence, which means that it does not move us to grasp something better or understand something more accurately but moves us to invent and to imagine. Rather than keeping something immobilized or canalizing its energy, inspiration keeps it in motion. Insofar as it remains an intractable force, a live wire, and an ever-renewable process in which one is in the throes of constantly pushing further—rather than a response to a ready-made reserve of energy—inspiration (rather than sublimation) is better suited as a concept to account for aesthetic transformations of the kind narrated by Haas. "You know," Haas says, commenting on the compositions of one particular colleague, "I never liked the music. . . [It felt] cold, elusive, it just never spoke to me. At one point, I read in his autobiography that he only composed when he felt relieved of sexual tension. And what I thought, a little wickedly, was, 'Yes, you can tell'" (Brown, 2016). Haas's statement raises interesting questions about sexual energy and its relationship to inspiration, suggesting that it is the circulation of energy rather than its canalization that ties to inspiration.

One would be justified to ask what makes it possible for someone to be more traumatophilic as opposed to traumatophobic. How does one bend their will to turn toward trauma's revisitation, and what are the circumstances, social, interpersonal, and intrapsychic, that may facilitate such a turn? Part of what hamstrings our ability to do different things *with* trauma is also the conceptual barricade set *around* trauma, such that trauma is only configured as harm and injury. Part of the difficulty of thinking traumatophilically, then, is that traumatophilic thinking can be itself painful, even itself a traumatism: it can wound our ideas about trauma, and it can wound those of us whose identities are organized around having survived violence. It is my contention that risking this wound is important and, even, necessary for transformation to happen. Is it sadistic to take a stance in favor of wounding? I suppose it is, though, as chapter 5 argues, this is an unusual kind of sadism, an exigent and deeply ethical one.

5

Exigent Sadism

In the documentary *The Artist and the Pervert*, made a couple of years into the Trump presidency, we find Mollena Williams-Haas and Georg Haas in a recording studio.[1] They have been developing a joint musical project, but Haas has been having trouble doing his work.[2] It is clear from their interactions that this is an unusual condition for him. At the end of the session, he looks dejected:

> MOLLENA WILLIAMS-HAAS: The thing is, I am sure you are not the only person for whom this is an issue. I am not saying you have to compromise your artistic integrity, but I am saying that doing shit like spending three hours on Facebook or getting upset about Austrian politics, and I am like, "Please don't do that. . . "
>
> GEORG HAAS: This I will stop. . . This I will stop. Darling, this is the real problem. And the only thing, frankly, why I am afraid not to get ready is Trump. I tell you why. It's a very egoistic point of view. I was so happy to leave fascist Austria and come to the States. Now I know there is no place to escape. And this [situation] really puts me down. Sorry. And I have to—
>
> MWH (*interrupting him*): I am sorry to be cruel, but I can't have any empathy for White people right now when it comes to this point of view. I can't. Like, I understand that you are upset, and I get it, but the hard truth is—welcome to the way that most of the people in the world have been living in forever. And you *cannot* let that be an impediment to you actually doing your work. It's not allowed. That is not allowed. *I did not give up my entire life so that you could mope about an election.* (emphasis to convey how these words were stressed in the video)

There is a lot that is noteworthy in this brief exchange, but let me first contextualize it some. By the time this scene appears in the documentary, we have been made aware of Haas's family history: his parents and his grandparents were Nazis who, after the war, understood themselves as a persecuted minority of "decent" people." We have also seen his mother speak explicitly about her beliefs against miscegenation, about her racial hatred, and about White superiority. And we also know that these authoritarian beliefs seeped into his childhood, with Haas having been beaten and emotionally abused. Haas has described his grandparents as murderers, his parents as the Führer and the Führerin, and he has laid out for us the painful impact of his early life on him. It is thus not hard to be sympathetic to the difficulty he is reporting: here is a man who fled to the United States to distance himself from his country's and his family's Nazism, only to then find the tide of right-wing White supremacy skyrocket during the Trump administration, thereby eliminating any hope of ever fully escaping fascism.

Williams-Haas listens attentively. She is not insensitive to his predicament, which is, perhaps, why she prefaces what she is about to tell him with, "I don't want to be cruel." She is aware that what she is about to say will be harsh and she does not want to hurt him. Still, she bends her will (we see her hesitate, then take a deep breath) and keeps at it. What does she tell him? I hear her telling him two things: First, she tells him that escaping from the brutality of the world is a fantasy, which is subtended by his Whiteness; what is harsh about that is not that she is "calling out" his privilege, though she is doing that too. The merciless truth is that escaping evil is not an option anywhere, ever, for anyone, however much his Whiteness might have thus far supported that illusion. Williams-Haas is underscoring the compensations that Whiteness has afforded him such that he could come to believe and expect that he would be protected from encroachment; Trump is where that illusion reaches its limit. What she is harshly telling him is something like, *all humans have to contend with horror, and that includes you: you are not special, you will not be spared the tragedies of being human.* The second thing she tells him is that in having accepted her as his "slave" in their BDSM arrangement, he has also assumed some responsibility toward her. What is that responsibility? Not to withdraw within himself (mope) but to show up: to remain present with her in their shared endeavors rather than to sink into or revel in the jouissance of his self-pity, which is no less than a narcissistic retreat.

To some people, it may appear that this is an instance of the bottom, here Williams-Haas, "getting the upper hand," taking control. But I argue that what Williams-Haas does is more layered, that it is, in fact, an exercise of a particular, queer kind of sadism that is independent of positionality (whether one is the top or the bottom). I have been referring to this ethical type of sadism throughout this book as exigent sadism, and it is the focus of this chapter.

What is queer about exigent sadism is that while it is, indeed, cruel, it also has some measure of care and support built into it.[3] To be able to name these hard truths to Haas, Williams-Haas has to bring some ruthlessness to the situation—even as she is not trying to hurt or destroy him. The element of care in exigent sadism is not delivered in its usual, recognizable form, that is, the care is not necessarily warm or offered with tenderness; it is stern and sobering. And yet Haas feels supported by her intervention enough not to close down, which may, perhaps, be why he is able to listen to her seriously and why he smiles in relief, even in admiration, as she speaks. This openness and receptivity, not presuming to already know what the other will say but leaving space for an encounter with the unexpected coming from the other, is also the space of the erotic. To put this differently, the quality of the relationship *between* Williams-Haas and Haas is critical to their having that kind of intimate exchange: but it would not be possible if Williams-Haas were not able to bend her will, to take this strange pleasure of pressing him, all the while risking hurting him, or if Haas were not able to allow his ego—that is, his self-understanding *and his relationship to his childhood and generational history*—to be wounded. In the documentary, this interaction happens very quickly, and the fleetingness of it speaks to my emphasis elsewhere that these bursts of self-sovereignty and overwhelm are not durational but arise in transient bursts.

Following Williams-Haas's comments, Haas tenderly rests his head against hers and thanks her. His thanking her feels heartfelt, and the scene is intimate and moving. The warm feeling it generates in the viewer, however, should not trick us into overlooking the high stakes in that exchange. It is not hard to imagine that a person in Haas's position might have felt hurt, invalidated, not seen by his partner: what Williams-Haas is going after, after all, is how Haas sees his traumatic history hampering him in the present. If the encounter does not explode into a conflict, it is also because of the way Haas responds to her unusual form of care: not by becoming defensive but by giving himself over to her, by making himself possible to her, by staying receptive to the foreignness she is bringing to him rather than closing up and becoming combative. Again, if you are tempted to imagine this as a moment when Haas, formally the Master in their arrangement, is topped by his slave, the position Williams-Haas has adopted, I ask you to slow down your thinking. Haas is not "allowing" her to reverse their roles. His consent to what is unfolding happens in real time, it materializes at the limits of his ego, and it is an internal affair: it has to do with him surrendering himself to the distance between what he was expecting to receive when sharing with Williams-Haas his traumatic response (perhaps compassion, sympathy, or validation) and what he actually received (a naming of what his racial positionality has afforded him). Limit consent, we are reminded, is not about maintaining control of a situation or protecting one's sense of self.

Neither the exercise of exigent sadism nor the capacity to become passible to it are affixed to power positionalities: that is, exigent sadism is not the domain of the Master (or, of the one with social or interpersonal power), nor is passibility the domain of the slave (or, the one who lacks social or interpersonal power). Said differently, I asked you to slow down your thinking because part of what I work toward in this chapter is to delink power positionality from the exercise of exigent sadism, from passibility, and from limit consent.

To better unpack these seeming contradictions, let us turn to theorizing exigent sadism.

Exigent Sadism: Neither Destructive nor Sensible

The mere mention of the term "sadism" tends to inspire moral panic, generating rushed judgments. This is, perhaps, why, in contrast to the concept of masochism, which has been rigorously and elegantly theorized both within psychoanalysis (e.g., Freud, 1924; Laplanche, 1987) and within queer of color critique (Musser, 2014, 2018; D. Scott, 2010), sadism has not enjoyed the same level of intellectual attention. I do not mean that sadism has not been critically discussed—in fact, I will shortly outline some of the philosophical ruminations it has generated, starting with the work of the Marquis de Sade, from whom the term is originally sourced. What I mean is that as a concept, sadism has become entrenched in a somewhat fixed binary: it is most often reflexively understood as a destructive force or, alternatively, as benign simulation (as in some BDSM theory). In this chapter, I make a call for carving space for a more rigorous and ambivalent querying of the currents of sadism.

The most commonly encountered meaning of the term "sadism" is tied to how it is given to us by the Marquis de Sade (1782/1966b, 1795/1966c). In his work, sadism appears as limitless destructiveness with no regard for the other, a grabbing of pleasure that is reliant on, if not engorged by, the other's detriment, which it causes. This reading of Sade is not the only one possible, but it is the predominant interpretation of his oeuvre, giving us a sadism that is overbrimming with fascist overtones, as we will explore. Within this version of sadism, the other becomes a mere plaything at the arbitrary and cruel whim of the sadist. This monstrous kind of sadism demands the complete obliteration of the other's humanity and subjecthood, and it is this barbaric form of sadism that frightens us and that we reflexively associate with the term "sadism."

At the other end, we encounter a relatively benign, mimetic sort of sadism that is deployed in the interest of pleasure-production, as given to us by some BDSM theory, some sex-positive activists, and some sex educators. This sadism is mimetic in nature—in the sense that it proceeds with all involved parties agreeing to act "as if" the sadist were engaging their cruelty or aggression while, in fact, they carefully dose simulated violence (or humiliation and so on) to pleasure the recipient, who, excepting situations of abuse, can trust that the sadist will not be *really* sadistic. Such sadism does not assume risks of the kind we have been exploring in previous chapters: neither the sadist nor their "victim" risks themselves, nor do they risk experience or wounding their ideas. The mimetic sadist proceeds, rather, through reasoned calculation and prudent moderation. This is the territory of worrying about things becoming "too much" and of ensuring a well-regulated interaction; this pretend sort of sadism is, therefore, more allied with attachment theory and with concerns about security, trust, and boundaries. Let us call this sadism "sensible sadism," to mark how it is signposted by reason, restraint, and self-temperance. This understanding of sadism draws from Enlightenment reasoning and harks back to a particular form of rationality whose sole purpose and intent is to dominate the unknown, rendering things predictable and calculable. Neoliberal sensibilities are also specific to sensible sadism, insofar as they emphasize the mastery that accompanies self-knowledge, aim to achieve satisfactory results for the participants, and insist on personal responsibility at the expense of risking something new, precluding encounters with opacity. Neoliberal sensitivities are also profoundly traumatophobic, and so is sensible sadism.

Both of these two sadisms aim toward mastery: destructive sadism is oriented around mastery in the sense of being in control of oneself and of the other, while sensible sadism, organized through the illusory promises of affirmative consent, forfeits the possibility of encountering the opaque by architecting carefully dosed encounters whose economies do not become overwhelming to either ego involved. As such, neither can make a bid for experiences that approximate the limit, and which may open up toward overwhelm states or sovereign experience. Rather than create traumatisms, destructive sadism inflicts trauma, crushing the other's subjectivity and injuring their autonomy. If destructive sadism goes too far, sensible sadism does not go far enough. Too asthenic to bend the will, it is unable to reach the energetic intensities (see chapter 2) required for the ego's rupture. In contrast, I want to offer a different parsing for thinking about sadism not as a location from which one exercises reign over the other, or that promises anticipable satisfactions, but as a way of fostering the other's self-sovereignty and as a place of immense vulnerability *for the sadist*. Expanding the term "sadism" to encompass the exigent sadist's own exposure and to flesh out the risk she undertakes may sound counterintuitive, so I will discuss at length why I think exigent sadism is worthy of our critical attention.

Sadism's Origins

The Marquis de Sade's erotico-philosophical writings preoccupied several key intellectual figures of the twentieth century. This preoccupation has a visible fault line. Prior to World War II, twentieth-century intellectuals read Sade for his iconoclastic and revolutionary potential. Sade was celebrated by Apollinaire as the freest spirit that ever lived (Lély, 1966), was crowned as one of Freud's most prominent forerunners (Hassan, 1969; Seaver, 1999; Wilson, 1962), was seen as anticipating the work of

Havelock Ellis and Richard von Krafft-Ebbing (Eisler, 1951; Taylor, 1954), and was even regarded an early precursor to modern psychodrama (Schutzenberger, 1966). Others have placed the value of his testimony on the radical obscenity and violence of his work, on his transgression of literary boundaries that had not previously been attempted, and on his having brought language to the limits of representation (Carter, 1978; Hénaff, 1986; Neboit-Mombet, 1972). Sade has also been carefully studied for his political philosophy, encountered in his libertines' famously long treatises on the nature of government, the social contract, human nature, and the church—often delivered in the breaks between their criminal erotic debauches.

But after World War II, the tide started to turn against Sade. Whereas he had been previously seen as "the eulogist of sexual liberation," philosophical thinking in the wake of catastrophe turned him into "the paradigmatic example of fascist desire" (Marty, 2016 p. 20). A canon of texts thus began to emerge in postwar France drawing a direct line from his philosophy to Nazism. Jacques Lacan, who originally saw in Sade the confirmation of the historical phenomenon of the death drive, showed in his seminal essay "Kant avec Sade" that Sade's philosophy may be regarded as the unconscious truth of Kant (1963/1989). For him, Sade pushed Kant's formalist ethics to their logical extreme, elevating willful evil to the level of universal law, effectively turning it into a categorical imperative.

In *The Dialectic of Enlightenment*, Max Horkheimer and Theodor Adorno (1987) also traced how Sade represented the extreme of Kantian reasoning. In pushing Enlightenment philosophy to its limit, Sade reduced people to no more than expendable, spare parts, thereby becoming the link, if not the gateway, to fascism. Sade's exhaustingly formalized systematization of carnal pleasures (e.g., 1782/1966b) was considered in light of the "special architectonic structure of the Kantian system [which finds its embodied expression in] the gymnasts' pyramids in Sade's orgies" (Horkheimer & Adorno, 1987, p. 69). Virtuosos of self-mastery, Sade's libertines run their passions through formalist reason, calculating, scheming, plotting, strategizing, preparing, devising, such that all aspects of their crimes may be precisely mapped and their results fully anticipated. Murderous depravities must be apathetically executed, and true libertinage is carried out in cold blood, with no trace of emotion. Unworthy of a libertine's respect, crimes of passion reflect a pathetic lack of self-restraint, an interest in the victim rather than in the execution of the crime itself. In Sade's stories, writes Simone de Beauvoir, "sensual pleasure [never] appear[s] as self-forgetfulness, swooning, or abandon. . . [The Sadean hero] never, for an instant, loses himself in his animal nature; he remains so lucid, so cerebral, that philosophic discourse, far from dampening his ardour, acts as an aphrodisiac" (1953, p. 33).

In this reading of Sade, torment is inflicted for the necessity of reason, not to grab some unexpected pleasure but as a dutiful execution of a plan that will yield calculated pleasures and pronouncedly indifferent to the other as a separate center of subjectivity—in contrast to Sacher von Masoch, who, as we will see, places emphasis on the contractual agreement with the other. Sade's libertines are governed by unbending principles, key among them a philosophy of *sang-froid*, an unemotional, impassioned submission to "perfect" crimes. It is not hard to see where Sadean principles and Nazism may meet: in the elevation of the cult of sovereignty; in the highly formalized, apathetic approach to crime; in the ruse of a superiority over those who are deemed expendable, a prescription that fascism formally racialized. Long before the Holocaust, of course, there existed another historical event, the Atlantic Slave Trade, that also employed Sadean principles, albeit for differently racialized subjects and for different ends: the apathetic accounting of bodies and of their properties to maximize labor and capital, the turning of humans into flesh (Spillers, 1987), and the sovereign exercise of control over Black people's lives and bodies easily rhyme with (this reading of) Sadean logic.

In *The History of Madness*, Foucault saw in Sade the face of resistance to psychiatric power, precisely because Sade, who was imprisoned and psychiatrically confined for most of his life, resists the psychological conceptualization of madness—all that before Foucault disavowed him. "Sade," he writes in 1975, "formulated an eroticism proper to a disciplinary society: a regulated, anatomical, hierarchical society whose time is carefully distributed, its spaces partitioned, characterized by obedience and surveillance. It's time to leave all that behind," he urged, "too bad for Sade: he bores us. He's a disciplinarian, a sergeant of sex, an accountant of the ass and its equivalents" (1975, pp. 226–227).

Foucault offers us, instead, a model of sadism and masochism that radically departed from Sade. "The idea that S/M is related to a deep violence," he says, "that S/M practice is a way of liberating that violence, this aggression, is stupid. We know very well [that] what all those people [S/M practitioners] are doing is not aggressive; they are inventing new possibilities of pleasure with new parts of their body" (Foucault, 1989, p. 209). Foucault did not by any means found the BDSM theory that relocated sadism from fascism to its infirm antipode, that is, sensible sadism, but he did help bolster it. "What strikes me with regard to S/M," he writes, "is how it differs from social power. . . Of course, there are roles but everybody knows very well that those roles can be reversed. Sometimes the scene begins with the master and slave, and at the end the slave has become the master. Or, even when the roles are stabilized, you know very well that it is always a game. Either the rules are transgressed, or there is an agreement, either explicit or tacit, that makes them aware of certain boundaries" (Foucault, 1989, p. 210).

Social structures, the BDSM activist Pat Califia writes, instate "compulsory sexual arrangements, wherein people can be labeled according to race, age, class and gender . . . with no choice, no safe word, no negotiation" (1988, p. 25). In S/M play, the argument goes, practitioners merely don on and don off social categories, jettisoning them by fiat and at the mere call of a word—giving us a sadism that is mostly affectation. Notice, for example, Califia's caution that because "the top's pleasure is dependent on the bottom's willingness to play," the sadist may be befallen by "a mild-to-severe case of performance anxiety" (1996, p. 232). Sadism thus becomes a pretend role to be adopted, compared to real power situations, which "involv[e] pain and cruelty where the consensual agreement to these roles is unacknowledged or absent" (Juicy Lucy, 1987, p. 30): at work here is a "play with power" (A. Stein, 1999, p. 51), as opposed to an exercise of power.

There is real power, this reasoning goes, and then there is BDSM-type power, which is not real but pretend power, a simulacrum (Byrne, 2015). BDSM, from that perspective, is something one performs, something one plays at, and we may remember here Susan Sontag's caution that there is theater in sadomasochism (1974). The play of sadomasochism, in this view, is a play of appearances. Here theatricality functions as alibi, something that represents rather than re-presents an actuality, something that symbolizes power but does not conduct its force in the encounter. The idea is that real power is blunt power, whereas the simulation of power, the play *of* power, is less consequential. But, as discussed throughout this volume, this neat divide is illusory: in the moment of aesthetic experience, what may look like simulated power converts, through limit experience, into real power, that is, into power that can act on us in ways that are actual and that linger. Think, for example, of the power of performance, like the power that *Slave Play* exerted on me; the power that Mia felt I had over her after a single session; the power that Jim assumed through Kaneisha's authorization which, as it turned out, exceeded her: all these start out as simulated power but end up kindling energies that are real and have material consequences. Aesthetic experience erodes the divide between real and simulated power, thereby "problematizing a binary division between artifice and authenticity" (Byrne, 2013, p. 152).[4]

Breaking Sadism and Masochism Apart from Sadomasochism

Krafft-Ebing's *Psychopathia Sexualis* (1866) described a convergence between sadism and masochism in a sadomasochistic complex involving experimentations with taking one role and then assuming the reverse, in a dialectical dynamic of giving and receiving pain. But the widespread misconception that sadism and masochism are complementary phenomena should be credited to Freud. His idea that "a person who feels pleasure in producing pain in someone else in a sexual relationship is also capable of enjoying as pleasure any pain which he may himself derive from sexual relations" (Freud, 1905b, p. 159) pooled sadism and masochism together in a singular concept, sadomasochism. Writing that a "sadist is always at the same time a masochist," he established that the two are not substantially different phenomena but mere inversions of each other, "active and passive forms" of the same libidinal current (Freud, 1905b, p. 159).

The unification of sadism and masochism under the unified concept of sadomasochism was criticized by Gilles Deleuze, who challenged the idea of their complementarity (1989)—and his critique also grounds my own thinking. Deleuze carefully parsed out the considerable differences between the project of the sadist and that of the masochist, returning to the texts of the Marquis de Sade and von Sacher Masoch. Deleuze points out that the sadist, as imagined through Sade's writings, has no interest in convincing, persuading, or educating her victim. As the ultimate sovereign agent, she acts against the other's consent. Caught in a hermetic universe of solitude, she boasts her omnipotence. In Masoch's novels, however, we find ourselves in the domain of a victim in search of a victimizer. The victim orchestrates their own violation, but to do so, they must first educate and enlist the consent of the torturer, who is contracted into her role as agreed-on abuser through the victim's solicitation. As such, "the masochist draws up contracts while the sadist abominates and destroys them," because any rule that is not under the sadist's full control stands to question her dominion and undermine her sovereignty (Deleuze, 1989, p. 22). The masochist, on the other hand, is "animated by a dialectical spirit" of enrolling the other in their masochistic contract. As a true dialectician, the masochist "knows the opportune moment and seizes it" (Deleuze, 1989, p. 33). We would thus be hard-pressed to recognize as truly sadistic the masochist's contractual partner, who mostly assents (and, at times, modifies) the scenario concocted by the masochist. Similarly, a masochist who wants to be abused is anathema to the Sadean sadist, for whom consent and shared inventiveness subvert her need for an absolute reign over the other that is uncompromised by their vision or desire.

It is only "careless reasoning," Deleuze notes (1989, p. 40), that destines these two—Sade's sadist and Masoch's masochist—to meet. Central to Masoch's script, we see, is not the will of the sadist but that of the masochist. Masoch's sadist ends up participating in a contract that is not of their own crafting wherein they are educated, trained, and incited as a doubled effect of *the masochist's will*. This form of masochism is not a relinquishment of the will but the will's execution—that is, it is only made to appear *as if* it involves submission, even though the masochist is not actually giving themselves over to the other. In other words, Masoch's masochist does not bend their will but, in fact, uses the masochistic contract to execute it, embroiling the "sadist" in it. I put "sadist" in quotation marks, to mark that Masoch's sadist exists in the realm of sensible sadism and to underscore that Masoch's masochist, by contractualizing the exchange, does not bend her will to give herself over to the sadist but, instead, works toward implementing her will.

The underlying premise, that power is constructed through a theatrics of signification, seeks to salvage, and in some case has succeeded in salvaging, sadomasochism from psychopathology. But, on the downside, it leaves us with an anemic sort of sadism. The "whole episode," writes Califia, can be called off with a word . . . by which the curtain can be dropped on the whole show should either party want to go home" (1988, p. 25). But our discussion of *Slave Play* suggests that things are not as straightforward: Jim's safe word does not "stop the show"; it puts things in motion, leading eventually to act 3. Of course, when Califia writes, "If you don't like being a top or bottom, you switch your keys. Try doing that with your biological sex or your race or your socioeconomic status" (1996, p. 232), what he wants to highlight is that in BDSM, positionality is consensually agreed upon rather than installed through social relations. The idea is that switching brings into sharp focus the contingent nature of social conditions.

Still, the subterfuge of sensible sadism defangs sadism. Here is the widely circulating trope, offered by Tonya Pinkins, in an interview with the *Slave Play* cast: "People have this misunderstanding about BDSM in that they think that the dom—they don't understand that the dom is the servant. . . What it means when you are a dom is that you have to look at the other person, what they are looking for, what do they want, and you are there to provide it" (Talks at Google, 2020). Such defanged sadism, however, begins to sound like sophistry. Sensible sadism makes no bids beyond satisfaction, and since it does not escalate toward the unbearable but stays within the tight perimeter of the other's affirmative consent, it relinquishes its potential to reach states of overwhelm. Neither sensible sadism nor its Sadean counterpart can bring us anywhere near sovereign experience: that is the purview of exigent sadism.

The Conceptual Architecture of Exigent Sadism

My project is interested in wresting conceptual space for a different sort of sadism, which I call exigent sadism—a genuinely frightening force that is subtended by the sexual drive and that cannot be easily embraced but that might enable overwhelm and sovereign experience. This force is sadistic, in that it taps into the anarchic, unbinding properties of the sexual drive, and it is exigent, in the sense that it has to do with following without reserve the draw toward opacity. It entails a recognition that one has to do what is necessary (though not in the utilitarian sense) to intervene against mastery, exerting a certain violence on the ego's tendency to bind. In exigent sadism, we enter into an adventure with all of ourselves, not to make something specific happen but risking the breaking down of our ego and/or curating aesthetic experience that may foster the other's overwhelm. Importantly, exigent sadism is not about controlling the outcome of an encounter—that is, it is not a "method" or a "technique"—it inflicts something at the limit of consent, unleashing forces beyond our grasp.

Consider Robert O'Hara's thoughts regarding the decision to withhold an intermission during *Slave Play*:

> You came to a play called *Slave Play*. You gonna have to sit and watch all of it. . . We're not gonna stop, like, "Y'all good? You got the pee out?" . . . And that's the challenge of this play . . . There are places for you to escape, but if you escape, there are consequences. . . If you want to see the rest of the play, there are consequences to that too. So it traps you in . . . We want you to digest the information, but *I also want you to choke a bit. . .* I want you to feel like . . . you may throw up some of it, *[and if you do] you will remember what it felt like.* (*Slave Play* discussions, March 11, 2022, emphases added)

If O'Hara sounds sadistic, it is because he is, but let us slow down a bit to note *how* he languages his sadism: the audience, of course, does not really *have* to sit and watch, and no one is physically trapped in the theatrical space. There are no restraints to keep people hostage, and, as we saw, many did get up and leave. What O'Hara is working toward is best understood as curating an experience where the audience, *if they are lucky, gets to have the experience of choking, of feeling like they may not be able to digest what is unfolding on the stage, and then of remembering how these indigestible bits felt in their body.*

For that to happen, however, two sets of criteria have to be met. First, O'Hara has to keep us "trapped" in our seats, which involves the artistry of his craft (i.e., that we may be seduced *to want to stay*), together with the ruthlessness of subjecting us to something genuinely ego-disruptive (otherwise, we will not feel "trapped" but merely "enjoy" the art) and, also, a measure of care (so that we are shattered but not damaged by the experience). To work this way entails vulnerability: O'Hara is taking a risk. Just like Williams-Haas, who did not know how Haas would bear her sadism, O'Hara too cannot know ahead of time what his sadism will evoke in the audience—and, as we have seen, some theatergoers felt traumatized, others that it went too far. Second, for the art to become an aesthetic experience, we, the audience, also have to bend our will, to make ourselves passible to its action on us. That involves more than just staying in the theater to experience the whole performance; it also involves tuning ourselves into the aesthetics of the terribly beautiful and, also, resisting the tendency to barricade ourselves into what we already think we know about what is unfolding onstage (as, for example, in feeling certain we "know" what happened in the closing act).[5]

And let us also note that O'Hara is taking much pleasure in this process: most exciting for him, he describes, was watching the audience walk into the theater, knowing "they have no idea what they are in for . . . and that's fun, that's the thrill of going to the theater" (Sunday discussions, March 11, 2022). Similarly, it is easy to discern in *The Artist and the Pervert* that Williams-Haas also derives some pleasure from this stern naming of Haas's White privilege. Said differently, the exigent sadist (here, O'Hara and Williams-Haas) is not self-sacrificing, nor are they "servicing" the other: they are entering an experiment that pleasures them, while also putting things they care about on the line (for O'Hara, the play, and for Williams-Haas, her relationship).

Exigent sadism, as these examples illustrate, retains Sade's commitment to self-sovereignty but not as something that is wielded over the other, nor as self-possession, but as a risk one also takes with oneself. Exigent sadism is not an imposition on the other but an offering, and it may or not be accepted. Williams-Haas's harsh comment was accepted, but the truth is that she took a risk: in saying something that could have hurt Haas (which she did not want), which may have angered him, or changed their relationship, she also made herself vulnerable, exposing herself to something unforeseen. What sets exigent sadism apart from more ordinary offerings of insight or of helpful observations, which are accompanied by tenderness, is that the odd care of exigent sadism is undergirded by ruthlessness, which can make it feel jolting to the receiver and weirdly pleasurable to the sadist herself.

The sadistic practice I am describing creates a space that can possibly bring in something really opaque, to open us to the wound in the other and to the wound in the self, but also may create, along with it, a form of support that is not in keeping with our usual understanding of consent or sadism. The exigent sadist is made vulnerable, not only to the other but to herself, since, in following the exigency of her sexual unconscious—that demand coming from "that imperious object . . . simultaneously undeniable and yet always impossible to grasp completely . . . incontestably sexual" (Laplanche, 2006a, p. 4)—she opens herself to her own opacity. And she also takes the risk of infiltrating the other's boundaries, bringing to them something really foreign and disturbing. What Williams-Haas offers Haas is ruthless; it wounds his ideas about his fixation on the fascist past (translation), and it puts his trauma back into circulation, turning it into a source of inspiration. In that sense, her sadism does not deny Haas's traumatic preoccupation with fascism; it helps jolt him out of how ossified his relationship to it has become. Part of what makes the disturbance introduced by this type of sadism deeply ethical is that it is also accompanied by some measure of caring support. This support is not of the ordinary kind as when we offer empathic reassurance or validation of the other's pain. Nor is it instrumental, intending to produce a specific effect, as that would be antithetical to the surrender to the unknown required of the exigent sadist. The support, rather, is distributed in the texture of the encounter itself: in the way space is held for the other's experience, in the physical sensorium of the sadist's address, and in her determination to remain in relation to the other come what may.

Exigent Sadism and the Touching of Wounds

Insofar as exigent sadism enables the touching of wounds, it can produce an intimacy that goes beyond conventional forms of bonding and closeness, cleaving eroticism from the vocabularies of the law, of healing, and of authority. Holding open space for such experiences is scary; and it imperils both parties, albeit in different ways. For one, the exigent sadist cannot guarantee a good outcome: instead, she steps into the fray with the other's marginal authorization (limit consent) and takes the leap because she believes that it is worthwhile to put oneself at risk for the sake of experience. Exigent sadism's only covenant is that the sadist will not try to exploit the other by breaking their will and that they will not try to control, or lay a claim on, the narrative of the other's experience. In this sense, both parties give themselves over to the other, though not to the other's subjectivity but to the other's opacity—and to the opacity in themselves. Both enter as full participants, and though the asymmetry of their positions is irreducible, each assumes responsibility for the encounter. In other words, unlike sensible sadism in BDSM, where the sadist is imagined to hold all the responsibility, exigent sadism and masochism do not jettison their ties to one's responsibility to oneself. Both participants, that is, surrender to a process that has a state of overwhelm as one possible outcome—though, I want to repeat here that overwhelm is not a "project" with a determinate end, as that would only reify the experience. In other words, this sadism does not proceed from the sadist's ego but from her very dispossession, that is, from her capacity to bend her will: this is one of exigent sadism's critical differences from destructive sadism. If through this process, the other comes undone, the sadist makes no claims as to what they will make of the experience, and no influence is exerted as to how the other will reconstitute themselves. This is also what gives this kind of sadism its ethical footing: the exigent sadist provides the conditions for sovereign experience but refuses to tell the other what to make of it and does not try to control how the other will understand it.

The experience that one curates for another through exigent sadism initiates something; it puts something in motion, though what exactly and how it will track cannot be known in advance. The sadist is, nevertheless, responsible for what they have put in motion, which means that they have to remain fully present in a way that forces them to invent. Such invention involves being open to the possibility of new forms of engagement. These new forms of engagement go beyond the clichés of the way we are supposed to interact interpersonally based on our identities. When one is required to invent, one has to reimagine: the exigent sadist thus has to say or do things that are not in books, in syllabi, or in workshops, things that do not draw on universals but that derive from her very being. She is required to be fully present and alert to the particular interpersonal relation. If something goes wrong, the sadist has to take responsibility, though responsibility here is not about shriveling in guilt: such shriveling is responsibility's narcissistic mutant, and it results in a turning away from the person wounded.

Responsibility entails staying present for the difficult moment, not to wilt out of fear or guilt but remaining responsive to the other. This is, in some way, what Gary in *Slave Play* wants from Dustin. Whereas Dustin is preoccupied with Gary's tears and worries about his postorgasmic collapse, Gary neither regrets the pain nor blames Dustin for it. What Gary wants, it seems to me, is to go through the experience *with* Dustin. This is an unusual, yet important, sort of intimacy, but such a stance cannot be a strategy or a method, it has to derive from one's being. Such intimacy requires tailor-made responses that derive from the current situation. There is no categorical imperative to help us navigate them, and no relationship "script" would help Dustin and Gary steer their way forward: they have to do it risking themselves, to stand disarmed before each other.

From this angle, we can see that exigent sadism requires work and effort and that it also offers care that is not conjugated in the terms we ordinarily understand as care, like "love," "recognition," "safety," or "respect." Such care also involves not using the other to disavow one's erotic vibration, which makes the acknowledgment of the sadist's own vulnerability of critical importance. Exigent sadism requires a radical form of commitment characterized by patience and waiting. Contrary to the destructive sort, it is neither rushed nor impulsive. Its intimacy is very particular. When two individuals appear before each other this way, experiences outside the habitual become possible: two distinct experiences in an intense moment of intimate connection.

The exercise of exigent sadism over another requires that one may first be able to exercise it over oneself. I do not mean this in the empathic sense of "knowing what it feels like." I refer to not allowing oneself to be inhibited by one's morals or even "good" politics in the aesthetic moment, not to wither under the fear of encountering opacity but to take a leap, following not logic but the poetics of being.

Erotics of the Monstrous: *The Night Porter*

Situated in 1957 postwar Vienna, *The Night Porter* traces the chance reunion, years after they first met at a concentration camp, of Max, a former SS guard now working as a night porter in a hotel, and Lucia, a former camp inmate, who is visiting the hotel with her new husband, an American composer. Their recognition of each other is instant and uneasy. "Blocks of memory return fluidly and continuously throughout the film" (Ravetto, 2001, p. 124), sparing neither them nor us, the viewers, from the more abject, vilifying dimensions of their shared past. Organizing the narration around a series of visual flashbacks from their previous erotic relationship, the film's director, Liliana Cavani, offers a portrayal of the grotesque intimacy that develops between Lucia and Max. The two rekindle a sadomasochistic erotic connection that, despite their changed circumstances, has distinctive similarities, both alluring and perplexing, with their origin story. An inscrutable "mutual tenderness and protection" (Brabender, 2008, p. 300) develops between them. In parallel, Max belongs to a group that meets privately: a lawyer with access to the archives of the war tribunals, a practicing psychoanalyst, and an established businessman all belong to a secret network of former Nazis who convene and coordinate their actions in order to conceal and destroy evidence that might implicate them in war crimes. Contrary to Lucia's previous position of powerlessness in the camps, she thus finds herself with the considerable power of being able to break their cover—something the Nazis become aware of and that becomes a problem that the couple negotiates through eroticism. Part of the frightening power of this film "lies in its characters' total abandonment to experience" (Houston & Kinder, 1975, p. 366).

Not everyone can sit through *The Night Porter* easily, or at all. With incomparable skill and relentless escalation—things get more difficult to watch and more perverse as the film goes on—Cavani does not just symbolically represent a challenging story; she re-presents it, subjecting us, too, to its erotic brutality. That we, as Robert O'Hara had said in relation to *Slave Play*, have come to watch means that we, too, the recipients of Cavani's exigent sadism, bear a share of responsibility and will have to reflect on the particulars of our participation.[6] But *The Night Porter* is not *Shoah*, *Schindler's List*, or *Sophie's Choice*: Cavani has imagined around this particular genre of Holocaust movies. It is, in fact, precisely this act of imagination on her part that becomes a problem in the film's reception. *The Night Porter* has been castigated as an exploitative attempt to titillate through offensive depictions and interpretations of the tortures suffered in the camps (Valentine, 2007). Others saw it as a "thinly disguised fascist propaganda film that glorifies sadism" and that, in the minds of some critics, attempts to "legitimize the death of millions of innocent victims at the hands of the Nazi machine" (McCormick & Giroux, 1977, p. 31). Some holocaust survivors vehemently criticized Cavani for muddying our sense of historical truth through the introduction of inappropriately sexualized renditions of power relations in the camps. None other than Primo Levi himself vociferously protested the nightmarish threading of the erotic with genocidal fantasy (1988).

Not everyone, of course, perceived *The Night Porter* as Nazisploitation. What makes Nazisploitation an ethically dubious genre is the situating of sex and violence "in flagrant inaccuracies and exaggerations" vis-à-vis the Holocaust (Hills, 2015, p. 188). But, says Italo Moscati, the writer of *The Night Porter*, the film "is not a history book, it is a fantasy, with the possibilities that that entails" (quoted in Hills, 2015, p. 200). The defense that the story in this film is not portrayed for reasons of historical fidelity, and the argument that we should not expect from an artistic object a one-to-one correspondence to the historical archive did little to assuage the turmoil that *The Night Porter* animated. When Primo Levi denounced the film as "beautiful and false," we may assume that by "false" he meant that it imagines scenarios that exceed—even violate—historiography. It may be precisely the fact, however, that the film dares fantasize *about* the monstrous past that generated the crisis of its reception. Savage and harrowing history, this reasoning goes, should be documented, reported, logged, chronicled, and archived—that is, kept intact, untouched, undisturbed—whereas fantasy, by putting immobilized trauma back in circulation, threatens to unseat memory.

The implication that an ethical relationship to history should be organized around commemoration, mourning, and a tending to wounds implies that there are proper protocols to the way we are to look at the past: to find therein what we already know, to confirm in our viewing the history that was already given to us. Looking in this way, though, can become insincere, a site for the performance of disbelief, horror, distress, and compassion. I do not make light of the fact that there are instances when the historical record is often vacated (as by Holocaust deniers), most of which involve harm that is caused to populations that are deemed disposable by virtue of their intersecting identities vis-à-vis race, gender, religious background, and ethnic belonging. What I want to do is flag the ecstatic anxieties that congregate around the question of *how* the past is to be remembered, what we are expected to find when we look at its representations, and whether we are permitted to fantasize about it in the first place. How that fantasy appears in public spaces when it also makes sexual use of unthinkable violence is where ethics, aesthetics, and perversity intersect.

Portrayals of the sort dared by *The Night Porter* do not minimize the horrors of the past; "on the contrary, they keep them relevant" (Waller, 1996, p. 269). By entwining aesthetic experience with traumatic memory, the film works to defamiliarize us with stories told about the Holocaust, those portrayed in the typical Hollywood narratives. *The Night Porter* departs from the usual framing of victim/victimizer as the organizing axis of the story. Why is that important? Because even the atrocious and the terrible can be far more complex than we want to know. "Cavani's love story," writes de Lauretis, "is not only the story of the relation between two individuals, but of the world around them, of the culture and history in which they exist, of the values, conflicts, and inner contradictions of a society which is, whether we want to see it or not, our own" (1976, p. 36). This, Cavani knows, is best conveyed not cerebrally—that is, through narration and critique—but as something that the viewer has to endure through the action of the film.

The setting of the film in 1957 Vienna means that the relationship between Max and Lucia unfolds after all Soviet occupation troops have pulled out of the city. Life in Vienna picks up, continuing as if the past has passed and life can simply go on. Yet the "heritage of fascism remained and festered in the dark tenement houses and luxury hotels of Europe. . . Lucia and Max," writes de Lauretis, "are two people involved in the Nazi infamy, albeit at opposite ends, who cannot forget" (1976, p. 37). Lucia and Max refuse to forget, resisting the glossing over of the traumatic past. They are, we might say, traumatophilic. And this is where the difficulty of the film resides: they do not remember as commemoration (that is, as translated remembering ordered through symbols provided by the dominant narratives in the mythosymbolic); their remembering is through the action of repetition and through a touching of wounds that is conjugated through the sexual. This, perhaps, is what also makes the film so spellbinding and mesmerizing: the film acts on us because it does not portray organized traces of mnemic recollection but offers remembering as the space for the emergence of the erotically perverse.

"I spoke to many different survivors," Cavani explains in describing her process of working on the film, "women from different backgrounds, who as young resistance fighters had been captured by the Nazis and sent to concentration camps. There was one woman who had become a teacher after the war and lived in Cuneo [in Northern Italy]. She told me that during the summer holidays, she would go back to Dachau . . . and spend a week there. I asked her something rather banal—why didn't she go to the beach instead? She told me she felt the need to be there, it was almost as if she was visiting another planet" (Iannone, 2021, p. 149). "[Another woman] was a middle-class woman from Milan, who had been captured and sent to Auschwitz. . . She finally agreed to speak to me and revealed how her family had told her to stop dwelling on what happened during the war. . . [What] she couldn't get past was how the war had exposed the darkest parts of her own personality. She had done things she never thought she'd be capable of, just to survive" (quoted in Iannone, 2021, p. 149). "What disturbed her most was the fact that in the camp she had discovered the depth of her own nature, that is to say, what good and evil she was capable of. She underlined the word *evil*. She said she could not forgive the Nazis for making her aware of people's capacity for evil. But she gave me no details; she only told me not to expect a victim to be always innocent because a victim too is a person" (quoted in de Lauretis, 1976, p. 36). In all these accounts, we see how the horror of the camps and the need to survive forced some people to encounter things in themselves that were terrible and forced—and that drove some survivors to later suicide.

Works like *The Night Porter* and *Slave Play* spin morality into a crisis. What is at stake in *The Night Porter* is not a struggle between whether history is remembered or refused but the struggle to conceive of the historical event as a sacred object that is expected to remain unpolluted by pleasure or intimacy (Ravetto, 2001). The worry is also that Nazi ideology is aestheticized and thus smuggled in through sex and pleasure (Sontag, 1964). Official histories (and I am only referring here to histories that do not deny the cruel barbarisms of the past) oftentimes prescribe which rememberings we may circulate and which relations to those rememberings we may entertain. Such proscription is its own barbaric, intromissive gesture—arriving to us through primary violence and as part of the mythosymbolic surround of the cultures (or microcultures) in which we become subjectivized. We have already seen how the question of which historical records are kept laminated and which are allowed to generate varied and complex stories, stories with difficulties and contradictions, is always already racialized. In the sphere of barbarism, we are told, the erotic is out of place (Douglas, 1966). What *The Night Porter* asks us to reflect on is whether thus encountering the erotic is polluting or pollinating, which is another way of asking whether the erotic makes bids to unfreeze immobilized trauma. The notion that it is sacrilegious to tend to surfaces excited by the terribly beautiful (Moten, 2003) forecloses our curiosity and freezes some subjects in their traumatic past, which is how traumatophobia works.

"The Nazis," Foucault writes, "worked with brooms and dusters, wanting to purge society of everything they considered unsanitary, dusty, filthy; syphilitics, homosexuals, Jews, those of impure blood, Blacks, the insane. It's the foul petit bourgeois dream of racial hygiene that underlies the Nazi dream. Eros is absent. That said," he then adds more ambivalently, "it's not impossible that locally, within this structure, there were erotic relationships that were formed in the bodily confrontation between victim and executioner. But," he retreats, if that happened, "it was accidental" (1975, p. 226). In Foucault's reading, eros is about purity.[7] Cavani shows that even in those conditions, there is a possibility for erotic relations that are not accidental but emerge precisely from the material circumstances that confound them. For those who are willing to endure performance or to enjoy art that takes us into the disaster (Adorno, 1970), the theatrical piece, the film, the photograph, even the analytic session can exert a sadistic force rendering them into traumatisms, setting in motion fresh translational activity.

"How could Nazism," Foucault protests, "have become everywhere today. . . in all the pornographic literature of the world, the absolute reference to eroticism? All the shoddiest aspects of the erotic imagination are now put under the sign of Nazism" (1974, p. 251). He goes on from there to advocate for the discovery of new ways to use the body to produce new pleasures. But repetition, writes Rebecca Schneider, is "a powerful tool for cross- or intra-temporal negotiation, even (perhaps) interaction or inter(in)animation of one time with another time" (2011, p. 31). The traumatophilic return to the site of the wound is not, as Foucault seems to suggest here, a problematic fixation with the past: it is not coming back full circle but a helicoid movement that revisits similar points along a different axis, propelling us forward (Laplanche, 2006a).

A few months ago, I was discussing *The Night Porter* with a group of analysts in a study group I run on Laplanche's work. We were all grappling with questions regarding Lucia's erotic involvement with Max: Was she too traumatized and thus compromised? Why would she be picking up a sexual thread that got thankfully dropped when she was saved from the camps? My colleague, Willa France, noted her impression that Lucia was just caught in something from which she could not escape.[8] Upon returning to the movie for a second viewing, however, she found herself "hard-pressed to see her [Lucia] as a victim." Lingering on Lucia's nonverbal cues—her glances, pauses, gestures—Willa felt that she was observing something much more nuanced, which extended beyond the yes/no dichotomy of consent. Willa's revised response was made possible by her having returned to the film again: it is obviously not everyone's intuitive inclination to view a difficult film twice or to give oneself over to repetition this way—nor does everyone have the nerve, or the appetite, for it. But what my relationship to *Slave Play* suggests and Willa's comment highlights is the relationship between repetition and passibility: repetition is part of how art can seize us.

Larisa, a colleague from the same group, was preoccupied with the horror she felt in relation to an especially difficult scene. During Lucia's internment, she has asked Max, on account of their "special relationship," to transfer another inmate who displeases her.[9] In the scene in question, Max presents Lucia with a box that contains, as we are startled to discover, the captive's severed head. The moment is shocking, especially because we do not see it coming. Was this Max's overzealous offering to her? His perverse interpretation of her wish? Was Lucia intending this terrible thing to happen? Some group members now seemed to vaguely recall that the expression on Lucia's face when receiving the "gift" was rather enigmatic. Larisa expressed that she would like to force herself to watch that scene again, to focus on Lucia's facial expression and bodily comportment at the moment she encountered the severed head. I asked Larisa what she was hoping to encounter there. She explained wanting "to return to the scene to see what else I might feel there." Larisa's wish captures the particular kind of ethical and aesthetic engagement I have been exploring in relation to exigent sadism—a repetition that is not easy to endure and that requires the bending of the will. Larisa imagines returning to the scene not to better scan Lucia's face for clues of what had "really" occurred but for the sake of inspiration, to see what may be kindled in herself. Is it ethical, one may ask, to return to a scene of a beheading "for inspiration"? I suppose it depends on what one means by "ethics." It also depends on what one imagines is accomplished if one turns away from a scene of that sort. Does it prevent the harm or undo the injury? Is the fear that by returning to look, one is complicit with the crime? Is it more ethical to be outraged, heartbroken, or horrified—and, if so, why?

In-Conclusion

The Night Porter and *Slave Play* are examples of art that "takes itself into the disaster . . . rather than merely protesting hopelessly against it" (Adorno, 1970, p. 19). Who, Adorno asks, "wants to stick around for that—to experience the disaster" (1970, p. 19)? Contrary to social life, where subjects do not get to choose if—and which—disaster befalls them, some art invites us into the wreckage. Not everyone has the bandwidth to look, or to look again, and not everyone will be able to look in order to eavesdrop on themselves, to tune in to what gets roused inside them. Those who do, meet the aesthetic object at the limits of their consent. Rather than ask, however, why someone would step willingly into the fray of the traumatic—to ask, that is, after their psychology, motivation, or intent—my project tries to raise a different set of queries that have to do with how such art and performance acts on us, how it "traps" us (O'Hara), what we have to grapple with in ourselves to respond to such a calling, and what kinds of states and possibilities this dangerous endeavor opens up to.

It can be hard to trust that there is power to be found in the self's and in the other's decentering. Certainly, this is not power of the conventional sort but of a more private kind—of an internal one that relates to one's autonomy. What I have wanted to illuminate is what it is we stand to lose when we only care about affirmation, what are we depriving ourselves and each other of if we only permit the people close to us to relate to us on our terms. I do not mean to diminish those who care about being seen and value being known—and we all do, at different moments.

These are not unworthy projects, nor are they unimportant. But they are projects with different stakes and that enable different possibilities.

At one of *Slave Play*'s Sunday discussions (December 12, 2021), I asked the play's intimacy director, Claire Warden, how she worked with actors around the extraordinarily intimate, trauma-filled work they were being asked to engage with almost every night. I did not know then that I was asking a question about the bending of the will: How did she, I wanted to understand, help them counter their resistances to subject themselves to the play again, to be possible to what it roused in their bodies? "I will say to actors when I work with them," Warden explained, "this isn't necessarily about being comfortable, that's certainly [the case] with this play, I don't need you to be comfortable, this will be uncomfortable. What we are looking for you is to feel . . . human." That the full range of humanity is not reachable through safety, control, or recognition but in daring to risk the excitement of danger, to tread into places that scare yet thrill us—assuming such risks despite not knowing what they will usher in yet throwing ourselves in the experience anyway: this has been the wager of this volume.

Epilogue

Like a Spider or Spit

In this book's introduction, I asked you to give yourselves over to me, preparing you for the fact that this book was written for readers who are willing to risk experience. As I, too, gave myself over to the writing of this book, I was startled to realize that this work was not about what I thought it was—overwhelm and limit consent—but, perhaps most importantly, about theorizing the currents of sadism. Exigent sadism can carry us beyond the dialectics of recognition—an analytic that oppressively dominates contemporary thinking—into the realm of the unconscious, that bizarre space that cannot be reckoned with via hermeneutics, where the incommensurable remains stubbornly and thankfully unresolved, a tension that excites and troubles us but that, as we have seen, also stands to inspire us. This tension has to do with what it means to be human, with what it means to be alive.

The essay titled "Formless" in Bataille's volume *Visions of Excess* reads,

> A dictionary begins when it no longer gives the meaning of words, but their tasks. Thus, *formless* is not only an adjective having a given meaning, but a term that serves to bring things down in the world. . . What it designates has no rights in any sense and gets itself squashed everywhere, like a spider or an earthworm. In fact, for academic men to be happy, the universe would have to take shape. . . On the other hand, affirming that the universe resembles nothing and is only *formless* amounts to saying that the universe is something like a spider or spit. (1929/1985a, p. 31; emphasis in original)

What would bringing down the world look like in the context of a universe replete with inequities, injustices, and violences? This volume has nothing to contribute to rectifying such wrongs. What I have tried to do, instead, is to suggest that opening ourselves to experiences that are opaque, allowing ourselves to be drawn into overwhelm, and accepting that it will cost us to do so may bring things down not in the world but in ourselves, delivering us to places that disrupt the terms by which we think what we think we know about ourselves—and each other.

In the pithy and provocative text just quoted, Martin Jay notes that what Bataille says argues for "the reduction of meaning . . . not by contradiction—which would be dialectical—but by putrefaction: the puncturing of the limits around the term" (1993, p. 66). In arguing for formlessness, Bataille is refusing "to place the world into categorical straightjackets, assigning everything a proper form" (Jay, 1993, p. 65). Bataille's outrageous claim that follows, that "affirming that the universe resembles nothing and is only *formless* amounts to saying that the universe is something like a spider or spit," is, for Jay, "not a truth claim in its own right, but rather an assault on all claims to reduce the world to formal truths" (1993, p. 65).

The notion that exciting and capacious possibilities inhere in engaging the gutter, the detritus, and the debased has run throughout this book. It is in Adam's disgusting, malodorous stranger; it can be found in Dean's unexpected, erotic astonishment in his piss-play bottoming; it is most certainly present in Gary Fisher, who begs to be called a "n*"; and it is present in Kaneisha, who wants to be made to eat off the floor like a dog. It is the positioning of the subject in its own refuse, which involves no less than a steadfast bending of one's will, that, I see now, marks my project. It is a rare and *fortunate* moment when an encounter with another or an encounter with art or performance may work on us at the very site of experience, enabling the actual to re-present itself and the traumatic to re-appear. To be traumatophilically disposed, then, is to be exposed to a forcefield "at the blindspot of understanding" (Bataille, 1957, p. 111); it is to encounter the other and to be summoned by art not on our own terms but in the jolting of our ego. Such "silenc[ing of] the incessant chatter of the ego" (Scarfone, 2015b, p. 75) may thereby offer us a peculiar kind of sovereignty, not over others but a most intimate relationship with ourselves.

In standing behind the claim that sovereign experience is worth what it will cost us and in carving out a conceptual space for exigent sadism, I have taken a risk *with you*. In some ways, I took that risk from the start, when I asked you to give yourselves over to me, which is to some degree what all books ask of the reader, though not all authors make the announcement. I finish this writing exposed and raw, but hopeful. Perhaps you, too, have felt raw and tender at times or even experienced some moments of wonderment.

ACKNOWLEDGMENTS

My father, Νίκος Σακετόπουλος, jumped out of airplanes for a living, or such is the story told in my family. I never bought that story: to me, it always looked like my dad jumped out of airplanes because he loved how it felt and because he wanted to experience that feeling that again and again. This is the backdrop against which this book has been written: my father's relationship to parachutes and to the unique blend of discipline and abandon they require has shaped my aesthetic relationship to risk. Not everyone has had the benefit of growing up surrounded by such robust faith in, and commitment to, risk. But anyone who has also knows that risk-taking requires an assortment of discipline, self-sovereignty, and surrender. All three are theorized in these pages, and they have all been required of me in the writing of this book. Κατά κάποιον τρόπο συνεπώς μπαμπά μου, την ικανότητα να γράψω αυτό το βιβλίο και την επιμονή που χρειάστηκε, μου τα καλλιέργησες εσύ.

My mother, Αντιγόνη Σωτηριάδου, *my Antigone*, has never questioned my choices, however unusual, surprising, or simply bizarre they have been. Από την μητέρα μου, είχα επίσης την σπάνια τύχη να πάρω περισσότερα απ᾽ όσα της είχαν δωθεί. To be given to this way is rare, and it is not without cost to the giver. Writing this book has also required of me a bending of my will and an eavesdropping on myself: και τα δύο τα έμαθα από εσένα μαμά. My mother also gave me the gift of inspiration, as it is in from her shelves that I plucked the book that first made me fall in love with psychoanalysis. Για αυτά τα σπάνια δώρα μαμά μου, σε ευχαριστώ.

My brother, Πέτρος Σακετόπουλος, separated by a year and by the many more miles of our different life paths, has taught me that love is a conjoint site of fierceness and tenderness—and that the integrity that is required to hold onto both is an ongoing project. Σε ευχαριστώ που πάντα επιστρέφεις, σε ευχαριστώ που πάντα ξαναβρισκόμαστε.

Muriel Dimen was the first mentor also talk to me about writing. Initially my teacher and supervisor, then friend, then family, Muriel taught me that one is always playing catch-up with one's ideas. A very early version of what has become chapter 1 in this book benefited from her comments. I think she would have liked this book and seen her impact on me in it, but, sadly, she will not read it. I was lucky to be holding her hand as she was dying. Experiencing her death was one of the most intimate experiences I have had. Velleda Ceccoli also started as my teacher and supervisor, taught me how to be an analyst, and became my Italian mother. Over the years, she has held my hope, my heartbreak, and my ambition with love, steadiness, and femme solidarity. You, too, Velleda mou are in these pages.

Cheryl Dumas, the consummate riding buddy and my beloved friend, offered care of many sorts, including the sustenance of helping me protect my emotional energy and time. Over long motorcycle trips and weekend rides, she talked to me about riding routes, gear, and aftermarket parts. Thank you Chaka, among other things, for the gift of balance. Let's keep riding GSes (and, as we are finding out, not only GSes!) again and again, all over the world!

Samantha Hill and Tim Dean have furthered my imagination and offered sturdiness. They each sat on my shoulders at different moments of this book's writing, inciting little devils that urged me to slam my foot on the pedal and not let go. I think of them as my writing tops, and I am indebted to them for their exigent sadism (a good sadism, as chapter 5 insists). Sam taught me the philosophy I needed, walking me through intellectual traditions that, in my training as a psychoanalyst, I was unprepared to tackle. She has been generous and kind even as many people jockeyed for her time when her biography of Hannah Arendt came out. It is to her that I owe the pleasure of having experienced Bataille again—including the pleasure of laughing and hearing her laugh. Tim trusted me enough to tear through early drafts with painful commentary, an offering for which I remain immensely grateful. Thank you, Tim, also for our multihour, middle-of-the-night calls, for discussing ideas, yours and mine, for talking about death almost as much as we have about life, and for going through the pandemic together—which is when this book was written.

My friend Mistress Blunt enabled my preoccupation with *Slave Play*, by forwarding links and interviews, alerting me to podcasts, and sending screenshots from Twitter. I owe her for her enthusiastic support, for her irreverence, and for her frequent and titillatingly indecorous comments.

Josh Chambers-Letson was my wonderful, and wonderfully supportive, corresponding editor at the Sexual Cultures Series. Informally, he was also my seducer, as it was at his invitation that I began imagining this volume. Thank you, Josh, for your razor-sharp read of multiple drafts and for the care you have taken to help me think my ideas. My thanks also to Tavia Nyong'o for his sustained excitement and conviction in my project, to Eric Zinner for his enthusiasm and trust (and for steering me clear of gerunds!), and to Furqan Sayeed for making sure that nothing fell through the cracks. Deep gratitude to Amber Musser for dazzlingly brilliant comments on my work, for the gift of opacity, and for her friendship.

While I was already trained when I started working with Andy Druck and Dominique Scarfone, I came into my own as a psychoanalyst during, and largely because of, their influence and friendship. Andy cheered me on from the start. He also taught me how to be direct and truthful with patients, not to be afraid to call things what they are by hiding behind theory or technique, and he also protected me. Thank you, Andy, for your astuteness and care. Dominique taught me my Laplanche and continues to nourish my faith in psychoanalysis as a magical, and magically weird, space. His conviction that one needs to follow what is exigent sustains me, and I have benefited from his teaching, which does not suffer the narcissism that usually befalls the psychoanalytic rock star.

Brent Zachery generously shared knowledge and resources, in addition to helping curate the fantastically interesting Sunday salons for "processing" *Slave Play*. My thanks also to mike bond, who contacted me upon publication of my work on *Slave Play*, for agreeing to be interviewed for this book despite his investment in disappearing from public discourse.

When I asked my friend Griffin Hansbury if some of the ideas in this book were too much, he mischievously replied, "Definitely!" Everyone should be graced with friends who savor too-muchness, but in Griffin, I also have an ally in thinking queerness with the complexity it deserves. I am grateful to him and to his partner, the wonderful Rebecca Levi, for long weekends of rest and play, which is what writing also needs. Harmeet Malhi was my first friend upon immigrating to the States, and she taught me how to navigate American exceptionalism with grace. Hemu, I owe you so much. Lara Sheehi has been able to see through my code-switching and to reach out to me immigrant to immigrant. She, more than any of my friends in the US, is attuned to my postcoloniality. Lara's fierceness is otherworldly, and her work on the liberation of Palestine, co-authored with her partner and my friend, Stephen Sheehi, makes me proud to be an analyst.

Much appreciation to the many friends and colleagues who talked with me about or read earlier versions of the ideas explored in this book: Velleda Ceccoli, Ken Corbett, Andy Druck, Lisa Duggan, Janet Jakobsen (always with Moxy's approval), Adrienne Harris, Jonathan House (who also shared Laplanchean knowledge and references with unrestrained generosity!), Eng-Beng Lim, Dominique Scarfone, and Kathryn Bond Stockton. Colleagues in my Laplanche study group, Bryan Batista-Thomas, Willa France, Diane Fremont, Sam Guzzardi, Susan Heimbinder, Diana Moga, Sonia Orenstein, Vera Osipyan, Ann Pellegrini, Romy Reading, Amy Smith, and Michael Waldon, have taught and challenged me. Special thanks to the anonymized "Larisa" and to Willa France for their permission to quote them in chapter 5.

To my family and friends back home, who have accompanied me through the decades, thank you for your love and steadiness στην Ναταλία Θεοδωρίδου, στον Κωστή Ψαλτόπουλο, στην Ιφιγένεια Μαυράκη, στον Φωτάκο μου και τις κότες του, στην Ιλιάδα Χαρλάφτη και την Ανδρομέδα μας, στην Στέλλα Χρήστου, στον ταλαντούχο Αλέξανδρο Κορομηλά, στην Αργυρώ Πετράκη, στον Γιάννη Προκοπάκη, και φυσικά, με πολλή αγάπη, στην Δήμητρα Πελτέκη! Special shout-out to Nancy Papathanasiou and to Elena Olga Christidi, my badass dyke friends who are changing the face of queer mental health in Greece—and to their love child, Orlando LGBT+, Greece. Νικόλ Ντελημάρη και Άννα Φωτίου σας ευχαριστώ για την φιλία σας, για το παράδειγμά σας, και για το φύλο μου. For friendship and camaraderie on this side of the ocean, thank you also to Yaakov Kader, Tobin Kramer, Monica Holmes, Paula van de Nes, Marco Posadas, Jack Pula, and Gabby Stein. Special gratitude of a different kind to Betty and Ralph Pellegrini, to Sevasti Michalopoulou, to Τάκης, Γιοχάννα, Χρήστος, και Θοδωρής, and also to Berty and Sheila, and to Denise, Traceigh, and Dina.

It goes without saying that I owe myself to my two psychoanalysts, L. and D. Thank-yous are insufficient for projects so vast.

Giannis Michalopoulos has been my rock και ο θυσαυρός μου. There are not enough words to capture what he has contributed to my work in this book by teaching me about profound vulnerability and about what it means to be disarmed before another. Γιάννη μου, ξέρεις.

Last, love, admiration, and endless gratitude to Ann Pellegrini. Ann is, simply put, the best human. Her fierce, erotic passion for ideas, for thinking, unthinking, and rethinking has benefited me far beyond this book. It is also Ann who should be credited for my obsession with *Slave Play*, having gifted me my first viewing of it, sharing nothing about the plot with me, guarding the experience for me as is my preference and as this play especially required. Ann also read and helped me think through multiple drafts without wrinkling my thinking, told me when it was time to stop revising, and was generous when I did not. Ann held me while I risked myself in the writing of this book. Thank you, Αννούλα μου, for all the sparks and for the kindness you bring to my life.

Early versions of chapters 2 and 3 were previously published in the *Journal of the American Psychoanalytic Association* and the *Psychoanalytic Quarterly* and are reproduced here in their reworked form, with permission.

NOTES

INTRODUCTION

1. Clinical material is shared with the permission of patients discussed in this book. Identifying details, including names, have been altered for confidentiality. In some instances, my patients have themselves chosen the pseudonyms used for them. The matter of how to disguise case materials in order to preserve patients' privacy in publishing case reports has long been debated in the field of psychoanalysis. The gold standard has been set by Gabbard (2000), who proposed three approaches. The first, thick disguise, involves disguising the clinical material so heavily that only the patient can recognize themselves. The second applies to cases where thick disguise would stand to eliminate important aspects of the case (for instance, race or gender cannot be easily swapped out without distorting the clinical situation) and stipulates that composites made up of different patients may be used as long as, in the analyst's estimation, they preserve the dynamic features of the case. Asking for the patient's consent is the third approach and has become the expectation. But even this is potentially distorting and distorted: consent inquiries are complicated by the patient's relationship to the analyst. For example, it may be hard to say no to one's analyst, especially for patients who pay lowered fees; the lure of being "useful" to the analyst's endeavor, or important enough for the analyst to want to write about you, may be too insurmountable a draw for assent to be meaningful; and so on. An analyst who does not explore the meaning of the patient's assent may have ticked the box of "obtaining patient consent" but has not substantively met the psychoanalytic standard.

2. Some of the notes in this book address questions or issues that are of special relevance to clinicians. I henceforth designate those with the initials "CN" (for "Clinical Notes") to simplify the engagement of the critical apparatus for different kinds of readers. I offer CNs to contextualize ideas in relation to theoretical and technical considerations—though not as a compendium of how to "apply" theory to the clinical situation (in other words, this book is not a clinical manual).

3. Nonclinical readers (and, sometimes, even clinical ones) may misunderstand case reports as being "real," as opposed to those derived from theater, film, or other artistic texts that are explicitly imaginary productions. It is important to understand, though, that while everything I describe vis-à-vis clinical case studies is truthful (i.e., it is not falsified), there are several reasons why clinical case reports are, to some degree, also fictional productions. For instance,

to protect confidentiality, I have had to disguise the material and the patient—and, thus, choose what I substitute in for what I have taken out. Further, what patients report to me is mediated by the patient's feelings about me, about the work, and about what the work brings up, which makes patients' statements not veridical in the everyday sense of the word. Last, my own personality, history, biases, etc. inflect what aspects of the patient and of the clinical process capture my attention and how they color my take on it, thereby introducing further meaningful distortions. Analysts take all these into account when working with patients, aware that the realm in which we work follows different logics than those of everyday life. I clarify this for non-analyst readers to explain why I analogize the clinical alongside the artistic. That is, I approach the characters in the performance, text, and art that I discuss not as textual figures who live only on the stage, page, or screen but as case studies that provide "evidence of experience" (J. Scott, 1991). My interest pertains to *how* these aesthetic objects hook onto *us*, how they have their effects on us: in other words, it is also the audience that is the psychic entity under scrutiny here.

4. Laplanche uses terms that the psychoanalytically savvy reader may be well-versed in to describe processes that are appreciably different from what is meant by other analysts, which makes it easy to presume that one understands his ideas. For example, his version of the unconscious is very different from (the canonical understanding of) Freud's—and this has significant implications for thinking about racialization, trauma, and performance. To help counter such conflations, I try to present Laplanche's concepts in as clear and crisp a way as possible, so that they are less likely to disappear into what a reader may already know.

5. This volume is packed with psychoanalytic jargon, but this should not daunt the interested reader. I will explain all the concepts I use from the ground up.

6. This is not to say that analysts do not get ensnared in trying to ferret out hidden meanings; it is only to underscore that we are also trained to tend to the way things get enacted and come alive in the clinical setting.

7. CN: The slap's "perfection," it is worth noting from a clinical perspective, was not recounted to me independently of the transference relation. By the time Carmen described this experience, she had shared with me that no one before me had ever understood her "so precisely." This "perfection" in understanding her both pleased and horrified her: in her mind, I became so idealized and dangerous that Carmen had trouble attending her sessions consistently. Because being so well "understood" by me felt so gratifying *and* jolting, the work we did around the "perfect" slap was, therefore, also closely related to the transference. The idea that to be understood could be disturbing or upsetting may sound counterintuitive to the nonclinical reader. And it also introduces issues of consent that are explored in the case of Mia, presented later in the introduction.

8. We can imagine someone else in this instance, for example, externalizing this upset and somehow blaming Ava. It is worth considering that, in some cases, consent "violations" may follow this logic. This is not to minimize the many and

frequent occurrences of actual violations, as in sexual harassment and sexual assault, it is only to add more complexity to our thinking on this difficult topic.

9. In psychoanalysis, largely due to the work of Jessica Benjamin (1988, 2004), Hegelian dialectics and particularly Alexandre Kojève's (1947) reading of Hegel have played an outsized role in thinking about the subject-object relation.

10. Laplanche is not referring to the pedophilic adult or the disturbed parent but sees sexual deviancy as a universal substratum in the human psyche. Chapter 1 explains these ideas in more detail.

11. We should be careful here, however, not to overgeneralize. It may be more accurate to say that it is not minority-group membership but *one's relationship* to one's minoritarian location that matters most. We all know, for example, people who manage the lived difficulties of their minority status by overidentifying with dominant ideas about minority subjects as a way to ward off the pain of being othered. The reverse also occurs, as with subjects who possess considerable social privilege and who want to jettison it in identification with minority culture. It is not just social positionality, then, but also one's relationship to it that factors into how these dynamics can play out.

12. Throughout this volume, I use the term "erotic" to refer to the polymorphously sexual in Freud's *Three Essays* and the *sexual* in Laplanche's theory. I am not using the word to avoid sexuality per se but, rather, to avoid its easy conflation with sex (as in Freud's notion of "instinctual sexuality") as having predetermined aims (heterogenital procreativity). Further, I do not mean "erotic" as derived from a defanged Eros, which is separated out from the more disquieting dimensions of the sexual. This point is taken up in depth in chapter 2.

13. In equating masochism with the self's contraction, I am thinking of more classical definitions of masochism rather than work by Black feminists who have complicated our thinking about it (e.g., Cruz, 2016; Musser, 2014, 2018). I take on these distinctions in more depth in chapter 5.

14. CN: Carmen has since converted this experience into an object of contemplation. Remembered melancholically and haunting subsequent erotic encounters as the "perfection" that no partner could ever again offer, the experience can be *both* painfully craved *and* kept at arm's length. It is, in that sense, mastered and more under her control.

15. The matter of "safe space" comes up routinely in psychoanalysis—and, also, in the classroom. I understand patients' requests for "safe space" in several ways: one is a very particular wish for privacy and confidentiality, for me not to deliberately abuse the power of my position and to be thoughtfully engaged in the way I listen and speak to those who seek my help. Such requests can issue from the patient's (oftentimes warranted) worry about the analyst harboring phobic attitudes about the patient's positionality, insufficiently understanding (and needing to be educated about) the patient's intersecting identities, and concerns about being treated without consideration for the particular life circumstances and social relations that animate the patient's lived experience. There is also, I think, another

dimension to that request. The plea, as I hear it, is, "As I am about to make myself vulnerable to you, promise me you won't hurt me." This is a plea that reverberates across all human relationships but that we do not articulate to each other except in the most intimate of circumstances. When patients bring up the idea of a safe space, I can promise to do my best—but when it comes to promising that I will not hurt them, the matter is infinitely more complicated. Even within the protections of a relationship that is conducted in small doses and with the benefit of reflective intentionality, the establishment of a safe space is, under the best of circumstances, highly dubious. That is not because I do not care if my patients feel hurt or because I am careless but because any encounter between two human beings carries the potential for injury. If the relationship sustains long enough, the potential for injury becomes an unintended inevitability. Where trauma has pre-existed, new injuries also carry the potential to activate the past by stumbling on its remnants, evoking anxiety and risking retraumatization. In that sense, I find the term "safe space" somewhat naïve. An analyst's consulting room is never a safe space. It is, in fact, one of the most terrifying places one can find oneself in, which is why patients are oftentimes frightened to come to treatment in the first place, as well they should be. The most terrible things get (re)visited in an analyst's office. And yet it is only under the false truth and necessary illusion of safety that one may make oneself vulnerable in the first place (as explored in chapter 2). With time also comes the mourning of the notion that any intersubjective space can ever be fully safe—and eventually the begrudging, always incomplete acceptance of the fact that placing ourselves among others always carries the risk of wound and injury. Knowing this is not merely an intellectual exercise—most of us, after all, "know" that others could well hurt us. To come to know this on an emotional level is a hard-won and painful truth.

16. "Candidate" is the term employed for analysts-in-training.

17. Clinically speaking, the question of when to first discuss one's fee with a patient can be tricky. Many patients will ask at the initial call, which makes it easier to be direct. Patients who do not usually belong to two categories: those for whom money is not of concern or individuals with an especially complicated relationship to money (and, it should be noted, the former does not preclude the latter). When the patient does not inquire, bringing up the fee on a first call can be delicate; the first call is a time when the patient is especially likely to be distressed, anxious, or overwhelmed. Will the patient feel like they are being reduced to a billable hour? Might they feel shame or anger if the fee is outside their range but, given the nature of the contact, they do not have the space to express it? If the patient needs a lower fee, discussing a different amount (assuming the analyst can afford to do so) could take over the initial call when it may be easier to discuss it in person. And so on.

18. What clinician, writes Allanah Furlong, has not faced "the full and recurrent import of the disappearing/return-of-the-repressed nature of consent?" (2003, p. 573), e.g., with patients who understand cancellation policies but then become

enraged at the expectation of payment for a missed session. Questions about consent abound in the clinical setting: What does it mean for a patient to consent to a psychoanalytic treatment when the information one needs to make informed decisions requires a knowledge of one's unconscious life that can only, and even then only partially, follow the treatment to which one is considering consenting? Or, conversely, what does an analyst consent to when they agree to treat a particular patient, since the course of an analysis cannot possibly be anticipated (see also Furlong, 2005, 2020).

19. The analyst's experience of the patient's action on the analyst is not an unmediated registration of the patient's impact. What the analyst registers as their experience of the patient (and what they can narrate about it) is mostly the effect of how the analyst responds to the force of the patient's repetition and that is also based on their (the analyst's) own psychic complexion. The analyst, as a social being with their own unconscious life, brings to the encounter a heterogeneous array of experiences that belong to their past and that include elements from their dream.

20. There is a wealth of literature in Black feminist studies that helps me articulate these links better now than I could have at the time. Discussing sexual crimes committed against slaves in the antebellum South, Saidiya Hartman notes that since "the opportunity for nonconsent is required to establish consent, consent is meaningless if refusal is not an option" (1997, p. 111). This, Hartman reasons, complicated the question of agency for Black enslaved subjects and, to varying degrees, their descendants. For Amber Musser, the fact that enslaved Black subjects could not withhold their consent does not just mark the denial of personhood but scrambles the terms by which we map consent. That the assumption of a liberal subjectivity has become a precondition to valid consent, she writes, "reveal[s] the racial privilege that inheres in this imbrication of agency and sexuality" (2016, p. 158). To say this differently, an understanding of agentic allowance that demands as its starting point unencumbered freedoms and subjects who are not constituted through trauma tells us less about which consent is valid and which is not and more about the racial fictions that are baked into our notions of consent.

21. CN: This, to me, is a more helpful approach to thinking about how to work with racial difference in the consulting room. Rather than naming the dyad's racialization and inquiring about the patient's feelings about it, as some analysts are wont to do (an approach that feels rather epidermal—if not unskilled—to me), clinicians may be better off being attuned to the way racial difference and racial history may *appear* in the relationship through action—as opposed to relying only on how it announces itself, through words or representations. This has to be balanced against White analysts' liberal anxieties about doing their "due diligence" of making sure that they check the box of "talking about race."

22. "Where in everyday life," Arnold Modell asks poignantly, "can you find persons who, for an agreed-upon period of time, will place their own needs and desires to one side and be there only to listen to you and who are more than usual punctual and reliable and can, for the most part, be counted on not to retaliate and to be free of temper tantrums?" (1991, p. 25).

23. CN: Psychoanalysis does not suffer the problem of not knowing well, and we should be very wary of believing that our field has come anywhere near resolving its problem with engaging opacity. Encounters with opacity are not merely a temporary forbearance of what is yet unknown, which we tolerate in the reassurance that it will become clear over time. Most often, analysts tackle the problem of not knowing by turning it into a temporal one: the not known is the *not yet* known. The demand for transparency is, thus, not relinquished but deferred. This has created a climate of "tolerating not knowing" as that which will be rewarded with future insight. Despite psychoanalytic thinking's affectations of humility, "not knowing" is thus exalted but then reified (i.e., we all "know" we do not know). From this angle, W. R. Bion's notion of negative capability (1970) can become an empty gesture, more a concept to be applied and less something to be endured.

24. CN: Let us remember how hard it was for Mia to come to treatment in the first place and her fears about talking about her childhood.

25. Glissant's "The Black Beach" offers us a startlingly beautiful, paradigmatic instant of this more benevolent reception of that relation (1990, pp. 121–130). I am thankful to Homay King, whose work has brought this particular essay to my attention (2021).

CHAPTER 1. TO SUFFER PLEASURE

1. It is worth remembering here an often overlooked idea in Freud's *Three Essays on the Theory of Sexuality* (1905b), where he posits shame as a par excellence sexual affect. For him, shame is sexual excitement that has become too much to bear, and it only secondarily recruits repressive social rules. While no doubt restrictive social rules can leave one ashamed of one's sexual desire, we should not forget that shame has its own sexual frisson.

2. Despite the nosological baggage of the term "perversion," I insist on retaining it to capture the phenomenology of sexual experience that involves anguish as well as pleasure. Further, as a term, "perversion" maintains vigorous ties with the exuberant physicality and the perplexing, inscrutable dimensions of the sexual's polymorphousness in a way that other terms do not. My commitment to this term is a luxury that I have only because others have already highlighted that psychoanalysis has not approached perversion with disinterested objectivity and have mounted strong critiques of the term's pejorative misuse and psychoanalysis's sexual conservativism (Blechner, 2009; Corbett, 2013; Dimen, 2001, 2005; Hansbury, 2017).

3. Freud deleted this quote in his 1920 revision of *Three Essays*. As such, it now appears only in a footnote, making it easy to miss (Van Haute & Westerink, 2016).

Rubin's intervention came amid the Sex Wars and the hotly debated conflicts about female sadomasochistic sexuality (see Duggan & Hunter, 2014).

4. Jakobsen and Pellegrini also put some pressure on "benign" in Rubin's phrase, arguing that even as "public recognition of 'benign sexual variation' is absolutely vital," giving in to the temptation that "sex is a purely personal affair . . . fits [all too] well with neoliberalism's distinction between private and public spheres" (2004, p. 138).

5. The term "sadomasochism" does not appear as a synthetic word in Freud's published works, but he is nonetheless responsible for the unification of the two under a single concept: by arguing that sadism and masochism are derivative forms of each other, he made popular the idea that the two are cooccurring phenomena. This assumption comes under considerable pressure in chapter 5 of this volume.

6. I am grateful to Muriel Dimen, who raised this point with me early in my training and then helped me discern its clinical implications across different patients whose treatments she supervised. In psychoanalytic circles, and to this day, this interchange between developmental theory and normalization continues to go mostly unnoticed, and because of that, developmental theory and attachment theory continue to evade the lacerating critique they deserve for injecting regulatory principles into the heart of psychoanalytic theorizing and technique (see Davis & Dean, 2022).

7. It is polymorphously perverse because it trades in masochism (the diver visits the octopus despite freezing temperatures) and sadism (in an unusual spurt of "noninterventionism," he watches closely as the octopus gets amputated by a shark); it is obviously voyeuristic but also exhibitionistic (he offers us a peephole into how his body both touches and retracts from the slime and suction of the octopus's dermis on his body); the pleasures of the encounter are diffuse, nongenital, nonprocreative, dispersed across the entire cutaneous surface, and so on.

8. See Musser (2014) for an explication as to how such a lens relies on an oversimplified notion of agency.

9. When "impulse can no longer find preestablished security in forms or content," Adorno writes, we are forced to invent, "compelled to experiment" (1970, p. 23).

10. The Law here is not used in its juridicolegal sense but references a set of socially inscribed directives, deviation from which invites collective sanctions and generates anxiety.

11. This statement is less true of the work of Jacques Lacan, who was quite interested in the amplificatory effects of limits on desire.

12. Contrary to Lacan, Laplanche is concerned with the concrete, caretaking adult (1987), not the Other who inaugurates the symbolic order.

13. Laplanche is explicit that the processes he describes are not contingent on a biological tie between the caretaking adult and the infant, making his theory especially hospitable to queer use.

14. Laplanche initially used the problematic locution "enigmatic signifier" to discuss enigma. This introduced a confusion into the theory, that there was a message *in*

enigma, a signification that, while hidden, could be discovered. Later in his life, Laplanche became aware of this problematic interpretation and clarified, "when I speak of an enigmatic message, I speak of messages 'compromised' by the unconscious" (2003b, p. 205); "the compromising of the adult message . . . is not in any way a copy of the adult unconscious" (2003b, p. 208). The notion that enigma is a message that can be deciphered, as if solving a puzzle, remains the most common misunderstanding of Laplanche's theory.

15. Laplanche uses the term *sexuel*, which in French is a neologism. In English, it is italicized to distinguish the unconscious from the more ordinary "sexual," but I forgo this convention here for the sake of simplicity and just speak about the "infantile sexual."

16. It is worth asking if "failure" is a suitable term given that the failure to translate is an ontological condition, rather than a particular subject's misfire. It is only from the ego's perspective that we could justify the locution that translation "fails."

17. CN: Analysts are particularly susceptible to a hypertrophied focus on "understanding," and my hope is that Glissant's contribution helps demonstrate that "understanding" is not benign and that it may involve contorting patients to fit our existing "scales and taxonomies, and measuring accordingly" (Glissant 1990, p. 190). His emphasis that "understanding" may involve a move that is also appropriative underscores how we, as analysts, could lose sight of the unintelligibility, impenetrability, and confusion that our patients bring to us *not as a problem for them but as a problem for the analyst.* I stress this point not to universalize the claims that Glissant makes about "understanding," which are specifically sutured to the postcolonial—such a gesture, after all, would simply return us to the very problem of appropriation that he is trying to move us away from. What I want is to show how useful his work can be for analytic theory and praxis.

18. Byrne (2013) interestingly traces "Nietzsche's notion that Dionysian self-shattering characterizes sexuality in general" as foreshadowing Bersani's proposition about sexuality being founded on the self-shattering that follows the mounting tension between pleasure and unpleasure. The Dionysian aesthetic, she writes, "expresses the bliss of destruction and pain, causing [and here she is quoting Nietzsche from *Birth of Tragedy*], 'subjectivity to vanish to the point of complete self-forgetting' where 'all memories of personal experience dissolve'" (Byrne, 2013, p. 83).

19. Laplanche uses the term "assignment" to gender to emphasize the primacy of the other in this process (of gender-becoming); this is the case, he says, "whether the first assignment is the declaration at the town hall, at the church or in some other official place, a declaration involving the assignment of a first name, the assignment to a place in a kinship network, etc., or very often the assignment to membership in a religion" (2003a, p. 173). Though he speaks of "first assignment," he also stresses that this identification of our gender by the other is "ongoing," a process that occurs not in a singular moment but as an ongoing "bombardment of messages" (2003a, p. 173). Where psychoanalysis has historically been mostly preoccupied with the way we identify *with* others, Laplanche

prioritizes the way we are identified *by* others and how such identifications are themselves enigmatically laced.

20. Several authors, like de Beauvoir and Habermas, who read Sade and Bataille as lacking political engagement see Sade as unhelpful in theorizing political life. Chapter 5 examines claims that link Sade and his project to nihilism and fascism and pursues lineages of Sadean thought that open up other critical paths.

21. Limit experience and inner experience are not synonymous concepts. Following my discussion of Bataille (and inner experience), I retain the former term in this section for the sake of uniformity of referents. Devoted readers of Bataille's and Foucault's work will rightly object that there are considerable differences. For one, Foucault fixes the point of transgression at a different place than Bataille does—as for Foucault, transgression involves a movement beyond the way we are constituted as subjects by discourse, collapsing our historically contingent subjecthood, which has no "true" core or essence.

22. We might say, then, that while Sade returns us to animality as part of his critique of bourgeois society, Bataille embraces animality as part of what it means to be fully human. Whereas Sade represents the extreme of Kantian humanism, Bataille topples it.

23. Samuel Delany's writing is a particularly good illustration of work that rides the sexual drive not to jar or disturb (1973, 1974) but to unapologetically describe, instead, the plenitudes of the sexual.

24. CN: Theorists from distinct psychoanalytic traditions (e.g., Balint, 1968; Ferenczi, 1938; Loewald, 1980; Milner 1969) have written about uninterrupted belonging as a regressive movement akin to what can happen in patients in intensive psychoanalytic treatments. But the self's unraveling is not regression in the sense that it defaults the subject to an earlier developmental stage of psychic operations. Nor is it a developmental relapse to a stage that should have been outgrown, to a condition one should have matured out of, or to a traumatic state one can work through. When the ego shatters, the subject that comes undone is not collapsing into a prior level of psychic organization in linear time but finds themselves in non-time or, if you prefer, in elongated time, where their experience is most intense. That is, ego shattering is not a return to the past but, rather, a spiral movement that "return[s] regularly to the same points of the vertical" that, "if flattened to a single lane," looks like a circle (Laplanche, 1979, p. 197). In three-dimensional space, this is a helicoid movement, a revisiting of what is exigent but that also propels us forward—though toward what, one cannot know ahead of time. Chapter 4 addresses this in depth.

25. CN: This state may appear dissociative, but it is not necessarily so. Rather than a transient fragmentation or disconnect, I see it as issuing more from contacts with opacity, rather than the *lack* of contact with aspects of the self, which is the main feature of dissociation.

26. CN: In the clinical setting, such vivisecting justifiably worries artistically inclined patients, who are concerned that by being overexamined, it will drain their inspi-

ration. Patients whose sex lives are richly textured and vibrant similarly hesitate to discuss them in analysis, justifiably concerned that a hypertrophied emphasis on meaning can hobble their drive. Clinically, we would do well to respect these anxieties, rather than dismiss them as merely defensive. My hope is that psychoanalysts may find inspiration in this book for other ways in which to sit with such experiences in their patients without forfeiting their symbolic meanings.

27. Chapter 2 tracks the way these "appearances" become dramatized within the analytic relationship.

CHAPTER 2. THE DRAW TO OVERWHELM

1. As psychoanalysts, our data set usually comes from analytic treatments. Observations from everyday life are more unusual, but they can also serve as helpful springboards for theorizing mental phenomena. Freud's description of the reel game and his theorizing of fort/da (1920) is a paradigmatic example. To protect this particular dyad's privacy, I have distorted identifying information and, as with the clinical cases, have changed both names.

2. As a reminder, throughout this book, I use the terms "perversity" and "perversion" not as a marker of pathological sexuality but in their original analytic meaning, to denote sexuality that is polymorphous, has exchangeable objects, is fragmenting, and is not organized reproductively or heterogenitally (Freud 1905b; Van Haute & Westerink 2016).

3. Queer of color critique offers many helpful conceptual tools with which to think about these distinctions, including suggestions by Cruz (2016), Musser (2014), Nash (2014), Rodríguez (2014), and D. Scott (2010). My suggestions here are broadly informed by these works but take a psychoanalytically informed direction. Their focus takes center stage in chapters 3 and 4.

4. We may remember my patient Mia from the introduction, who, feeling that I "screwed" her, could only see working with me as submitting to my will—and my fee. Let us also recall her inventive solution that we would be working together against her consent, which permitted us both to "surrender" to each other so that we could begin an analysis.

5. For this concept in relation to Levinas, see Scarfone (2015b).

6. Part of my project is to draw a distinction between different forms of sadism (normative, sensible, destructive, and exigent) and, more importantly, to break apart exigent sadism from the sadomasochistic complex.

7. Medical experimentation in the concentration camps and on populations of color whose consent was not informed are prime examples of this (see, for example, Snorton, 2017).

8. Consent—as in when it comes up, who can grant it and under what circumstances, who should be asking for it and how, when it can be treated as valid versus coerced, how it is reliably communicated, etc.—has been hotly debated throughout the history of feminisms and especially during the "Sex Wars" (see Duggan & Hunter, 2006; Duggan, 2021).

9. For more in-depth discussion, see DePereira, Messina, & Sansalone (2012); Gentile (2015); Saketopoulou (2011a).

10. CN: The possibility of the adult's infantile sexuality becoming inflamed is especially likely when involving a child because, as we have seen, the adult's exposure to the child's radical helplessness agitates the adult's sexual unconscious.

11. Hegel (1807/1977) made this argument in his exploration of the Master/Slave (Lord/Bondsman) dialectic. Jessica Benjamin (1988) offered an analytically informed adaptation of Hegelian sublation that has magnetized psychoanalytic theorizing (2004). Gayle Salamon (2016) has incisively critiqued these elements specifically in Benjamin's engagement with *The Story of O*.

12. CN: This parallel deserves a separate exploration, but I can only address now how I think it relates to limit consent. Also, while I emphasize the parallels, there are important differences that should be mentioned: in the earlier example, the patient is an adult, while Lumi is a child; the cognitive capacity, embodied experiences, and psychic makeup of an adult create landscapes vastly different from the child's relating to a parental figure; and so on.

13. I am not saying this to infantilize patients but because clinical experience shows that what occurs in the consulting room, even as early as the first session, can arouse forces and replay dynamics that could not have been anticipated ahead of time.

14. For an in-depth discussion of the ethics of what the analyst can and must disclose at the beginning of a treatment without compromising its scaffolding, see Saks and Golshan (2013).

15. From a rhetorical perspective, it can appear paradoxical that Freud started first with the sexual aberrations and theorized their foundations thereafter.

16. See the section "Jean Laplanche: The Fundamental Anthropological Situation" in chapter 1.

17. It is telling in this regard that Freud never posited a separate energy source for the death drive, as an analogue to the sexual drive's libido. It was Edoardo Weiss (1934) who first proposed the idea of *destrudo* as the death drive's correlative to the libidinal energy reserves of the life drive. Freud, to the contrary, continued to flounder trying to demonstrate that the libido's variable transformations propelled the death drive.

18. CN: In the third section of this chapter, I explore the technical implication of this point and note how the analyst's anxiety at such moments might spur them to interject questions or interpretations that disrupt the patient's move toward overwhelm. This can also happen when the analyst dials things back by recoiling too early from difficult material, lest it overwhelm the patient.

19. CN: At such moments, what analytic treatment can offer are the conditions for freed-up enigma to become restitched into new translations rather than to become repressed. To an analysand, the forging of new translations can be a transformative experience, offering the mobility of novel psychic configurations.

20. Privacy considerations prevent me from sharing more information about Isabela's race and ethnicity, as well as other important aspects of her identity.

21. The reader might remember that Adam had described an experience of this sort as well, and Megan Rundel (2015) offers a similar clinical description. For hypotheses on these overlaps between Adam, Isabela, and Rundel's patient, see Saketopoulou (2015).

22. For such work on the intergenerational transmission of trauma, see Atlas (2021).

23. This, at best, can only be asymptotic; one can never *durably* get out from under these forces. (Chapter 4 discusses self-sovereignty as offering short-lived escape from under them).

CHAPTER 3. RISKING SEXUALITY BEYOND CONSENT

1. I am playing here with Stockton's felicitous description of the queer child as growing up sideways (2009).

2. On most Sundays throughout the play's two Broadway runs, the production held open-ended conversations between members of the cast/production and anyone interested in attending them. While new people joined the conversation at each meeting, a self-selected core group of theatergoers soon emerged who returned to the space week after week to process some of the most bracing parts of the play with the cast and production team—and with each other.

3. CN: To clarify, the notion of the "primal" does not refer to what comes chronologically first. Laplanche underlines that the primal "is present from the beginning, concretely, at the origin of the human being, in other words: in the nursling." It most centrally refers to "what is ineluctable, what is truly independent of all contingencies, even the most general. . . The primal situation is the confrontation of the newborn—of the infant, the infans in the etymological sense of the term: the one who does not yet speak—with the adult world" (1987, pp. 101–102).

4. Consider as an example a person who identifies as a butch woman and for whom the proliferation of trans discourses enables new translations of their gender experience. Let us imagine that this person comes to see themselves as trans. This new translation ("I am trans") can retroactively reveal the original translation of their gender (the original "I am a butch woman") as the effect of primary violence, since it was shaped through the translational restriction of binary gender (Laplanche and Aulagnier). Some trans subjects may thus only retroactively come to experience the initial mandate that they arrange themselves into a neat male/female classificatory divide as traumatic [this has implications for a critique of the category of rapid-onset gender dysphoria, for the problematic notion of "core gender identity" and for de-transitioning that I cannot go into here but see Saketopoulou (2018b, 2020) and Hansbury and Saketopoulou (forthcoming)]. This is different from having always experienced oneself as trans and being pained about having had to present as cis all along, in that, the injunction to normative gender may *become traumatic after discursive shifts have occurred*, that is, only after—and because of—the encounter with enlarged possibilities afforded by new translational codes. And it it is only then that the original translational tools are revealed as having exerted a violence, that is experienced as traumatic only in the après-coup.

5. CN: We know, of course, that that can also occur, e.g., when the caretaker suffers from pathology or is traumatized. In this case, we would be closer to what Aulagnier described as "secondary violence," and to what Laplanche called "intromission." Secondary violence and intromission are traumatic because they impose meaning, prohibiting the infant from carrying out its independent, creative meaning-making work.

6. Exploring this point in depth would take us too far afield. Briefly, subcultural life can offer expansive possibilities for nonnormative subjects—not only by providing support and validation for minoritized subjects but, as importantly, by offering a collective infrastructure of alternative discourses that may, in turn, become its own translational funnel yielding translations that better fit the subject's being (Saketopoulou, 2017a).

7. In that respect, while for Laplanche, it is the term "intromission" that denotes violence insofar as intromission imposes meaning (1987), I maintain that, of the two, it is actually *implantation* that is more durably traumatic. This is because implantation is an ordinary, routine, and noncontingent occurrence. Intromission has a chance of being identified as being of foreign origin, as having infiltrated us from the outside, whereas implantations, because they are constitutive to the sense of "being" or "having" a self, can never be marked as having invaded the subject from without. The implications of this claim are fleshed out in chapter 4.

8. Depending on the circumstances, the absence of consent may not be equivalent to the violation of one's consent.

9. We know (and Freud probably did too) that the *Project's* neurological models are mistaken. Nevertheless, the insights yielded in the *Project* were reworked in *The Interpretation of Dreams*, where, disaggregated from biology, they became foundational to Freudian metapsychology.

10. CN: For example, the ego's disinvestment of its representations may lead to depersonalization (de M'Uzan, 2013). I do not linger in those clinical dangers as much in this volume, but see Hansbury (2017) for a powerful clinical example handled with great sensitivity made possible *because* of how Hansbury avails himself of subcultural translational tools circulating in queer communities.

11. I am grateful to Dominique Scarfone for alerting me to this passage and to Jonathan House for generously sharing with me the original French text, which has yet to appear in English.

12. CN: I do not have space here to explain my selective use of her concept of the anarchic, which Zaltzman conceived as a drive unto itself but which I see as more related to Laplanche's sexual drives of life and death (1984a, 1995).

13. Antonino Ferro (2005) and Maria Grazia Oldoini (2019) have also used the term traumatophilia but with a different emphasis to describe the attraction to trauma's repair and redress. I am granting here a more enlarged scope to traumatophilia in that I see it as working to enliven overly rigid ego structures, instead of repairing trauma.

14. There are significant implications for thinking about trigger warnings here and what it is we do, or are asking others to do, in shielding us from wounding. Exploring this is beyond the scope of this volume, but see Saketopoulou (2014).

15. It is one of Whiteness's operations to understand everything as self-referential, as, for example, in Jessica Derschowitz's treatment of the play (2019). Nevertheless, this play is not aimed at educating White people, even as many White people have been educated by it. This lack of address is not specific to *Slave Play*; it is the domain of aesthetic experience overall. While the artist may have an imaginary interlocutor in mind, the work is not intended *for* them (Lyotard, 2002). Just like the infant perceives enigma as a message addressed to them, it is we, the audience, who imagine that a performance is crafted for our benefit or should be.

16. See Frank, Romano, & Grady (2019) and MacDonald (2019) for exceptions.

17. All quotes from *Slave Play* are based on the first edition of the *Slave Play* script from the New York Theatre Workshop production, unless explicitly noted otherwise.

18. The stereotyped implication that Black men are well-hung and the historical fact that Black men were hung from trees as part of the envy stirred by that very fantasy (Poulson-Bryant, 2005) highlight the imbrication of racialized violence's brutality with the erotic. Being reduced to a part object can feel offensive and injurious. And because, as discussed in chapter 1, part objects are the purview of the infantile sexual, it can also be an erotic elixir, arousing enthralling appetites (Dimen, 2017).

19. I have given a lot of thought to the ethical issues that arise as I, a person who is neither Black- nor POC-identified, think with these complex materials and as I work in this volume with words that have been, and in most contexts continue to be, offensive, violent, and painful. The n* word is a word with a searing history. Its evocation will, no doubt, have different effects on differently racialized readers. To soften this effect as much as I can without turning away from the material and, also, to mark my own location, I have decided on the following convention: where I quote the work or words of others, I preserve their wording as it appears in the original text or as it was said to me. Where I reference someone else's use of the word in my own voice (i.e., when I am not quoting), I use "n*" instead of spelling out the word. If I were to be reading this text out loud, I would be choosing to say "n* word" throughout; that is, I would not enunciate the word even when quoting someone else. In that instance, some of the distinctions I am trying to draw— between others' words and my own—would, in a spoken text, require constant and ongoing clarification. I might say, for instance, something like, "Harris's text spells out the n* word fully, but I won't say it out loud." This no doubt is an imperfect solution, at the very least because it reproduces to some degree the racial dynamics I am also laboring to flesh out in this volume. There may be better ways to handle this that I have not conceived of. To some degree, this endnote, as well as the issues that the use of the word raises in the first place, also reflect the difficult juncture that US politics—and US psychoanalysis—are at in this particular

historical moment. Said differently, talking about race, racism, and racialization has to involve a willingness to let oneself become immersed in the messiness of social relations and to find oneself in the "shitty place" that Powell (2020) invokes in her work on interracial encounters. This is especially important for those of us who are not Black- or POC-identified and for whom it is easier to avoid getting one's hands dirty. For me, the decision not to side with safety but to take the risk of speaking about these difficult matters even as I know that I may get it wrong is a matter of psychoanalytic ethics, especially so at a time when psychoanalysis is so anxiously struggling to "get it right" when it comes to race. In this sense, White analysts' worry about "getting it right" can get in the way of the very work that psychoanalysis (and psychoanalytic institutions) *need* to be doing.

20. Intending to make an intervention in thinking about colorism, *Slave Play* includes two White-passing partners; one of the two cotherapists turns out to be Latina, and one of the two men in the gay couple is of non-White heritage, though the specifics are deliberately kept vague. On the one hand, the play seeks to center the experience of Black people, on the basis of the particular history of slavery in this country. On the other, however, it can also be read as flattening the experience of non-Black people of color into White adjacency, overlooking the complex histories of colonial oppression and discrimination that non-Black people of color suffer (Sunday discussions, January 16, 2022). Nor do all Black people share a history of slavery. As such, while any Black person can be subject to police brutality, discrimination, and dehumanization, slavery is centered as the master signifier, ignoring how colonial logics have also wielded traumatic impacts.

21. While this was true of the first Broadway production, when the play returned to Broadway for the second run, audiences seem to have been more "prepared." At the Los Angeles production in 2022, where audiences were again newly exposed to the play, theatergoers also got up and left the play during the first act.

22. The implication that the therapeutic endeavor is itself littered with the logics of White supremacy are not very fleshed out in the dialogic exchange, but they are dramatized through the interactions among the therapists and the patients. Psychoanalysts are still struggling with these ideas in our literature (Holmes, 2019; Powell, 2018). Lara Sheehi and Stephen Sheehi's work on "psychoanalytic innocence" trenchantly illuminates these problems (2021).

23. In fact, while desexualization appears in the play only in the second act, the reception of the play was incredibly split on this point. In the Sunday salons, attendees often seemed dumbfounded when the play was described as pornographic. Students in my classes are continuously met with surprise when they mention to friends and colleagues that they are reading *Slave Play* as part of a psychoanalytic course on psychosexuality as opposed to, say, on "cultural competence." Many theatergoers, it seemed, would rather think that their enjoyment of *Slave Play* obtained from the play calling out White people on their racism. Of course, holding onto this desexualized framework requires doing considerable scotomizing work: the play traffics in graphic sexual acts; there is nudity; a huge black dildo is bran-

dished onstage; an actor wears a corset and high-heeled leather boots; there is a sensuous boot-licking scene; there are orgasms; safe words are used; BDSM sex is negotiated; a couple meets on FetLife. Harris has repeatedly acknowledged the role of BDSM theory in his work (e.g., when asked about it at a town hall at the Black National Theatre), and the full mirror that literally forms the play's scenic backdrop is inspired by porn (Sunday discussions, January 5, 2020). The sexual dimension was, of course, not lost on those who objected to and protested the play; for them, it was precisely the mingling of the erotic with slavery's iconographies that made the play offensive.

24. In the *Underground Railroad Game*, a play negotiating similar themes as *Slave Play*, the playwright Jennifer Kidwell describes such inhibitions as follows: "Most of the time around white men I can feel their assholes just tighten up. Like this little nervous fear that if they're not careful, they're going to slide right back into history and start ordering me around or asking me to clean their house" (Fisher Center at Bard, 2019).

25. While *Slave Play* was playing on Broadway, Harris wrote, produced, and performed in a new play under the handle @GaryXXXFisher. That play, *Black Exhibition*, turned the heat even higher than *Slave Play* and included Harris reading excerpts from Gary Fisher's work.

26. This line of thinking comes into unavoidable tension with some of the main premises of Afropessimism's insistence that the Black subject has never been part of the human and that the very fact of the Black person's exclusion from the human helps set up the White subject's always already humanization (Wilderson, 2020). The question that Fisher raises, however, is less about whether the Black subject is included or excluded from the category of the human and more about how the very category of humanization is itself restrictively imagined to begin with: as being organized through dignity, not abjection, through respect and not the pleasures of humiliation.

27. We may recall here my encounter with Mia. Initially, neither of us "recognized" her reality in the other: for me, Mia was being somewhat unreasonable; for her, I had screwed her.

28. Mollena Williams, a Black woman and prominent race-play activist, explains that what underwrites these arguments is the worry that open discussion—or depiction—of such sexual desires will function as "a gateway drug for racism" (2009a): "because, then, of course, ALL white people will feel ALL POC are fair game" (2009c). But, she adds sardonically, "the thing is this: ignorant fuckers have been doing inappropriate shit for YEARS" (2009c).

29. In an interview, the actor playing Gary, Ato Blankson-Wood, has described undergoing a personal transformation process alongside his character during the play's run. See endnotes 9 and 12 in chapter 4.

30. Agency that is unconstrained by trauma is impossible for *any* subject since the unconscious is constituted *through* trauma (implantation). This is more pronounced for subjects who have toiled through historical and structural trauma.

Musser has aptly called fantasies of liberal agency, "white fantasies" to mark how they are always already racialized (2016). Chapter 4 explores in more depth how Whiteness builds its density around imagining itself as untraumatized and as capable of unconstrained agency.

31. What Harris describes as versatility is also what some Black women have found to be the most offensive aspects of the play (e.g., Pinkins, 2021). But as Robert O'Hara and Antoinette Crowe-Legacy comment, people concerned about Black women and what the play did to them have not bothered to ask the Black women in the play. "Kaneisha is fucked up. She is a fully fucked-up individual," Crowe-Legacy explains, "and it's glorious to see that and know that you can be Black, be a woman, and be fucked up! And see yourself in all of its fucked-upness in front of your face" (Sunday discussions, March 11, 2022).

32. In an interview with Michaela Coel, the writer, producer, and protagonist of the show *I May Destroy You*, Harris addresses concerns around putting in circulation difficult stories. "One of the reasons I write the way I do," he says, "is because I don't think Black authors have been historically allowed to make people uncomfortable." Coel, whose own work also tackles thorny matters around race, gender, and sexuality, responds, "We [Black people] deserve to be made uncomfortable, too, and that discomfort is so raw and so outrageous. The audience should be allowed to feel those things. We shouldn't make work that simply panders to whatever the political norm is right now" (Coel, 2020). Harris and Coel argue that Black artists have historically been constrained from raising urgent but politically inexpedient questions for fear that their work imperiled the way Black people were regarded, compromising the narratives of racial uplift or progress that have been felt to be necessary to counter negative racial stereotypes (see Musser, 2014; and Nash, 2014, for in-depth explorations of these ideas). The problem is that there are so few genres of Black stories available to White audiences that each one has to carry the responsibility for them all. This is what Viet Thanh Nguyen calls "narrative scarcity," the opposite of "narrative plenitude" (2018).

33. CN: This is what Scarfone (2015b) calls the "unpast."

CHAPTER 4. TOWARD A THEORY OF TRAUMATOPHILIA

1. Traumatophobia, I want to be clear, is not bad or dismissible; different people need to orient their attention toward different things in their lives and are prepared for different sets of explorations at different times. In making my intervention regarding traumatophilia, I do not want to diminish that; what I want to do is highlight the impossibility of eliminating the imprint of psychic trauma and to emphasize that traumatophilia is *a way of relating to trauma*.

2. Psychoanalysis, as Ann Pellegrini has argued, operates not outside but under the auspices of precisely such economies (2021).

3. See Nasheed (2018); Owens (2022); and Change.org (n.d.).

4. An interesting detail is worth drawing attention to. In the first production of the play at the New York Theatre Workshop in downtown Manhattan, Kaneisha

protests Jim's tepid participation in the sexual scenario with these lines: "The fact that . . . The minute I express what I need from him. How I need it. He shut down. Made a half step . . . Even after all the prep on Day Two and Day Three . . . He—I—made a fool of myself . . ." (Harris, 2018, p. 74). The script was minutely revised for the Broadway production. That particular passage newly reads, "Even after all the prep on Day Two and Day Three . . . *the flash cards, the vocabulary words, those fucking movies!* He—I—made a fool of myself . . ." (Harris, 2019, p. 86; emphasis added to highlight the changes, ellipses in original). This addition accentuates how rigorously the Black partners applied themselves to prepare the White and White-passing partners to participate in the erotic slave scenes with historical verisimilitude.

5. "When I heard about this play *Slave Play*," Tonya Pinkins describes, "I was like, 'Yeah, I am not goin' to see that. That is going to upset me . . . [I went out of] respect for [my intern who recommended it] . . . and as soon as it started, I was like, 'OMG, Jeremy is writing my life! How does he know my personal life?' . . . Not everyone liked [the play]. Some young queer people told me they felt traumatized by it. . . I think that the truth is always polarizing. . . There is going to be people who love and people who hate it, and for me, that's honestly the test of the truth." In the same conversation, a Black woman from the audience comments, "So often on Broadway, shows are windows, rather than mirrors, for me, so the extent to which I was able to see myself in the show was so magical" (BUILD Series, 2019). Similarly, Sullivan Jones, a biracial man who played Phillip in the first Broadway production, described how the play helped him reflect on his romantic relationship, "A lot of questions that were raised for me were, What is the public presentation of being with a person of a different race? So in your private relationship, it's one thing, right? . . . But when you walk out of the house and all of a sudden it's you and as a six foot four Black man and a White person next to you, what does that mean in midtown, versus what it means in Bed-Stuy, versus what it means in Connecticut, etc., etc.? I live in Bed-Stuy . . . and it's a predominantly Black neighborhood, and when I walk through Bed-Stuy with a White person, I feel—I felt—I feel a certain amount of shame. Because there is a history of brothers who, as soon as they get successful, they date White women, and we can talk about whether that's real or true or not. . . But I would be in Bed-Stuy and sort of be with my White lady and be like, 'Fuck, I'm *that* dude.' And feeling shame about that. And seeing the looks in people's faces, particularly Black women in the neighborhood being like, 'This nigger, man, is out here with a White woman?' And having to wrestle with that. And what the play did for me. . . what it made me do, the conclusion I came to was, only you as an individual knows what saves your life, if it's the music you listen to, the food you like, the people that you are with. And this person, I decided, is the kind of person who is saving my life, is a source of salvation for me. And if people can't handle that, be they White or Black, then that's their problem. So, when I walk down the street now, when I am with my lady and I am in front of Black people, I can absorb that, whatever's coming from them. I

acknowledge it and I absorb it, but I also say, 'This is my truth. I am happy about it, and I am living my life . . . So the play made me double down on that, which is crazy because you would almost think it would take you in an opposite direction" (Talks at Google, 2020).

6. Roundtable discussion on *Slave Play*, Black National Theatre, Harlem, NY, December 9, 2019.

7. We do not know if her scratching him is excited engagement or the beginning of her saying no. Because we read that moment in the aftermath of what comes next (her pushing him off), it is easy to retroactively interpret it as the beginning of her withdrawing her consent. But this may or may not be what is happening for Kaneisha in real time.

8. In an interview with Samuel Delany, Harris admits that one of his goals "was to make people feel turned on in the theater again. But also to have them be confused about why they were turned on" (Fernandez, 2020).

9. In response to Kaneisha's monologue about the ancestors, Ashley Ray tweeted, "My elders, my ancestors did not 'lay' with demons. They were forced by demons, raped by demons, hurt by demons, some of them were children, little girls who had everything taken from them by demons in a way i can never experience having consensual sex with a white person" (Owens, 2022). But, as we saw in mike bond's words in chapter 3, the question of whether the ancestors need to give their blessing for race play to proceed is by no means settled. Asked about this, Mollena Williams sharply retorts, "I have spoken with the ancestors, they are delighted that I can FUCKING CHOOSE to do [race play] for a few bloody hours" (2009a).

10. Affirmative consent is too unrefined a conceptual tool when it comes to desires that have arisen through the very denial of personhood. Harris prods us to see that neither the assent of the Black partners' "yes" nor the refusal of Jim's "no" can be taken at their word. Sexuality, to be considered appropriate, Amber Musser writes, is expected to go "hand in hand with liberal subjectivity. . . Autonomy and agency are integral to having an appropriate sexuality" (2016, p. 156). But, although autonomy and agency may be the hard-earned outcomes of projects of self-actualization for White people, for Black people, embarking on such projects involves having to first wrest autonomy and agency out of the hands of White supremacy, to gear up self-definitions that answer to one's own coordinates. Affirmative consent, once again, is shown to be inapposite when it comes to the erotic lives of people whose freedoms were, and continue to be, curtailed. The consent models we are currently urged to adopt may be too whitewashed to help our thinking (Musser, 2016).

11. That laughter is also where some Black audiences' difficulty with the play arose; see A. Harris (2019).

12. The charge that *Slave Play* pandered to White people never felt true to me. In the course of my engagement with the play and following critical responses to it, I have heard many Black and BIPOC people rave about the play's impact on them, and the members of the cast themselves have also been vocal on this. Chalia LaTour,

who played Tea, one of the therapists, expressed this: "I am a fair-skinned Black woman, and in my family, this skin tone isn't by way of any purposeful interracial partnership; this is by way of generations of slavery and children who've been abandoned, and that's how I get my skin tone. And a lot of my family does not talk about the 'why' of this color. And I know through this play that it's given me the opportunity to break down these arguments, questions, and confusions, to where I sit in the diaspora, with so much lack of history or connection, like who means family and who doesn't. I know that there are conversations that I've had with my mother, who is much fairer than I am, who has never talked to me about her experience with race in any real depth until she saw this play. And then she could tell me, 'No, in high school I felt like Philip, and at this point I felt, like Kaneisha, and here I felt like Dustin, and I think I was Patricia here . . . And that's been a huge gift for me, realizing how many of us are still trying to find context to speak about ourselves and each other, and that's going to take time, and the offering up of so many examples." The actor Ato Blankson-Wood, who played Gary, describes that "at the time I first encountered Gary, I did not see myself as prized. I didn't feel prized by the world around me. And I didn't prize myself. And I think that that was a huge challenge, that I had been walking through the world devaluing myself, buying into a lot of ideas that White supremacy projects at Black people, like especially Black queer people. . . I feel that saying that line ["No motherfucker, *I* am the prize!"] every night has been like me healing myself, casting this spell on myself, reminding myself that I have value, real value, and that, no matter what is projected at me, that value comes from within. And that's just something I am going to walk away from this experience with" (Talks at Google, 2020). For Antoinette Crowe-Legacy, *Slave Play* "felt so deeply and irrevocably true": "It felt like my therapy, like, 'we may be wrong, but we will *try*' . . . I *needed* this play. . . I felt I could see myself in it" (Sunday discussions, December 19, 2021).

13. CN: In using the term "microdosing," I am not implying that traumatophilia is a psychic protocol or that traumatophilia can be executed as a method. This microdosing has to come from the subject; it is not something the other implements.

14. CN: The expression "come into contact" is imprecise: one is never really in direct, unmediated contact with the drive. It makes more sense actually to think of it not as contact but as a contact zone. This description is consistent with a psychoanalytic estimation of what it might be like to find oneself in the proximity of the bare drive—a "proximity," as the drive can only be approached asymptotically/obliquely (Laplanche, 1984).

15. In "The Solar Anus," Bataille (1931/1985b) speaks to the luminosity of sovereign experience, likening it to the blinding impact of the sun. He encourages us not to turn away from the intensities that aesthetic experience can call forth in us but, instead, to make ourselves passible to their heliotropic tug. When we do not refuse such radiant exposures but let ourselves be carried—and carried away—by them, when they are turned into a taste, we stand to come into an encounter with the limits of ourselves.

16. The piece thus defangs the strangeness of Williams-Haas's and Haas's challenging sexualities. This avoidance rhymes too well with what Muriel Dimen (2003), André Green (1995), and Tim Dean (2009) have noted regarding the arc of psychoanalytic theorizing around sexuality—a move from the heat of the psychosexual to the cooled-off domain of object relations that we discussed in depth in chapter 1. Such a move also diverts us from the sadomasochistic properties of the sexual drive and its annexations of trauma to the yardstick of socially acceptable and productive sublimations.

17. For mike bond, "a white woman [has] to like you first before [she will] beat you or call you racial names" (Hernandez, 2004). Chapter 5 takes up this paradoxical requirement, that one would have to "like" someone to dominate them.

CHAPTER 5. EXIGENT SADISM

1. This chapter continues the discussion of the documentary *The Artist and the Pervert* from chapter 4, which chronicles some aspects of the BDSM Master/slave relationship between Mollena Williams and Georg Haas. By the time of the documentary, Williams uses her married name Williams-Haas. I retain "Williams" when referencing work of hers (publications, interviews, etc.) completed before her name change.

2. The work, titled *Hyena*, is composed by Haas and tells of Williams-Haas's struggle with alcoholism. It has since been completed and received critical acclaim.

3. In *Slave Play*, we see the measure of care in Harris's exigent sadism in the curating of shared conversational spaces for audiences to think about the play and its emotional impact and, also, in the placing of therapists in New York Theater Workshop's lobby, where *Slave Play* was first produced, so that theatergoers who felt triggered could get emotional support. His goal, Harris explains, was to disturb but also to "take care of people. . . to create spaces of care around [the] audience" (Tang, 2019).

4. CN: This thinking has serious implications for how we practice psychoanalysis. For the psychoanalyst Humphrey Morris, the stakes of whether we see power in the consulting room as real or simulated are ethical: "For me, an ethics of psychoanalysis begins in an acknowledgment of the way we can slip into pretending to ourselves that analysis is somehow pretend, pretending to ourselves that what happens in analysis is fundamentally in some way not real. . . Let's be honest: . . . analysis is not as-if life, not a pretend or metaphorical or virtual version of some other life. . . [It is] a practice of living. . . [not] some kind of rehearsal" (2016, p. 1175).

5. All of these points have already been discussed at length in chapters 3 and 4, and as such I do not repeat them here.

6. This is different with film than it is with theater, in which the audience's embodied presence "fills" the room, having a reciprocal effect on actors and thus also the action unfolding on the stage.

7. I leave aside an in-depth exploration of whether it is a search for purity versus the libidinal excitements of power that animated the energies put into the Shoah.

8. I am using my colleague's comment and real name with her permission.

9. "Larisa" is a pseudonym chosen by the analyst herself, when granting me permission to quote her.

REFERENCES

Adorno, T. W. (1965). *Lectures on Negative Dialectics*. Cambridge, UK: Polity.

Adorno, T. W. (1966). *Negative Dialectics*. New York: Continuum.

Adorno, T. W. (1970). *Aesthetic Theory*. Minneapolis: University of Minnesota Press.

Ahmed, S. (2004). Affective economies. *Social Text*, 22(2), 117–139.

Allison, D. (1992). *Bastard out of Carolina: A Novel*. New York: Plume.

Anonymous. (2017). *The Incest Diary*. New York: Farrar, Straus and Giroux.

Archard, D. (1995). *Sexual Consent*. Boulder, CO: Westview.

Atlas, G. (2021). *Emotional Inheritance: A Therapist, Her Patients, and the Legacy of Trauma*. New York: Little, Brown.

Aulagnier, P. (1975). *The Violence of Interpretation: From Pictogram to Statement*. London: Routledge.

Bach, S. (1994). *Narcissistic States and the Therapeutic Process*. New York: Aronson.

Balint, M. (1968). *The Basic Fault: Therapeutic Aspects of Regression*. London: Brunner/Mazel.

Barber, D. (2017, September 18). On Black negativity, or the affirmation of nothing: Jared Sexton, interviewed by Daniel Barber. *Society + Space*. www.societyandspace.org.

Barthes, R. (1975). *Pleasure of the Text*. New York: Hill and Wang.

Bataille, G. (1928). *Story of the Eye*. San Francisco: City Lights.

Bataille, G. (1934). Abjection and miserable forms. In S. Lotringer (Ed.), *More & Less* (pp. 87–101). Los Angeles: Semiotext(e).

Bataille, G. (1954). *Inner Experience*. Albany: State University of New York Press.

Bataille, G. (1956). *My Mother, Madame Edwarda, The Dead Man*. New York: Marion-Boyars.

Bataille, G. (1957). *Erotism: Death and Sexuality*. San Francisco: City Lights.

Bataille, G. (1973). *Literature and Evil*. London: Calder and Boyars.

Bataille, G. (1976). *The Accursed Share: An Essay on General Economy, Volumes 2–3*. New York: Zone Books.

Bataille, G. (1985a). Formless. In *Visions of Excess: Selected Writings, 1929–1937* (pp. 31–32). Minneapolis: University of Minnesota Press. (Original work published 1929)

Bataille, G. (1985b). The solar anus. In *Visions of Excess: Selected Writings, 1929–1937* (pp. 5–9). Minneapolis: University of Minnesota Press. (Original work published 1931)

Benjamin, J. (1988). *The Bonds of Love: Psychoanalysis, Feminism, and the Problem of Domination*. New York: Pantheon Books.

Benjamin, J. (2004). Beyond doer and done to: An intersubjective view of thirdness. *Psychoanalytic Quarterly*, 73, 5–46.

Benjamin, J., & Atlas, G. (2015). The "too muchness" of excitement: Sexuality in light of excess, attachment and affect regulation. *International Journal of Psychoanalysis*, 96, 39–63.

Berlant, L., & Edelman, L. (2014). *Sex, or the Unbearable*. Durham, NC: Duke University Press.

Bersani, L. (1986). *The Freudian Body: Psychoanalysis and Art*. New York: Columbia University Press.

Bersani, L. (1987). Is the rectum a grave? *AIDS: Cultural Analysis / Cultural Activism*, 43, 197–222.

Bion, W. R. (1970). *Attention and Interpretation*. London: Karnac Books.

Blanchot, M. (1969). *The Infinite Conversation: Theory and History of Literature*. Minneapolis: University of Minnesota Press.

Blanchot, M. (1980). *The Writing of Disaster*. Chicago: University of Chicago Press.

Blechner, M. (2009). *Sex Changes: Transformations in Society and Psychoanalysis*. New York: Routledge.

Booth, P. (2018). Waves of fandom in the fan studies classroom. In K. A. Howell (Ed.), *Fandom as Classroom Practice* (pp. 113–125). Iowa City: University of Iowa Press.

Brabender, V. (2008). Sociopathy and groups: Insights from the film *The Night Porter*. *International Journal of Group Psychotherapy*, 58(3), 297–301.

Brown, J. A. (2016, February 4). Decades: An interview with Georg Friedrich Haas. *Van*. https://van-magazine.com.

BUILD Series. (2019, October 18). The castmates of "Slave Play" have a conversation about the profound Broadway play. YouTube. www.youtube.com/watch?v=axclVxCoyMI.

Butler, J. (2005). *Giving an Account of Oneself*. New York: Fordham University Press.

Butler, J. (2011). Sexual consent: Some thoughts on psychoanalysis and law. *Columbia Journal of Gender & Law*, 21(2), 3–11.

Byrne, R. (2013). *Aesthetic Sexuality: A Literary History of Sadomasochism*. New York: Bloomsbury.

Byrne, R. (2015). Sadistic aestheticism: Walter Pater and Octave Mirbeau. *Criticism*, 57(3), 403–429.

Califia, P. (1988). *Macho Sluts*. Los Angeles: Alyson Books.

Califia, P. (1996). Feminism and sadomasochism. In S. Scott & S. Jackson (Eds.), *Feminism and Sexuality: A Reader* (pp. 230–237). Edinburgh: Edinburgh University Press.

Carson, A. (1986). *Eros, the Bittersweet*. Princeton, NJ: Princeton University Press.

Carter, A. (1978). *The Sadeian Woman and the Ideology of Pornography*. New York: Pantheon Books.

Celenza, A. (2000). Sadomasochistic relating: What's sex got to do with it? *Psychoanalytic Quarterly*, 69, 527–543.

Chambers-Letson, J. (2020). The body is never given, nor do we actually see it. In S. D. Colbert, D. A. Jones, & S. Vogel (Eds.), *Race and Performance after Repetition* (pp. 270–289). Durham, NC: Duke University Press.

Change.org. (n.d.). Shutdown Slave Play. www.change.org.

Chetrit-Vatine, V. (2014). *The Ethical Seduction of the Analytic Situation: The Feminine-Maternal Origins of Responsibility for the Other*. London: Karnac.

Chude-Sokei, L., Cruz, A., Musser, A. J., Nash, J. C., Stallings, L. H., & Wachter-Grene, K. (2016). Race, pornography and desire: A TBS Roundtable. *The Black Scholar*, 46(4), 49–64.

Cimatti, F. (2016). From the message to the image: How to come out of the enigma. In C. Dejours & F. Votadoro (Eds.), *La séduction à l'origine: L'oeuvre de Jean Laplanche* (pp. 201–225). Paris: PUF.

Civitarese, G. (2013). The inaccessible unconscious and reverie as a path of figurability. In H. B. Levine, G. S. Reed, & D. Scarfone (Eds.), *Unrepresented States and the Construction of Meaning: Clinical and Theoretical Contributions* (pp. 220–239). London: Karnac Books.

Clare, E. (2015). *Exile and Pride: Disability, Queerness, and Liberation*. Durham, NC: Duke University Press.

Cobb, J. (2022, January 23). Saw the *Slave Play* last night. Consulting my *lawyers* first thing tomorrow morning. Twitter [deleted]. https://twitter.com/jelani9?ref_src=twsrc%5Egoogle%7Ctwcamp%5Eserp%7Ctwgr%5Eauthor.

Coel, M. (2020, November 18). Michaela Coel is not afraid to make you uncomfortable. *W*. www.wmagazine.com.

Colbert, S. D., Jones, D. A., & Vogel, S. (2020). Introduction: Tidying up after repetition. In S. D. Colbert, D. A. Jones, & S. Vogel (Eds.), *Race and Performance after Repetition* (pp. 1–27). Durham, NC: Duke University Press.

Collins, P. H. (2000). *Black Feminist Thought: Knowledge, Consciousness, and the Politics of Empowerment*. New York: Routledge.

Corbett, K. (1997). Speaking queer: A reply to Richard C. Friedman. *Gender and Psychoanalysis*, 2(4), 495–514.

Corbett, K. (2009). Boyhood femininity, gender identity disorder, masculine presuppositions, and the anxiety of regulation. *Psychoanalytic Dialogues*, 19, 353–370.

Corbett, K. (2013). Shifting sexual cultures: The potential space for online relations, and the promise of psychoanalytic listening. *Journal of the American Psychoanalytic Association*, 61, 25–44.

Cruz, A. (2016). *The Color of Kink: Black Women, BDSM, and Pornography*. New York: New York University Press.

Dailey, A. C. (2014). Abject or autonomous? Patient consent to psychoanalytic treatment: Review of *Informed Consent to Psychoanalysis: The Law, the Theory, and the Data*, by E. R. Saks & S. Golshan. *Journal of the American Psychoanalytic Association*, 62, 1119–1132.

Daniels, K. F. (2019). Rising playwright Jeremy O. Harris addresses backlash over controversial *Slave Play*. *The Root*. www.theroot.com.

Davies, J. M. (2001). Erotic overstimulation and the co-construction of sexual meanings in transference and countertransference experience. *Psychoanalytic Quarterly*, 70, 757–788.

Davis, O., & Dean, T. (2022). *Hatred of Sex*. Lincoln: University of Nebraska Press.

Dean, T. (2008). The frozen countenance of perversions. *Parallax*, 14(2), 93–114.

Dean, T. (2009). *Unlimited Intimacy: Reflections on the Subculture of Barebacking*. Chicago: University of Chicago Press.

Dean, T. (2012). The biopolitics of pleasure. *South Atlantic Quarterly*, 111(3), 479–497.

Dean, T. (2014). Uses of perversity: Commentary on Saketopoulou's "To Suffer Pleasure." *Studies in Gender and Sexuality*, 15, 269–277.

Dean, T. (2015). The art of piss. *Animal Shelter*, 4, 121–129.

Dean, T. (in press). Freud's ménage à quatre. In M. Steinkoler & P. Gherovici (Eds.), *Psychoanalysis, Gender, and Sexuality*. Cambridge: Cambridge University Press.

de Beauvoir, S. (1953). *Must We Burn Sade?* Sommerset, UK: Peter Nevill.

Delany, S. R. (1973). *Tides of Lust*. New York: Savoy Books.

Delany, S. R. (1974). *Dahlgren*. New York: Vintage Books.

de Lauretis, T. (1976). Cavani's *Night Porter*: A woman's film? *Film Quarterly*, 2, 35–38.

de Lauretis, T. (2017). The queerness of the drive. *Journal of Homosexuality*, 46(14), 1913–1926.

Deleuze, G. (1968). *Difference and Repetition*. New York: Columbia University Press.

Deleuze, G. (1989). Coldness and cruelty. In G. Deleuze & L. von Sacher-Masoch, *Masochism: Coldness and Cruelty, and Venus in Furs* (pp. 15–140). New York: Zone Books.

de M'Uzan, M. (2003). Slaves of quantity. *Psychoanalytic Quarterly* 72:711–725.

de M'Uzan, M. (2013). *Death and Identity: Being and the Psycho-Sexual Drama*. London: Karnac.

DePereira, A. R., Messina, V. A., & Sansalone, P. A. (2012). Informed consent as a prescription calling for debate by analysts and researchers. *International Journal of Psychoanalysis*, 93, 963–980.

Derschowitz, J. (2019, December 31). How Jeremy O. Harris' *Slave Play* shook Broadway's status quo. *Entertainment Weekly*. https://ew.com.

Dimen, M. (1999). Between lust and libido: Sex, psychoanalysis, and the moment before. *Psychoanalytic Dialogues*, 9, 415–440.

Dimen, M. (2001). Perversion is us? Eight notes. *Psychoanalytic Dialogues*, 11(6), 825–860.

Dimen, M. (2003). *Sexuality, Intimacy, Power*. Hillsdale, NJ: Analytic.

Dimen, M. (2005). Sexuality and suffering, or the eew! factor. *Studies in Gender & Sexuality*, 6, 1–18.

Dimen, M. (2011). Lapsus linguae, or a slip of the tongue? A sexual violation in an analytic treatment and its personal and theoretical aftermath. *Contemporary Psychoanalysis*, 47, 36–79.

Dimen, M. (2016). Rotten apples and ambivalence: Sexual boundary violations through a psychocultural lens. *Journal of the American Psychoanalytic Association*, 64(2), 361–373.

Dimen, M. (2017). Part-objects and perfect wholes: Clinical stances on perversion. *Canadian Journal of Psychoanalysis*, 25(1), 172–188.

Douglas, M. (1966). *Purity and Danger*. London: Routledge.

Doyle, J. (2013). *Hold It against Me: Difficulty and Emotion in Contemporary Art*. Durham, NC: Duke University Press.

Dray, P. (2003). *At the Hands of Persons Unknown: The Lynching of Black America*. New York: Modern Library.

Dufourmantelle, A. (2019). *In Praise of Risk*. New York: Fordham University Press.

Duggan, L. (2021, December 6). Me too déjà vu. *Boston Review of Books*. https://bostonreview.net.

Duggan, L., & Hunter, N. D. (2006). *Sex Wars: Sexual Dissent and Political Culture*. New York: Routledge.

Edelman, L. (2004). *No Future: Queer Theory and the Death Drive*. Durham, NC: Duke University Press.

Eisler, R. (1951). *Man into Wolf: An Anthropological Interpretation of Sadism, Masochism, and Lycanthropy*. New York: Greenwood.

Eng, D. L. (2001). *Racial Castration: Managing Masculinity in Asian America*. Durham, NC: Duke University Press.

Eng, D. L. (2010). *Queer Kinship: Queer Liberalism and the Racialization of Intimacy*. Durham, NC: Duke University Press.

Eng, D. L., & Han, S. (2019). *Racial Melancholia, Racial Dissociation: On the Social and Psychic Lives of Asian Americans*. Durham, NC: Duke University Press.

English, D. (2010). *How to See a Work of Art in Total Darkness*. Cambridge, MA: MIT Press.

Epstein, M. (2004). *Thoughts without a Thinker*. New York: Basic Books.

Evzonas, N. (2020). Gender and "race" enigmatic signifiers: How the social colonizes the unconscious. *Psychoanalytic Inquiry*, 40(8), 636–656.

Faden, R. R., & Beauchamp, T. L. (1986). *A History and Theory of Informed Consent*. New York: Oxford University Press.

Fanon, F. (1952). *Black Skin, White Masks*. New York: Grove.

Fanon, F. (1961). *The Wretched of the Earth*. New York: Grove.

Ferenczi, S. (1938). *Thalassa: A theory of genitality* (H. A. Bunker, Trans.). London: Karnac.

Fernandez, T. (2020, February 26). Sex in the theatre: Jeremy O. Harris and Samuel Delany in conversation. *Paris Review*. www.theparisreview.org.

Ferro, A. (2005). *Seeds of Illness, Seeds of Recovery: The Genesis of Suffering and the Role of Psychoanalysis*. London: Routledge.

Fischel, J. J. (2016). *Sex and Harm in the Age of Consent*. Minneapolis: University of Minnesota Press.

Fischel, J. J. (2019). *Screw Consent: A Better Politics of Sexual Justice*. Berkeley: University of California Press.

Fischel, J. J., & O'Connell, H. R. (2015). Disabling consent or reconstructing sexual autonomy. *Columbia Journal of Gender & Law*, 30, 428–528.

Fisher, G. (1996). *Gary in Your Pocket: Stories and Notebook of Gary Fisher*. Durham, NC: Duke University Press.

Fisher Center at Bard. (2019, October 4). Underground Railroad Game | Conversation with Jennifer Kidwell and Scott R Sheppard. YouTube. www.youtube.com/watch?v=clJ1CZp5TCUR.

Fletcher, J. (2000). Gender, sexuality, and the theory of seduction. *Women: A Cultural Review*, 11(1–2), 95–108.

Fletcher, J. (2007). Seduction and the vicissitudes of translation: The work of Jean Laplanche. *Psychoanalytic Quarterly*, 76(4), 1241–1291.

Fonagy, P. (2008). A genuinely developmental theory of sexual enjoyment and its implications for psychoanalytic technique. *Journal of the American Psychoanalytic Association*, 56, 11–36.

Fonagy, P., Gergely, G., Jurist, E., & Target, M. (2002). *Affect Regulation, Mentalization, and the Development of the Self*. New York: Other.

Foucault, M. (1974, July–August). Interview. *Cahiers du cinéma*, 251–252.

Foucault, M. (1975). Sade: Sergeant of sex. In *Aesthetics, Method, and Epistemology* (pp. 223–227). New York: New Press.

Foucault, M. (1977). A preface on transgression. In D. F. Bouchard (Ed.), *Language, Counter-Memory, Practice: Selected Essays and Interviews* (pp. 29–52). Ithaca, NY: Cornell University Press. (Original work published 1963)

Foucault, M. (1989). Power affects the body. In E. Lotringer (Ed.), *Foucault Live: Collected Interviews, 1961–1984* (pp. 207–213). New York: Semiotext(e).

Foucault, M. (1991). *Remarks on Marx: Conversations with Duccio Trombadori*. New York: Semiotext(e).

Foucault, M. (1997). *Ethics: Subjectivity and truth*. New York: New Press.

Foucault, M. (2000a). Interview with Michel Foucault. In J. Faubion (Ed.), *Power: Essential Works of Michel Foucault* (Vol. 3, pp. 239–297). New York: New Press.

Foucault, M. (2000b). Sex, power, and the politics of identity. In P. Rabinow (Ed.), *Essential Works of Foucault 1954–1984* (pp. 163–173). Harmondsworth, UK: Penguin Books. (Original work published 1984)

Frank, A., Romano, A., & Grady, G. (2019, December 5). Reckoning with *Slave Play*, the most controversial show on Broadway. *Vox*. www.vox.com.

Freud, S. (1895). *Project for a Scientific Psychology*. In J. Strachey (Ed. & Trans.), *The Standard Edition of the Complete Psychological Works of Sigmund Freud* (Vol. 1, pp. 281–391). London: Hogarth.

Freud, S. (1905a). *Jokes and Their Relation to the Unconscious*. In J. Strachey (Ed. & Trans.), *The Standard Edition of the Complete Psychological Works of Sigmund Freud* (Vol. 7, pp. 1–247). London: Hogarth.

Freud, S. (1905b). *Three Essays on the Theory of Sexuality*. In J. Strachey (Ed. & Trans.), *The Standard Edition of the Complete Psychological Works of Sigmund Freud* (Vol. 7, pp. 123–246). London: Hogarth.

Freud, S. (1912). Recommendations to physicians practicing psycho-analysis. In J. Strachey (Ed. & Trans.), *The Standard Edition of the Complete Psychological Works of Sigmund Freud* (Vol. 7, pp. 109–120). London: Hogarth.

Freud, S. (1914a). On narcissism: An introduction. In J. Strachey (Ed. & Trans.), *The Standard Edition of the Complete Psychological Works of Sigmund Freud* (Vol. 14, pp. 67–102). London: Hogarth.

Freud, S. (1914b). Remembering, repeating and working through. In J. Strachey (Ed. & Trans.), *The Standard Edition of the Complete Psychological Works of Sigmund Freud* (Vol. 12, pp. 145–156). London: Hogarth.

Freud, S. (1915a). Observations on transference-love. In J. Strachey (Ed. & Trans.), *The Standard Edition of the Complete Psychological Works of Sigmund Freud* (Vol. 12, pp. 157–171). London: Hogarth.

Freud, S. (1915b). The unconscious. In J. Strachey (Ed. & Trans.), *The Standard Edition of the Complete Psychological Works of Sigmund Freud* (Vol. 15, pp. 159–215). London: Hogarth.

Freud, S. (1920). Beyond the pleasure principle. In J. Strachey (Ed. & Trans.), *The Standard Edition of the Complete Psychological Works of Sigmund Freud* (Vol. 18, pp. 1–64). London: Hogarth.

Freud, S. (1923). The ego and the id. In J. Strachey (Ed. & Trans.), *The Standard Edition of the Complete Psychological Works of Sigmund Freud* (Vol. 19, pp. 1–66). London: Hogarth.

Freud, S. (1924). The economic problem of masochism. In J. Strachey (Ed. & Trans.), *The Standard Edition of the Complete Psychological Works of Sigmund Freud* (Vol. 19, pp. 155–170). London: Hogarth.

Freud, S. (1932). The acquisition and control of fire. In J. Strachey (Ed. & Trans.), *The Standard Edition of the Complete Psychological Works of Sigmund Freud* (Vol. 22, pp. 183–194). London: Hogarth.

Furlong, A. (2003). Review of the book *Negotiating Consent in Psychotherapy*, by P. O'Neill. *Canadian Journal of Psychoanalysis*, 11, 567–576.

Furlong, A. (2005). Confidentiality with respect to third parties: A psychoanalytic view. *International Journal of Psychoanalysis*, 86, 375–394.

Furlong, A. (2020). Consenting and assenting to psychoanalytic work. *Journal of the American Psychoanalytic Association*, 68, 583–613.

Gabbard, G. O. (2000). Disguise or consent: Problems and recommendations concerning the publication and presentation of clinical material. *International Journal of Psychoanalysis* 81, 1071–1086.

Gentile, K. (2015, September). Affirmative consent and neoliberal bodies: The individual yes vs. the social no. Public Seminar. https://publicseminar.org.

Ghent, E. (1990). Masochism, submission, surrender—masochism as a perversion of surrender. *Contemporary Psychoanalysis*, 26, 108–136.

Glissant, É. (1990). *Poetics of Relation*. Ann Arbor: University of Michigan Press.

González, F. (2020). First world problems and gated communities of the mind: An ethics of place in psychoanalysis. *Psychoanalytic Quarterly*, 20 (4), 741–770.

Green, A. (1995). Has sexuality anything to do with psychoanalysis? *International Journal of Psychoanalysis*, 76, 871–883.

Green, J. (2019, October 6). Review: *Slave Play*: Four times as big and just as searing. *New York Times*. www.nytimes.com.

Greenberg, J. R. (1986). Theoretical models and the analyst's neutrality. *Contemporary Psychoanalysis*, 22, 87–106.

Haag, P. (1999). *Consent: Sexual Rights and the Transformation of American Liberalism*. Ithaca, NY: Cornell University Press.

Hansbury, G. (2017). The masculine vaginal: Working with queer men's embodiment at the transgender edge. *Journal of the American Psychoanalytic Association*, 65, 1009–1031.

Hansbury, G. & Saketopoulou, A. (Forthcoming). Sissy Dance, $1: The more and more of gender. *Psychoanalytic Review*.

Halperin, D. M. (1995). *Saint Foucault: Towards a Gay Hagiography*. Oxford: Oxford University Press.

Harris, A. (2019, October 7). What it's like to see *Slave Play* as a Black person. *New York Times*. www.nytimes.com.

Harris, J. O. (2018). *Slave Play*. New York: New York Theatre Workshop.

Harris, J. O. (2019a). *Slave Play*. New York: Theatre Communications Group.

Harris, J. O. (2019b, December 16). Spotlight on Broadway's *Slave Play*. YouTube. www.youtube.com/watch?v=ZyS6MxGA-LU.

Hartman, S. V. (1997). *Scenes of Subjection: Terror, Slavery, and Self-Making in Nineteenth-Century America*. New York: Oxford University Press.

Hassan, I. (1969). Sade: prisoner of consciousness. *Tri-Quarterly*, 15, 23–41.

Hegel, G. W. F. (1977). *Phenomenology of Spirit*. Oxford: Oxford University Press. (Original work published 1807)

Hénaff, M. (1986). Naked terror: Political violence, libertine violence. (L. R. Schehr, Trans.). *Sub-stance*, 86, 5–32.

Hénaff, M. (1999). *The Invention of the Libertine Body*. Minneapolis: University of Minnesota Press.

Hennefeld, M., & Sammond, N. (2020). Not it, or the abject objection. In M. Hennefeld & N. Sammond (Eds.), *Abjection Incorporated: Mediating the Politics of Pleasure and Violence* (pp. 1–24). Durham, NC: Duke University Press.

Hernandez, D. (2004, December 21). Playing with race. *ColorLines*. www.colorlines.com/articles/playing-race.

Hills, A. (2015). Viennese fantasies, Austrian histories: space, fantasy and fascism in Ingeborg Bachmann's *Malina* and Liliana Cavani's *The Night Porter*. In S. Araujo, M. P. Pinto, & S. Bettencourt (Eds.), *Fear and Fantasy in a Global World* (pp. 185–209). Amsterdam: Rodopi.

Holdren, S. (2019, October). *Slave Play* nearly demands a conversation. So we had one. *New York*. www.vulture.com.

Holland, S. P. (2012). *The Erotic Life of Racism*. Durham, NC: Duke University Press.

Hollibaugh, A. L. (2000). *My Dangerous Desires: A Queer Girl Dreaming Her Way Home*. Durham, NC: Duke University Press.

Hollier, D. (1979). *Le Collège de Sociologie (1937–1939)*. Paris: FOLIO.

Holmes, D. E. (2019). Our country 'tis of we and them: Psychoanalytic perspectives on our fractured American identity. *American Imago*, 76(3), 359–379.

Holtzman, D., & Kulish, N. (2012). Introduction. In D. Holtzman & N. Kulish (Eds.), *The Clinical Problem of Masochism* (pp. 1–14). Lanham, MD: Aronson.

Horkheimer, M., & Adorno, T. W. (1987). *Dialectic of Enlightenment*. Stanford, CA: Stanford University Press.

House, J. (2017). The ongoing rediscovery of après-coup as a central Freudian concept. *Journal of American Psychoanalytic Association*, 65(5), 773–798.

House, J. (2019). Commentary on Saketopoulou. *Journal of American Psychoanalytic Association*, 67(1), 169–183.

Houston, B., & Kinder, M. (1975). *The Night Porter* as daydream. *Literature/Film Quarterly*, 3(4), 363–370.

Jakobsen, J., & Pellegrini, A. (2004). *Love the Sin: Sexual Regulation and the Limits of Religious Tolerance*. New York: New York University Press.

Jay, M. (1993). *Force Fields: Between Intellectual History and Cultural Critique*. New York: Routledge.

Jay, M. (2005). *Songs of Experience: Modern American and European Variations on a Universal Theme*. Berkeley: University of California Press.

Johnson, D. (Ed.). (2013). *The Art and Performances of Ron Athey*. London: Live Art Development Agency.

Johnson, V. (1994). Playing with racial stereotypes: The love that dare not speak its name. *Black Leather in Color*. Retrieved March 21, 2019, from www.leatherweb.com.

Joseph, B. (1971). A clinical contribution to the analysis of perversion. *International Journal of Psychoanalysis*, 52, 441–449.

Joseph, B. (1982). Addiction to near-death. *International Journal of Psychoanalysis*, 63, 449–456.

Juicy Lucy. (1987). "If I ask you to tie me up, will you still want to love me?" In SAMOIS (Ed.), *Coming to Power: Writings and Graphics on Lesbian S/M* (pp. 29–41). Boston: Alyson.

Kahn, L. (2018). *Psychoanalysis, Apathy, and the Postmodern Patient*. London: Routledge.

Kahn, L. (n.d.). Nothing takes place between them except that they talk to each other. *Psychoanalysis.today*. Retrieved November 20, 2021, from www.psychoanalysis.today.

Kai, M. (2019, September 10). "It should cost you something": Playwright Jeremy O. Harris sets the record straight on *Slave Play* as it debuts on Broadway. www.theroot.com.

Kernberg, O. F. (1995). *Love Relations: Normality and Pathology*. New Haven, CT: Yale University Press.

Khan, M. M. R. (1979). *Alienation in Perversions*. Madison, CT: International Universities Press.

King, H. (2010). *Lost in Translation: Orientalism, Cinema, and the Enigmatic Signifier*. Durham, NC: Duke University Press.

King, H. (2021). *Why Laplanche Matters in 2021* [Paper presentation]. Laplanche in the States: The Sexual and the Cultural, online.

Klein, G. S. (1961). Freud's two theories of sexuality. In M. M. Gill & P. S. Holzman (Eds.), *Psychology versus Metapsychology: Psychoanalytic Essays in Memory of George S. Klein* (pp. 14–70). New York: International Universities Press.

Klossowski, P. (1967). *Sade, My Neighbor*. Evanston, IL: Northwestern Universities Press.

Kojève, A. (1947). *Introduction to the Reading of Hegel: Lessons in the "Phenomenology of Spirit."* Ithaca, NY: Cornell University Press.

Krafft-Ebbing, R. (1866). *Psychopathia sexualis*. New York: Arcade.

Kristeva, J. (1982). *Powers of Horror*. New York: Columbia University Press.

Kulick, D., & Rydström, J. (2015). *Loneliness and Its Opposite: Sex, Disability and the Ethics of Engagement*. Durham, NC: Duke University Press.

Lacan, J. (1989). Kant with Sade (J. Swenson, Trans.). *October*, 51, 55–75. (Original work published 1963)

Laplanche, J. (1979). A metapsychology put to the test of anxiety. In *The Unfinished Copernican Revolution: Selected Works, 1967–1992* (pp. 197–216). New York: Unconscious in Translation.

Laplanche, J. (1980). *Problématiques III: Sublimation*. Paris: Presses Universitaires de France.

Laplanche, J. (1984a). The death drive in the theory of the sexual drives. In *The Unfinished Copernican Revolution: Selected Works, 1967–1992* (pp. 351–366). New York: Unconscious in Translation.

Laplanche, J. (1984b). The drive and its source-object: Its fate in the transference. In *The Unfinished Copernican Revolution: Selected Works, 1967–1992* (pp. 293–312). New York: Unconscious in Translation.

Laplanche, J. (1987). *New Foundations for Psychoanalysis*. New York: Unconscious in Translation.

Laplanche, J. (1989). Temporality and translation. In *The Unfinished Copernican Revolution: Selected Works, 1967–1992* (pp. 401–422). New York: Unconscious in Translation.

Laplanche, J. (1991). Masochism and the general theory of seduction. In *The Unfinished Copernican Revolution: Selected Works, 1967–1992* (pp. 541–561). New York: Unconscious in Translation.

Laplanche, J. (1992a). Interview: Jean Laplanche talks to Martin Stanton. In J. Fletcher & M. Stanton (Eds.), *Jean Laplanche: Seduction, Translation, Drives* (pp. 3–20). London: Institute of Contemporary Arts.

Laplanche, J. (1992b). The unfinished Copernican revolution. In *The Unfinished Copernican Revolution: Selected Works, 1967–1992* (pp. 3–40). New York: Unconscious in Translation.

Laplanche, J. (1995). The so-called death drive: A sexual drive. In *The Temptations of Biology* (pp. 159–182). New York: Unconscious in Translation.

Laplanche, J. (1999). *Essays on Otherness*. London: Routledge.

Laplanche, J. (2000a). Drive and instinct: Distinctions, oppositions, supports, and intertwinings. In *Freud and the Sexual* (pp. 5–26). New York: Unconscious in Translation.

Laplanche, J. (2000b). Sexuality and attachment. In *Freud and the Sexual* (pp. 27–51). New York: Unconscious in Translation.

Laplanche, J. (2003a). Gender, sex and the sexual. In *Freud and the Sexual* (pp. 159–202). New York: Unconscious in Translation.

Laplanche, J. (2003b). Three meanings of the term "unconscious" in the framework of the General Theory of Seduction. In *Freud and the Sexual* (pp. 203–222). New York: Unconscious in Translation.

Laplanche, J. (2006a). *Après-coup*. New York: Unconscious in Translation.

Laplanche, J. (2006b). Exigency and going astray. *Psychoanalysis, Culture and Society*, 11, 185–189.

Laplanche, J. (2014). Traumatic temporality: An interview with Jean Laplanche. In C. Caruth, *Listening to trauma: Conversations with leaders in theory and treatment of catastrophic experience* (pp. 25–45). Baltimore: Johns Hopkins University Press. (Originally published 1994)

Laplanche, J. (2015a). Forces at play in psychical conflict. In *Between Seduction and Inspiration: Man* (pp. 107–122). New York: Unconscious in Translation. (Originally published 1994)

Laplanche, J. (2015b). Goals of the psychoanalytic process. In *Between Seduction and Inspiration: Man* (pp. 183–201). New York: Unconscious in Translation. (Originally published 1996)

Laplanche, J. (2015c). Narrativity and hermeneutics: a few propositions. In *Between Seduction and Inspiration: Man* (pp. 245–251). New York: Unconscious in Translation. (Originally published 1998)

Laplanche, J. (2015d). Response and responsibility. In *Between Seduction and Inspiration: Man* (pp. 123–144). New York: Unconscious in Translation. (Originally published 1994)

Lély, G. (1966). Preface to the letters. In Marquis de Sade, *Selected Letters* (pp. 21–30). New York: October House.

León, C. (2020a). Curious entanglements: Opacity and ethical relation in Latina/o aesthetics. In P. Zurn & A. Shankar (Eds.), *Curiosity Studies: A New Ecology of Knowledge* (pp. 167–187). Minneapolis: University of Minnesota Press.

León, C. (2020b, May 13). Ep. #117: Curious entanglements with Christina León. *Choose to Be Curious* (Sound Cloud). https://soundcloud.com.

Levi, P. (1988). *The Drowned and the Saved*. New York: Summit Books.

Levine, H. B. (2012). The colourless canvas: Representation, therapeutic action, and the creation of a mind. *International Journal of Psychoanalysis*, 93, 607–629.

Levine, L. (2016) A mutual survival of destructiveness and its creative potential for agency and desire. *Psychoanalytic Dialogues* 26:36–49.

Lewis, S. (2021, Winter). My octopus girlfriend: On erotophobia. *n+1*, 39, https://nplusonemag.com.

Lindsey, T. B., & Johnson, J. M. (2014). Searching for climax: Black erotic lives in slavery and freedom. *Meridians: feminism, race, transnationalism*, 12(2), 169–195.

Loewald, H. W. (1980). Ego and reality. In *Collected Papers in Psychoanalysis* (pp. 3–19). New Haven, CT: Yale University Press.

Lorde, A. (1982). Interview with Audre Lorde, by Susan Leigh Star. In R. R. Linden (Ed.), *Against Sadomasochism: A Radical Feminist Analysis* (pp. 66–71). East Palo Alto, CA: Frog in the Well.

Lowenfeld, H. (1941). Psychic trauma and productive experience in the artist. *Psychoanalytic Quarterly*, 10, 116–130.

Lyng, S. (2004). *Edgework: The Sociology of Risk-Taking*. New York: Routledge.

Lyons-Ruth, K. (1999). The two-person unconscious: Intersubjective dialogue, enactive relational representation, and the emergence of new forms of relational organization. *Psychoanalytic Inquiry*, 19, 576–617.

Lyons-Ruth, K. (2006). Play, precariousness, and the negotiation of shared meaning: A developmental research perspective on child psychotherapy. *Journal of Infant, Child & Adolescent Psychotherapy*, 5, 142–159.

Lyotard, J. F. (1991). *The Inhuman: Reflections on Time* (G. Bennington & R. Bowlby, Trans.). Stanford, CA: Stanford University Press. (Original work published 1988)

Lyotard, J. F. (2002). Emma: Between philosophy and psychoanalysis. In H. J. Silverman (Ed.), *Lyotard: Philosophy, Politics and the Sublime* (pp. 23–49). London: Routledge.

MacDonald, S. S. (2019, April 23). Believe it or not: Two new plays feature modern characters volunteering to be slaves-forget plausible, is it defensible? *The Undefeated*. https://theundefeated.com.

MacKinnon, C. (2007). *Are Women Human?* Cambridge, MA: Harvard University Press.

Marks, S. (2019, October 6). *Slave Play* is a funny, scalding walk along the boundary between black and white in America. *Washington Post*. www.washingtonpost.com.

Martin, L. H., Gutman, H., & Hutton, P. H. (1988). *Technologies of the Self: A Seminar with Michel Foucault*. Amherst: University of Massachusetts Press.

Marty, E. (2016). Why did the 20th century take Sade seriously? *Journal of the International Network of Sexual Ethics and Politics*, 4(1), 19–26.

Martyn, D. (2003). *Sublime Failures: The Ethics of Kant and Sade*. New York: Columbia University Press.

McBride, D. (2005). *Why I Hate Abercrombie & Fitch: Essays on Race and Sexuality*. New York: New York University Press.

McCormick, R., & Giroux, H. (1977). Two views on *The Night Porter*. *Cinéaste*, 6(4), 30–34.

McDougall, J. (1995). *The Many Faces of Eros: A Psychoanalytic Exploration of Human Sexuality*. New York: Norton.

McDougall, J. (2000). Sexuality and the neosexual. *Modern Psychoanalysis*, 25, 155–166.

Meltzer, D. (1973). *Sexual States of Mind*. Perthshire, UK: Clunie.

Miles, M. (2021). *On Memory, Tears, and Meditation*. London: Bloomsbury Academic.

Miller, J. A. (1993). *The Passion of Michel Foucault*. New York: Doubleday.

Milner, M. (1969). *The Hands of the Living God*. London: Karnac.

Mitchell, S. (2003). *Can Love Last?* New York: Norton.

Modell, A. H. (1991). The therapeutic relationship as a paradoxical experience. *Psychoanalytic Dialogues*, 1(1), 13–28.

Morris, H. (2016). The analyst's offer. *Journal of the American Psychoanalytic Association*, 64(6), 1173-1187.

Moten, F. (2003). Black mo'nin'. In D. Kazanjian & D. Eng (Eds.), *Loss: The Politics of Mourning* (pp. 59–76). Berkeley: University of California Press.

Moten, F. (2018). *Stolen Life*. Durham, NC: Duke University Press.

Muñoz, J. E. (2019). Race, sex and the incommensurable: Gary Fisher with Eve Kosofsky Sedgwick. In *Cruising Utopia: The Then and There of Queer Futurity*, 10th Year Anniversary Edition (pp. 193–206). New York: New York University Press.

Musser, A. J. (2014). *Sensational Flesh: Race, Power, and Masochism*. New York: New York University Press.

Musser, A. J. (2016). Queering sugar: Kara Walker's sugar sphinx and the intractability of black female sexuality. *Signs: Journal of Women in Culture and Society*, 42(1), 153–174.

Musser, A. J. (2017). Consent, capacity, and the non-narrative. In G. Cipolla, K. Gupta, D. A. Rubin, & A. Willey (Eds.), *Queer Feminist Science Studies: A Reader* (pp. 221–232). Seattle: University of Washington Press.

Musser, A. J. (2018). *Sexual Excess: Queer Femininity and Brown Jouissance*. New York: New York University Press.

Nash, J. C. (2014). *The Black Body in Ecstasy: Reading Pornography, Reading Race*. New York: New York University Press.

Nash, J. C. (2019). *Black Feminism Reimagined: After Intersectionality*. Durham, NC: Duke University Press.

Nasheed, T. (2018, December 16). *Slave Play*. YouTube. www.youtube.com/watch?v=L Mw5Jm503gM&feature=youtu.be&t=1253

Neboit-Mombet, J. (1972). A logician of unreason. *Europe*, 522, 48–53.

Newmahr, S. (2011). *Playing on the Edge: Sadomasochism, Risk, and Intimacy*. Bloomington: Indiana University Press.

New York Daily News. (2019, October 6). Broadway review: *Slave Play* is a frank, challenging drama on race and sex. www.nydailynews.com.

Nguyen, Viet Thanh. (2018, August 21). Asian-Americans need more movies, even mediocre ones. *New York Times*. www.nytimes.com.

Nigro, R. (2005). Experience of the self between limit, transgression and the explosion of the dialectical system: Foucault as reader of Bataille and Blanchot. *Philosophy and Social Criticism*, 31, 649–664.

Novick, K. K., & Novick, J. (2012). Some suggestions for engaging with the clinical problem of masochism. In D. Holtzman & N. Kulish (Eds.), *The Clinical Problem of Masochism* (pp. 51–76). Lanham, MD: Aronson.

Nyong'o, T. (2010). Trapped in the closet with Eve. *Criticism*, 52(2), 243–251.

Oldoini, M. G. (2019). Abusive relations and traumatic development: Marginal notes on a clinical case. *Psychoanalytic Quarterly*, 88(2), 251–275.

Owens, E. (2022, February 15). How "Slave Play" author Jeremy O. Harris lost an epic Twitter fight. *Daily Beast.* www.thedailybeast.com.

Pellegrini, A. (1997). *Performance Anxieties: Staging Psychoanalysis, Staging Race.* New York: Routledge.

Pellegrini, A. (2007). "Signaling through the flames": Hell House performance and structures of religious feelings. *American Quarterly,* 59(2), 911–935.

Pellegrini, A. (2021, April 10). Neoliberal necropolitics: Not your uncle Sigmund's death drive [Conference presentation]. The Intersection of Gender, Sexuality and Our Current Crises: The Psychological Impact of Race, Politics, Economics, and COVID, IPA, CFS and COWAA (presented online).

Pellegrini, A., & Shimakawa, K. (2018). Reenactability. In A. Sarat, L. Douglas, & M. M. Umphrey (Eds.), *Law and Performance* (pp. 101–121). Amherst: University of Massachusetts Press.

Pérez, P. (2015). *A Taste for Brown Bodies: Gay Modernity and Cosmopolitan Desire.* New York: New York University Press.

Phelan, P. (1993). *Unmarked: The Politics of Performance.* London: Routledge.

Pinkins, T. (2021). *You Can't Say That!* [Podcast]. Episodes 11 and 12.

Phillips, J. (2001). *Sade: The Libertine Novels.* London: Pluto.

Poulson-Bryant, S. (2005). *Hung: A Meditation on the Measure of Black Men in America.* New York: Doubleday.

Powell, D. R. (2018). Race, African Americans, and psychoanalysis: Collective silence in the therapeutic conversation. *Journal of the American Psychoanalytic Association,* 66, 1021–1049.

Powell, D. R. (2020). From the sunken place to the shitty place: The film *Get Out,* psychic emancipation and modern race relations from a psychodynamic clinical perspective. *Psychoanalytic Quarterly,* 89, 415–445.

Ravetto, K. (2001). *The Unmaking of Fascist Aesthetics.* Minneapolis: University of Minnesota Press.

Réage, P. (1977). *The Story of O.* New York: Ballantine Books.

Reid-Pharr, R. F. (2001). *Black Gay Man.* New York: New York University Press.

Reis, B. (2009). Performative and enactive features of psychoanalytic witnessing: The transference as the scene of address. *International Journal of Psychoanalysis,* 90(6), 1359–1372.

Reis, B. (2020). *Creative Repetition and Intersubjectivity.* New York: Routledge.

Rodríguez, J. M. (2014). *Sexual Futures, Queer Gestures, and Other Latina Longings.* New York: New York University Press.

Rubin, G. S. (2011). Thinking sex. In *Deviations: A Gayle Rubin Reader* (pp. 137–181). Durham, NC: Duke University Press. (Original work published 1984)

Rundel, M. (2015). The fire of Eros: Sexuality and the movement toward union. *Psychoanalytic Dialogues,* 25, 614–630.

Sade, D. A. F., Marquis de. (1966a). *Justine.* In A. Wainhouse & R. Seaver (Eds. and Trans.), *Justine, Philosophy in the Bedroom and Other Writings* (pp. 455–743). New York: Grove. (Original work published 1797)

Sade, D. A. F., Marquis de. (1966b). The one hundred and twenty days of Sodom. In A. Wainhouse & R. Seaver (Eds. and Trans.), *The One Hundred and Twenty Days of Sodom and Other Writings* (pp. 191–674). New York: Grove. (Original work published 1782)

Sade, D. A. F., Marquis de. (1966c). Philosophy in the bedroom. In A. Wainhouse & R. Seaver (Eds. and Trans.), *Justine, Philosophy in the Bedroom and Other Writings* (pp. 185–367). New York: Grove. (Original work published 1795)

Saketopoulou, A. (2011a). Consent, sexuality, and self-respect: Commentary on Skerrett's "Beyond 'Consent.'" *Studies in Gender and Sexuality*, 12(4), 245–250.

Saketopoulou, A. (2011b, July 1). Unpacking consent psychoanalytically through race play: A clinical case [Conference presentation]. In panel Renovating psychoanalysis: Clinical meets theoretical, Changing Psychoanalysis for a Changing Society, Annual IARPP Meeting.

Saketopoulou, A. (2014, December 6). Trauma lives *us*: Affective excess, safe spaces and the erasure of subjectivity. *Bully Bloggers*. https://bullybloggers.wordpress.com.

Saketopoulou, A. (2015). Sexual rapture, ego rupture and the role of transgression: A discussion of Megan Rundel's "The Fire of Eros: Sexuality and the Movement toward Union." *Psychoanalytic Dialogues*, 25(5), 631–637.

Saketopoulou, A. (2017a). Between Freud's second and third essays on sexuality: Commentary on Hansbury. *Journal of the American Psychoanalytic Association*, 65(6), 1033–1048.

Saketopoulou, A. (2017b). Structured like culture: Laplanche on the translation of parental enigma. *DIVISION/Review*, 17, 51–52.

Saketopoulou, A. (2018a, June 16). Queer: The anti-identity identity [Conference presentation]. 16th IARPP Conference, New York.

Saketopoulou, A. (2018b, October 11). Using psychoanalysis to understand #metoo memories. *New York Review of Books*. www.nybooks.com.

Saketopoulou, A. (2020). How the world becomes bigger; implantation and intromission in the après-coup: Discussion of House. In D. Braucher & P. Sauvayre (Eds.), *The Unconscious: Contemporary Refractions in Psychoanalysis* (pp. 174–184) New York: Routledge.

Saks, E. R., & Golshan, E. (2013). *Informed Consent to Psychoanalysis: The Law, the Theory, and the Data*. New York: Fordham University Press.

Salamon, G. (2016, December 4). Broken open by experience: Thoughts on Avgi Saketopoulou's "Perversion's aspiration: A bid for the enigmatic" [Conference presentation]. Second Story, Brooklyn.

Scarfone, D. (2011). Repetition: Between presence and meaning. *Canadian Journal of Psychoanalysis*, 19(1), 70–86.

Scarfone, D. (2013). A brief introduction to the work of Jean Laplanche. *International Journal of Psychoanalysis*, 94(3), 545–566.

Scarfone, D. (2014). The three essays and the meaning of the infantile sexual in psychoanalysis. *Psychoanalytic Quarterly*, 83, 327–344.

Scarfone, D. (2015a). *Laplanche: An Introduction*. New York: Unconscious in Translation.

Scarfone, D. (2015b). *The Unpast*. New York: Unconscious in Translation.

Scarfone, D. (2016). Fantasme et processus de fantasmatisation. *Revue Francaise de Psychosomatique*, 50, 47–68.

Scarfone, D. (2017). Foreign bodies: The body-psyche and its phantoms. In V. Tsolas & C. A. Anzieu-Premmereur (Eds.), *Psychoanalytic Exploration of the Body in Today's World* (pp. 146–158). London: Routledge.

Scarfone, D. (2019). The feminine, the analyst and the child theorist. *International Journal of Psychoanalysis*, 100(3), 567–575.

Scarfone, D. (2021, October 2). The message, the body, and the drives in psychoanalysis [Conference presentation]. Laplanche in the States: The Sexual and the Cultural (virtual conference).

Scarfone, D. (in press). *The Reality of the Message*. New York: Unconscious in Translation.

Schechner, R. (1985). *Between Theater and Anthropology*. Philadelphia: University of Pennsylvania Press.

Schneider, R. (2011). *Performing Remains: Art and War in Times of Theatrical Reenactment*. New York: Routledge.

Schutzenberger, A. A. (1966). Marquis de Sade, a French precursor of psychodrama. *Group Psychotherapy*, 19(1–2), 46–48.

Schwartz-Cooney, A. (2018). Vitalizing enactment: A relational exploration. *Psychoanalytic Dialogues* 28:340–354.

Scott, D. (2010). *Extravagant Abjection: Blackness, Power, and Sexuality in the African American Imagination*. New York: New York University Press.

Scott, D. (2021). *Keeping It Unreal: Black Queer Fantasy and Superhero Comics*. New York: New York University Press.

Scott, J. (1991). The evidence of experience. *Critical Inquiry*, 17(4), 773–797.

Seaver, R. (1999). Prologue. In D. A. F. de Sade, *Letters from Prison* (pp. 3–44). New York: Arcade.

Sebree, C. (2019). *Mistress*. Kalamazoo, MI: New Issues.

Sedgwick, E. (1996). Afterword. In G. Fisher, *Gary in Your Pocket: Stories and Notebook of Gary Fisher* (pp. 273–291). Durham, NC: Duke University Press.

Sharpe, C. (2016). *In the Wake: On Blackness and Being*. Durham, NC: Duke University Press.

Sheehi, L. & Sheehi, S. (2021). *Psychoanalysis under Occupation: Practicing Resistance in Palestine*. London: Routledge.

Sinfield, A. (2004). *Sexuality and Power*. New York: Columbia University Press.

Slavin, J. H., Oxenhandler, N., Seligman, S., Stein, R., & Davies, J. M. (2004). Dialogues on sexuality in development and treatment. *Studies in Gender and Sexuality*, 5, 371–418.

Smith, H. (2019, December 1). "Slave Play" is a performance filled with "intrigue and surprise." Interview with Jeremy O. Harris. *Today* (NBC). www.today.com.

Snorton, C. R. (2017). *Black on Both Sides: A Racial History of Trans Identity*. Minneapolis: University of Minnesota Press.

Sontag, S. (1964). Notes on "camp." *Partisan Review*, 31(4), 515–530.

Spillers, H. J. (1987). Mama's baby, papa's maybe: An American grammar book. *Diacritics*, 17(2), 64–81.

Srinivasan, A. (2021). *The Right to Sex: Feminism in the Twenty-First Century*. New York: Farrar, Straus and Giroux.

Stallings, L. H. (2015). *Funk the Erotic: Transaesthetics and Black Sexual Cultures*. Urbana: University of Illinois Press.

Stein, A. (1999). Without contraries there is no progression: S/M, bi-nary thinking, and the lesbian purity test. In D. Atkins (Ed.), *Lesbian Sex Scandals: Sexual Practices, Identities, and Politics* (pp. 45–60). New York: Harrington Park.

Stein, R. A. (1998). The poignant, the excessive and the enigmatic in sexuality. *International Journal of Psychoanalysis*, 79, 253–268.

Stein, R. A. (2005a). Skimming the milk, cajoling the soul: Embodiment and obscenity in sexuality: Commentary on Muriel Dimen's paper. *Studies in Gender and Sexuality*, 6, 19–31.

Stein, R. A. (2005b). Why perversion? "False love" and the perverse pact. *International Journal of Psychoanalysis*, 86(3), 775–799.

Stein, R. A. (2006). Unforgetting and excess, the re-creation and re-finding of suppressed sexuality. *Psychoanalytic Dialogues*, 16, 763–778.

Stein, R. A. (2008). The otherness of sexuality. *Excess: Journal of the American Psychoanalytic Association*, 56, 43–71.

Steiner, J. (1982). Perverse relationships between parts of the self: A clinical illustration. *International Journal of Psychoanalysis*, 63, 241–251.

Stockton, K. B. (2006). *Beautiful Bottom, Beautiful Shame: Where "Black" Meets "Queer."* Durham, NC: Duke University Press.

Stockton, K. B. (2009). *The Queer Child, or Growing Sideways in the Twentieth Century*. Durham, NC: Duke University Press.

Stockton, K. B. (2015, March 8). Reading as kissing, sex with ideas: Lesbian "barebacking"? *Los Angeles Review*. https://v2.lareviewofbooks.org.

Stockton, K. B. (2019). *Avidly Reads Making Out*. New York: New York University Press.

Stoller, R. J. (1975). *Perversion: The Erotic Form of Hatred*. London: Karnac.

Sullivan, H. S. (1953). *The Interpersonal Theory of Psychiatry*. New York: Norton.

Talks at Google. (2020, February 3). Slave Play | Broadway | Talks at Google." YouTube. www.youtube.com/watch?v=J96ODbxRcdE.

Tang, E. (2019, November 22). "Let's take the play to where the people are": Jeremy O. Harris in conversation with Lynn Nottage. *Vogue*. www.vogue.com.

Target, M. (2007). Is our sexuality our own? *British Journal of Psychotherapy*, 23, 517–530.

Tariq Radio. (2018, December 16). Tariq Nasheed: Slave Play. YouTube. www.youtube.com/watch?v=LMw5Jm503gM&feature=youtu.be&t=1253.

Taylor, R. E. (1954). The Marquis de Sade and the first *Psychopathia Sexualis*. In D. Geddes (Ed.), *An Analysis of the Kinsey Reports on Sexual Behavior in the Human Male and Female* (pp. 193–210). New York: Dutton.

Tessier, H. (2020). *Rationalism and Emancipation in Psychoanalysis: The Work of Jean Laplanche*. New York: Unconscious in Translation Press.

Tyler, I. (2013). *Revolting Subjects: Social Abjection and Resistance in Neoliberalism*. London: Zed Books.

Valentine, M. (2007). "Those that the Gods want to destroy, they first make mad": An analytic discussion of the depiction of sado-masochism in the film *Night Porter*. *British Journal of Psychotherapy*, 23(3), 445–457.

Vance, C. S. (Ed.). (1992). *Pleasure and Danger: Exploring Female Sexuality*. London: Pandora.

Van Haute, P., & Westerink, H. (2016). Sexuality and its object in Freud's 1905 edition of *Three Essays on the Theory of Sexuality*. *International Journal of Psychoanalysis*, 97, 563–589.

Vestal, L. (2018, December 30). Slave Play, hell no! *Evolving Man Project*. https://lornet-tvestal.com.

Wade, S. (2019). *Foucault in California*. Berkeley, CA: Heyday.

Walker, A. (1971). *You Can't Keep a Good Woman Down*. Orlando, FL: Harcourt Books.

Walker, A. (1982). A letter of the times, or Can this sado-masochism be saved? In *Against Sadomasochism: A Radical Feminist Analysis* (pp. 205–208). East Palo Alto, CA: Frog in the Well.

Waller, M. (1996). Signifying the Holocaust: Liliana Cavani's *Portiere di Notte*. In M. O. Marotti (Ed.), *Italian Women Writers from the Renaissance to the Present: Revising the Canon* (pp. 259–270). University Park: Pennsylvania State University Press.

Weinstein, l. (2007). When sexuality reaches beyond the pleasure principle. In D. Diamond, S. J. Blatt, & J. D. Lichtenberg (Eds.), *Attachment and Sexuality* (pp. 107–136). New York: Analytic.

Weiss, E. (1934). Bodily pain and mental pain. *International Journal of Psychoanalysis*, 15, 1–13.

Weiss, M. (2011). *Techniques of Pleasure: BDSM and the Circuits of Sexuality*. Durham, NC: Duke University Press.

White, K. P. (2002). Surviving hating and being hated: Some personal reflections about racism from a psychoanalytic perspective. *Contemporary Psychoanalysis*, 38(3), 401–422.

Wilderson, F. B. (2020). *Afropessimism*. New York: Norton.

Williams, M. (2009a, April 7). Race play interview—Part I. *Mollena*. www.mollena.com.

Williams, M. (2009b, April 7). Race play interview—Part II. *Mollena*. www.mollena.com.

Williams, M. (2009c, April 8). Race play interview—Part III. *Mollena*. www.mollena.com.

Williams, M. (2009d, April 9). Race play interview—Part IV (conclusion). *Mollena.* www.mollena.com.

Williams, M. (2010). *Playing with Taboo.* Pasadena, CA: Greenery.

Wilson, C. (1962). *The Strength to Dream: Literature and Imagination.* Boston: Riverside.

Woodard, V. (2014). *The Delectable Negro.* New York: New York University Press.

Woolfe, Z. (2016, February 24). A composer and his wife: Creativity through kink. *New York Times.* www.nytimes.com.

Zaltzman, N. (1979). *Η Αναρχική Ενόρμηση* (The Anarchic Drive). Athens: Hestia Books. (George Karabelas, Trans.).

Zurn, P. (2021). *Curiosity and Power: The Politics of Inquiry.* Minneapolis: University of Minnesota Press.

INDEX

abjection, 25–28, 51, 52, 113, 164–65

the actual, 156

Adorno, Theodor, 13–14, 17–18, 37, 175, 192

adult-infant relationship: in attachment theory, 38; implantation of adult's sexual unconscious in, 8–9, 40–41, 45–46, 70–71, 92, 134, 160–62; perversity implicated in, 40; subjectivation of the infant self through, 8–9, 40–42, 45–47, 70–71, 92–94, 134; violence in, 93–94

aesthetics/aesthetic experience: avoidance of understanding or resolution in certain works of, 13, 17; bending of the will and, 29; defined, 14; ego's stability challenged by, 10; eroticism associated with, 4–5; ethics and, 15–17, 29; exigency of, 136–38; exigent sadism and, 14, 140; Fisher's notebooks and, 116–17; infantile sexuality linked to, 53; "intended audience" a misconception in, 218n15; limit consent and, 3, 18, 146–47, 192; *The Night Porter* as case example of, 192; opacity in relation to, 13; otherness encountered in, 14; overwhelm associated with, 10, 76, 130; perversity and, 5, 31; photograph of Emmett Till as case example in, 14–17; pleasure associated with, 15; power in, 178; psychoanalysis as, 22; psychological depths affected by, 4, 13, 17, 140; repetition and, 132, 191; Sade and, 5; sexual drive in relation to, 17; *Slave Play* as case example of, 22, 109, 130, 132, 150–51, 192; and subjectiv-

ity, 5; suffering as component of, 5, 13; trauma put in circulation by, 14; as traumatisms, 190; and the unconscious, 12, 16–17, 29; vulnerability of, 4, 12. *See also* performance; *Slave Play*: audiences' experiences of; author's experience of

affirmative consent: BDSM and, 180; in case studies, 62; concept of, 3, 57; critique of, 3, 62–63, 96, 223n10; ethics of, 96; limit consent contrasted with, 3, 6–8, 57–58, 62–64, 68–69, 96, 127; medical version of (informed consent), 62, 66; perversity and, 78; *Slave Play* and, 157–58; transparency and communicability ascribed to, 6, 7, 8, 57, 63, 96

Afropessimism, 135, 220n26

agency: associated with minoritarian identities, 123, 209n20, 223n10; associated with Whiteness, 123, 221n30, 223n10; bending of the will contrasted with, 11; enabled by new translations, 87; traumas' constraints on, 123, 220n30

aggression, 72–74, 130, 146

Allison, Dorothy, *Bastard out of Carolina*, 32

Amistad (film), 157

anarchic drive, 101

Annunciation, Oratory of San Giorgio, Padua, 155–56

anti-Blackness, 112, 117–20, 124, 126, 141

Apollinaire, Guillaume, 88

après-coup, 12, 64, 85, 86, 122, 127, 149, 162

Aristotle, 17

unraveling of the self/ego: aesthetic experience as means to, 10; bending of the will to permit, 11; in case studies, 78–80, 85; defenses against, 6, 10, 50; detranslation as, 45–46, 49–50, 75–76, 100; eroticism and sexuality as means to, 10–11, 52–54; exigent sadism as means to, 181; experiences of pleasure with pain leading to, 45–46; Fisher and, 115, 117–18; intensity of experience in, 213n24; limit consent as means to, 54, 64, 102; not regressive, 213n24; as opportunity for new meaning-making, 49–51, 54, 58, 76, 86–87, 100, 104, 134, 151–52, 162, 196, 213n24, 215n18; overwhelm and, 58, 75–76, 99, 151; political implications of, 102; psychic effects of, 45–46, 75–76, 192; risk of, 99–100; sovereign experience and, 152–54. *See also* overwhelm; shattering

violence. *See* primary violence; secondary violence
vulnerability: of aesthetic experience, 4, 12; in bending of the will, 65; in case studies, 18–19; in clinical encounter, 67–68, 208n15; in limit consent, 63, 65; of psychoanalysts in clinical practice, 67; of writing and reading this book, 22. *See also* risk

Walker, Alice, 108–9
Warden, Claire, 193

Weiss, Edoardo, 215n17
White, Kathy, 120
Whiteness: agency associated with, 123, 221n30, 223n10; in case studies, 26–27; as dominant social location, 10, 47–48, 83, 135–36; Fisher's fantasies involving, 32, 114, 118; interracial eroticism and sexuality involving, 14, 16, 26–27, 32, 106–14, 118–19, 122–29, 142–46, 158–59, 163–66, 169–72, 222n5; mythology of, 135; psychic defenses of, 10, 27, 50, 123, 135–36; purity associated with, 27; *Slave Play* and, 106–13, 122–29, 141–42, 147, 223n12. *See also* White supremacy
White supremacy, 9, 48, 83, 102, 106, 111, 118, 125, 135, 170, 223n10
Williams, Mollena, 127, 132, 144, 158–60, 163–66, 169–72, 182–83, 220n28, 223n9
Williams-Haas, Mollena, *See* Williams, Mollena
Woolfe, Zachary, 158
wounds: opening of, 67, 116, 134, 182–83; pleasure associated with, 121; sadism in relation to, 168; the self's constitutive/fundamental, 116, 123, 135; touching/exploring, 50, 127, 130, 132–34, 160–61, 165–66, 183–85, 188; urge to heal, 67. *See also* curing; trauma

Zaltzman, Nathalie, 101
Zeno's paradox, 13
Zurn, Perry, 31

Originally from Greece and from Cyprus, AVGI SAKETOPOULOU immigrated to the United States to train as a psychoanalyst. She is in private practice in New York City and is a member of the faculty of the NYU Postdoctoral Program in Psychotherapy and Psychoanalysis. Her scholarship has received the Ruth Stein Prize, the JAPA Essay Prize, and Division 39's Scholarship Award, and she is the co-recipient of the IPA's first Tiresias Paper Prize. Still, few things give her as much pleasure as riding her motorcycle.

www.ingramcontent.com/pod-product-compliance
Lightning Source LLC
Chambersburg PA
CBHW020249030426

42336CB00010B/686